BTEC

HNC *HND* *Business*

Core module four:

Managing Finance and Information

PUBLISHING

BTEC HNC & HND BUSINESS

First edition June 1996

ISBN 0 7517 7013 2

British Library Cataloguing-in Publication Data

A catalogue record for this book
is available from the British Library

Published by

BPP Publishing Limited
Aldine House, Aldine Place
London W12 8AW

Our thanks are due to:

Colin Clark and David Badrick for assistance in
developing the open learning aspects of the text.

Genesys Editorial for additional editorial and
production work.

Printed in Great Britain by
Ashford Colour Press, Gosport, Hampshire

Contents

Preface

The HNC and HND qualifications in Business are very demanding. The suggested content, set out by BTEC in guidelines for each module, includes sophisticated topics which are normally only covered at degree level. Students therefore need books which get straight to the heart of these topics, and which relate them clearly to existing knowledge derived from school, college or work experience. BPP's series of textbooks is designed to meet that need.

This book has been written specifically for Core Module 4 *Managing Finance and Information*. It covers the BTEC guidelines and suggested content in full, and includes the following features.

(a) The BTEC guidelines

(b) A study guide, which explains the features of the book and how to get the most out of it

(c) A glossary and index

Each chapter contains

(a) An introduction and study objectives

(b) Summary diagrams and signposts, to guide you through

(c) Numerous activities, topics for discussion, definitions and examples

(d) a chapter roundup, a quick quiz with answers, answers to activities and an assignment (most with answer guidelines at the end of the book).

BPP Publishing have for many years been the leading providers of targeted texts for professional qualifications. We know that our customers need to study effectively, and that they cannot afford to waste time. They expect clear, concise and highly-focused study material. We believe that this series of study texts for HNC and HND Business Studies fulfils those needs.

BPP Publishing
June 1996

If you would like to send in your comments on this book, please turn to the review form on the last page.

Managing Finance and Information

DESCRIPTION OF THE MODULE

This module is concerned with managing information and financial systems within organisations. The two are interrelated in that the effective management of any resources, including financial, requires good information on which to base decision making.

This module has two sections.

Section One: Managing Finance

On completion of this section students will be able to:

- identify and analyse organisational financial resources
- identify and evaluate alternative sources of finance
- use financial information and procedures to support decision making
- evaluate the financial performance of organisations

Suggested content

Sources of finance: major sources; advantages and disadvantages; implications for organisations

Finance as a resource: cost of finance; flow; importance to decision making, types of asset and liability

Sources of financial information: analysis of costs, monitoring budgets and cash flow; cost benefit analysis

Financial performance: profit and loss account, balance sheet, cash flow statements; accounting ratios; comparison to market and company analysis

Section Two: Managing Information

At the end of this section students will be able to:

- evaluate the scope, key areas within and purposes of a Management Information System
- use information technology to store, retrieve and analyse information
- review systems for monitoring and providing management information
- evaluate the relevance and appropriateness of information generated from a Management Information System

Suggested content

MIS: implementing an organisational MIS; major information needs and flows; computerised systems; cost and benefits of an MIS; applications of MIS in different forms and sizes of organisations

Techniques: use of statistical techniques for compiling and presenting data; interpretation of data

Review: systems for monitoring and providing management information in the context of organisational needs and how these change

Evaluating information: accuracy, relevance, value and importance, data capture, ommisions

Study Guide

As well as giving comprehensive coverage of the BTEC guidelines, this book includes several features which are designed specifically to make learning efficient. The features are these.

(a) At the start of each chapter, there is a summary diagram which maps out the ground covered by the chapter. There are more detailed summary diagrams at the beginning of each main section of each chapter, giving more detail on the contents of the section.

(b) After the summary diagram there is an introduction, which sets the chapter in context. This is followed by learning objectives, which show you what you will have achieved by the time you reach the end of the chapter.

(c) Throughout the text, there are special aids to learning. These are indicated by symbols in the margin as follows.

Signposts guide you through the text, showing how each section is connected with the next one.

Definitions give the meanings of key terms. The *glossary* at the end of the text consolidates these.

Activities allow you to consolidate and test your learning. An indication of the time required for each is given (don't worry too much if you take a longer or shorter time). Answers are given at the ends of the chapters.

Topics for discussion are for use in seminars. They give you a chance to share your views with your fellow students.

(d) The wide margin at the outside edge of each page is for your notes. You will get the best out of this book if you engage in a dialogue with it. Put in your own ideas. Many things in business are matters of opinion, so do not be afraid to disagree with what you read.

(e) At the end of each chapter, there is a chapter roundup, a quiz with answers and an assignment. Use these to consolidate your knowledge. The chapter roundup summarises the chapter. The quiz tests what you have learnt (the answers often refer you back to the chapter so you can look over subjects again). The assignment (with a time guide) allows you to put your knowledge into practice - your teacher will let you know how for exam assignments you prepare is suitable as actual assessment material. Answer guidelines for most assignments can be found at the end of the text.

(f) The text ends with a glossary of key terms and an index.

Part A

MANAGING FINANCE

Chapter 1

SOURCES OF FINANCE

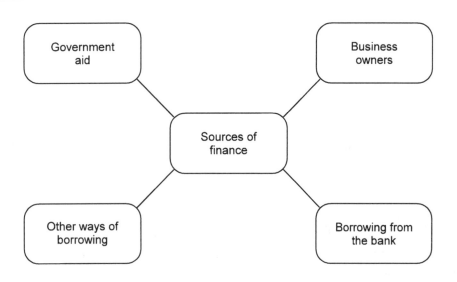

Introduction

Finance is at the very centre of business and management. Even if you have no direct responsibility for managing financial resources you ought to be aware that anything that anybody does in a business organisation either costs money, or generates money, or both.

In this chapter we are going to begin by looking at where that money comes from and the implications of obtaining money from different sources. In the next chapter we look more specifically at the sources of finance available to larger organisations (almost invariably companies).

This chapter introduces a number of topics, such as cash flow management, that are explored in greater depth later on in Part A of this book.

Your objectives

After completing this chapter you should:

(a) be able to identify and evaluate alternative sources of finance;

(b) be aware of the importance of ownership to the financing of a business;

(c) be able to suggest when and for what reasons a bank loan might be available;

(d) be able to describe other ways of borrowing money;

(e) be aware of a variety of grants that are available.

1 SOURCES OF FINANCE

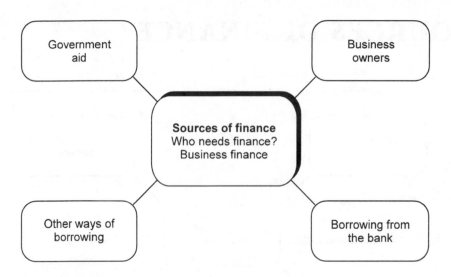

1.1 Who needs finance?

Finance means money. We all need it and use it every day, and we are all very interested to know where we can get more of it.

Let's begin by thinking about where you or I might get money from (short of stealing it) if we wanted some right now.

(a) We might use *our own* money - money in the bank or in our pocket or purse, that we have saved for later use.

(b) We might *borrow* from a friend, or use a credit card. If we wanted lots of money we might get a loan from a bank or building society.

(c) We might be *given* some money: the government would give us money if we were entitled to some form of benefit.

(d) We might *earn* some money by doing something or selling something to someone else.

For discussion

Depending on your background, experiences and beliefs you probably feel differently about these different ways of getting money. Assuming you are not a criminal, for example, you would not dream of stealing money. Do you feel uncomfortable about the welfare state? Do you think that people should be allowed to have unlimited savings? Do you mind being in debt? What would you not be willing to do to earn money?

The word *finance* is usually used in a bigger sense than just 'money'. It is any arrangement that you make in exchange for the ability to do all the different things you want to do.

(a) If you want to buy a Mars bar and a newspaper you finance your snacking and reading activities with the cash in your pocket.

(b) If you want to listen to the new REM CD now, but pay for it out of next month's salary, you finance this with your credit card.

(c) If you want to drive a car and can't pay for it in cash you get a 3 year loan from the bank to finance yourself: you probably never see the actual money.

However, because your savings and day to day cash have to come from somewhere, and because people you borrow from expect to be paid back eventually, you have to do something that *generates* income. If you are very lucky - if you win the National Lottery say - you may be able to live off the interest generated by your savings. Most people, though, have to *go to work* to generate income. They have to *sell* their time and talents to an employer, or become self-employed.

Personal finance is an interesting and complex subject in its own right. However, in this book we are interested in how businesses manage their finances.

1.2   Business finance

Businesses are set up with the object of making profits for their owners. A business, whether it be the local newsagent or a massive company like W H Smith's, has exactly the same need for, and sources of, finance as you and I.

(a) *The business has some money of its own*

If you started up a newsagent's business, say, you would probably have to put in some money from your savings to buy your initial stocks of sweets and cigarettes and newspapers and to pay bills like rent and electricity.

A company like W H Smith has money of this sort in the form of what people paid when they bought *shares* in the company. The money is owned by the 'company' of shareholders.

(b) *The business borrows money from the bank*

The newsagent might get his bank to agree to let him have an overdraft some of the time to tide him over periods when he has paid for stock but not yet sold it on to customers.

W H Smith might *borrow* millions of pounds from the bank over a term of many years to finance the building of new shops.

(c) Some businesses are helped out with their financing by *Government grants*, especially new businesses and businesses in deprived areas.

(d) All businesses will generate money by making *sales*. Some of this money will then be used to pay interest to the bank on its lending and to pay off part of the amount loaned.

We hinted above that the idea of ownership of a business is important to the subject we are discussing. We had better look at this in a little more detail.

2   BUSINESS OWNERS

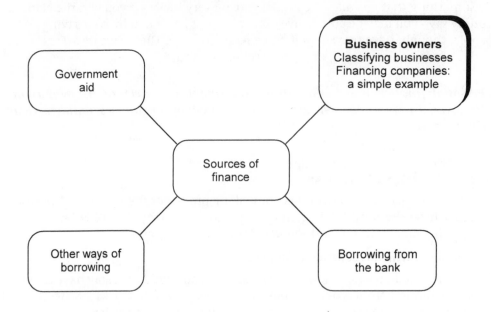

2.1   Classifying businesses

There are several different ways of classifying a business: for example, is it big or small; is it a service provider like a bank, a manufacturer like a car maker or a trader like a shop?

Activity 1   [15 minutes]

Divide into groups of three to four students. Each group should brain-storm to list as many businesses with a local presence that they can think of in, say, three minutes. Then the group should sub-divide the businesses into traders (wholesale and retail), service businesses and manufacturers; also, the group should rank them as large or small businesses, and discuss whether they are purely local businesses or part of large national or multinational businesses. This will enable you to start relating your studies to the world around you.

From the point of view of finance the most important distinction is the ownership of the business. This is partly a matter of how many people own the business, and partly a matter of the legal status of the business.

One owner: sole traders

A sole trader is a business that is owned by one person. This does not necessarily mean that only one person works for the business: a newsagent will typically be a sole trader but he will often have shop assistants working for him.

However, a sole trader is directly involved in the running of the business, he provides the money to start up the business (the *capital*), and all the profits that it makes belong to him.

For example, a self-employed plumber typically does all the plumbing work himself, he buys all the tools needed and a van to get about in, and the money he is paid goes directly into his pocket.

Two or more owners: partnerships

A partnership is an agreement between two or more persons to engage in business in common with a view to profit. It is desirable that partners have a written partnership agreement outlining important points such as the agreed shares of capital contributions and shares of profit, but there is nothing in law to say that any such written agreement is required.

Many small businesses are partnerships: three plumbers might get together in this way, for example, to share office space, or to offer a wider range of services to the same customers, or so that they can afford, and make full use of, expensive specialised equipment.

The 'professions' of law, medicine and accountancy are also often set up as partnerships (doctors and solicitors are not allowed to operate in any other way).

Two or more owners: companies

A company is a form of business that has two or more owners (although it can have only one) but which is separate in law from the people who own and control it.

This is quite a hard concept to understand when you first encounter it. You need to be aware that the law recognises not just individual human beings as persons, but also 'corporate bodies', in other words, companies. (An individual human being is called a *natural person*; a company is called an *artificial person*).

If a 'person' is recognised as such in law, the person then has certain legal rights and certain legal obligations.

(a) The most important *right* that a person has in the context of finance is the right to own property, for example money or machines.

(b) The most important *obligation* in this context is that a person has the responsibility for paying back financial debts.

A limited company is one whose owners' liability to pay back debts is limited to the amount that they put in. This is an advantage to the investor in a limited company, who knows that if the company in which he invested is hugely successful, he may get back many times the amount he invested. If the business "goes broke", he may lose his investment, but his house, car and other personal possessions are safe.

Note that it is the *shareholder's* liability that is limited. The company is a separate person in law and its liability is *unlimited*.

The company is the most important form of business. Let's look at a simple example to make sure that the implications of trading as a company are clearly understood.

2.2   Financing a company: a simple example

A limited company is owned by shareholders. For example:

(a) Zosie, Adam and Shiva want to set up a holiday home business, and they have £100,000 between them with which to do so. They go to a solicitor, and ask the solicitor to incorporate a company, which they decide to call Ecalpimos Ltd.

(b) Ownership of a company, by and large, is determined by the number of shares a person owns. Let's assume that the legal documents by which Ecalpimos Ltd is brought into existence state that the: 'authorised share capital of the company is to be £100,000 shares of £1 each'. This means that ownership is divided into 100,000 units with a face value of £1. It is decided that Zosie, Adam and Shiva will purchase all the shares.

If Zosie puts in £40,000 and Adam and Shiva each contribute £30,000, and the shares are purchased at their nominal value (ie £1 each) then Zosie will own 40% of Ecalpimos and the other two will own 30% each.

(c) The £100,000 now belongs to Ecalpimos Ltd, as it has been exchanged for the shares. If the money is used to buy a rundown property, that property belongs to Ecalpimos Ltd, not to Zosie, Adam and Shiva.

(d) Imagine that Ecalpimos Ltd makes a profit in the first year of trading of £1,000. This is distributed to the shareholders according to the size of their shareholding: Zosie will get £400, and Adam and Shiva will get £300 each. Such a distribution is called a dividend.

(e) Also, if Zosie, Adam and Shiva disagree on some issue relating to the management of the company, then Zosie has 40% of the votes, and Adam and Shiva 30% each.

(f) Most importantly, imagine you have lent Ecalpimos Ltd a sum of money with which to buy a hotel. Unfortunately the hotel burns down and, because it was not insured, Ecalpimos Ltd has no money to pay you back. You cannot get Zosie, Adam and Shiva to pay up from their own personal fortunes: the debt was owed by the company, not the individuals. This fact has a significant effect on the way the company's transactions are recorded and presented.

Definitions

Capital is used with a number of slightly different meanings.

(a) Capital is the money with which a business starts up - your life savings, for example, or a large redundancy payment might be used to set up a business.

(b) Capital is the also the name given to the assets that are used in a business. If you use your redundancy money to buy a pub and all its contents, then the building, the furniture, the beer stocks and so on are all your capital.

(c) Sometimes capital is the name given to money invested, for example £10,000 savings in a building society or £10,000 worth of ICI shares.

An *asset* is something owned by a business, for example a factory or a van.

A *liability* is a debt owed by a business, for example an overdraft at the bank.

Activity 2 [15 minutes]

The definitions in the box above are very important so make sure you understand them. Label the following items as 'capital', 'asset', 'liability', or 'none of these'.

(a) Cash in the bank

(b) A computer, bought on hire purchase

(c) An amount owed to a hire purchase company

(d) A rented building

(e) A factory full of machinery

(f) An employee

(g) Profits made by the business in previous years and not paid out to shareholders as dividends

(h) A tax bill

(i) Cash paid to settle the tax bill

On the next two pages we set out in tabular form the advantages and disadvantages of these basic kinds of financial and legal structure. (Any terms that you don't understand will be explained shortly.)

OWNER / MANAGER FINANCE - SOLE TRADERS AND PARTNERSHIPS

	Advantages for the business	*Disadvantages for the business*
FORMATION	Relatively simple and cheap to set up; no need to publish accounts (see 'shareholder finance')	With no track record, it could be hard to get credit from suppliers and bank
CAPITAL STRUCTURE	Owner(s) provide capital and the business is totally independent	Owner has total liability for debts. (Partners have total liability for *all* debts of the firm.) Owners may not have sufficient personal or business resources for growth. Borrowing required to finance expansion and also to cover times when there is a delay in collecting cash from customers. Finance is limited by maximum number of partners (20 except for some professional firms) but this is not usually a problem.
MANAGEMENT	Sole trader has total control over the management of the business, which enables him to offer a personal service to customers and potential customers. In a partnership, cover for sickness and holiday is available. Partners may be made responsible for different areas of the business, so specialisation is possible.	Could result in overwork for owner and difficulties in management, particularly as the business grows. The presence of more than one 'manager' could give rise to dangers of disagreement or slow decision-making between the partners. Continuity of the business could be a problem with the death or retirement of a key partner. One partner's word in business matters is binding on all other partners.
PROFITABILITY	Profits are distributed only to the owner(s); tax advantages over being an employee	Potentially a loss of business/profit during sole trader's absence from the business, eg due to sickness or holiday.

SHAREHOLDER FINANCE - LIMITED COMPANIES

	Advantages for the business	*Disadvantages for the business*
FORMATION	None	Complex and expensive to set up. Greater legal controls on management, eg submission of annual accounts to the companies' registry.Published accounts may give away sensitive trading information
CAPITAL STRUCTURE	Large potential membership to provide capital and resources. Shareholders' liability is limited to the amount asked by the company for their shares. Ownership of the company is transferable by selling share-holding	
MANAGEMENT	Day-to-day management can be made the responsibility of 'expert' managers.	
PROFITABILITY	Profits can either be distributed to shareholders as dividends or retained in the business to help future activities	Shareholders may demand larger dividends than the business can afford.

THE IMPLICATIONS OF DIFFERENT SOURCES OF FINANCE

Shareholder finance	*Owners/manager finance*
Separate legal entity (company)	Partners grouped in a relationship, ie no separate entity
Shareholders' iiability limited	Liability for business debts usually unlimited
Company (not its members) owns its assets	Partners jointly own partnership property, sole traders own property personally
Capital subscribed by shareholders may only be repaid to them under rules designed to protect interests of creditors	Owners may (by mutual agreement) withdraw capital as they wish - but unpaid creditors of the business may claim against them personally
A company must have one or more directors. A shareholder has no involvement in management (unless he is also a director or employee)	Owners are entitled to participate in management
A company always has a written constitution (memorandum and articles of association)	A sole trader or partnership may exist without any written partnership agreement
A company must usually deliver annual accounts, annual returns and other notices to Companies Registry and maintain registers - all open to public inspection	A partnership must disclose the names of the partners. But no one except a partner has any right to inspect accounts (although accounts have to be given to the tax authorities. Likewise sole traders.
A company may offer potential lenders of finance security by way of a 'charge' over its assets including current assets	Partners and sole traders cannot provide security by a charge on goods

We shall consider the financing of companies in much more detail in the next chapter. In the rest of this chapter we shall discuss ways of borrowing money and ways of getting people to give you money.

For most businesses the bank is the first place to turn to if the owners do not have enough ready cash to set up the business and keep it running.

3 BORROWING FROM THE BANK

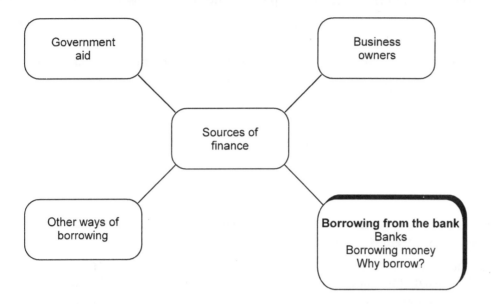

3.1 Banks

There are different types of banks which operate within the banking system, and you will probably have come across a number of terms which describe them.

(a) Clearing banks are the banks which operate the so-called 'clearing system' for settling payments (eg payments by cheque by bank customers).

(b) The term 'retail' banks is used to describe the traditional High Street banks, Barclays, Nat West, etc. The term 'wholesale' banks refers to banks which specialise in lending in large quantities to major customers. The clearing banks are involved in both retail and wholesale banking but are commonly regarded as the main 'retail' banks.

(c) Merchant banks are banks which offer services, often of a specialised nature, to corporate customers - companies.

All but the smallest businesses make extensive use of banks. The main functions and activities of banks can be summarised as follows:

(a) providing a payments mechanism ie a way in which individuals, firms and government can make payments to each other. The 'clearing system' of the clearing banks is the major payments mechanism in the UK, and it enables individuals and firms to make payments by cheque. The banks are also a source from which individuals and firms can obtain notes and coins;

(b) providing a place for individuals, firms and government to store their wealth, for example in current accounts or deposit accounts. Banks compete with other financial institutions to attract the funds of individuals and firms;

(c) lending money in the form of loans or overdrafts;

(d) acting as 'financial intermediaries': they accept deposits from people who have surplus wealth and lend it to those that need to borrow;

(e) providing customers with a means of obtaining foreign currency, or selling foreign currency, whenever they require it.

For the moment we are concerned with item (c), getting the bank to lend money to a business. Let's think about the circumstances in which a bank might be prepared to do this.

11

3.2   Borrowing money

If you want to borrow money the people lending it to you will usually only be prepared to do so if:

(a) they are sure they will be repaid within a reasonable time;

(b) they will make more for themselves by lending it to you (and making you pay interest) than they would from doing something else with their money.

For discussion

You have £10,000. You can put it in the building society and earn 6% interest. Alternatively you can lend it to a friend who says she is willing to pay 7% interest.

What further information would you want before you decide what to do?

Banks do not lend their money to anybody who happens to walk through the door. They apply certain well-tested principles of lending:

(a) They look at the *character* of the person or business asking for the loan. Can they be trusted - for example have they borrowed and repaid money in the past?

(b) Is the borrower *able to repay*? If it is a business, is it a profitable one and are there enough spare profits to be able to afford the interest and the periodic repayments of portions of the loan?

(c) Will the bank *make money* out of the loan? If the bank itself has to pay out 5% interest to people who deposit money in their accounts then it will have to charge more than 5% interest to people who borrow money.

(d) The bank will want to know the *purpose* of the loan. They won't lend you money so that you can engage in drug-dealing, for example. If you intend to gamble the money you want to borrow on the 3.30pm at Cheltenham the bank will not take the risk. The main reasons for borrowing are discussed in a moment.

(e) The *amount* of the loan is partly dependent on whether the borrower can afford to repay capital and interest and what *security* there is available (see below). For many business loans, however, the bank prefers the customer to have a significant personal stake in whatever the loan is for - the bank will put up £10,000 to help buy a new machine, say, if the business puts up the remaining £10,000 needed.

(f) The bank will need some form of *security* which it can turn to if the loan is not repaid. This is just like a mortgage: if you can't afford your mortgage repayments your house (the security) will be repossessed. Likewise, a bank will take some sort of charge over a business's assets. This means that the bank has a legal right to seize the assets if the loan is not repaid.

Clearly you can't just go along to a bank and ask for wads of money with which to do what you like. Here are the most typical and legitimate reasons for tapping the bank as a source of finance.

3.3   Why borrow?

Broadly speaking, a business will wish to borrow from the bank for one or more of three purposes:

(a) to purchase a business as a whole;

(b) to fund the purchase of fixed assets (capital finance) like buildings or cars; or

(c) to fund day-to-day activities ('working capital' or 'trading finance').

Buying a business

The two main circumstances in which a business might be bought are:

(a) as a totally new venture, possibly starting from scratch.

(b) as an expansion of an existing business.

New ventures are risky undertakings for businessmen: 80% of all new small businesses fail within the first five years. However, the new ventures of today may turn out to be tomorrow's Body Shop, so a bank will always consider lending in order not to miss an excellent future customer, and so as not to have a reputation for being unsupportive of enterprise and initiative.

An existing business, say a small retailer, may see a good opportunity for expansion when the chance arises to purchase another business, such as a warehousing operation. This is a form of new venture, but is probably less of a risk for the bank because the borrower has more experience of running a business.

In addition to new ventures and takeovers there are other circumstances in which a business is purchased:

(a) professional people, such as doctors, dentists or accountants, seeking to set up in practice;

(b) a management buyout, where the managers of a business purchase it from its existing owners; and

(c) purchasing a franchise for instance an individual might wish to set up a fast-food outlet within the framework of an international organisation which grants franchises.

For discussion

Why might managers be interested in buying the business they work for?

Think about issues like ownership, control and rewards. You might find it helpful to consider what advantages and disadvantages there would be for you if you were offered the chance to be one of the owners of your own employer.

Buying fixed assets

Another very common reason for a business to borrow is in order to finance the purchase of new fixed assets. These are things like machines or premises that are used to generate income for a business over a long period of time. Banks try to ensure that the loan in some way matches the asset's life.

Hence a loan to purchase computer equipment will be *short term* (since computer systems become rapidly out of date, particularly in an expanding business) whilst one to purchase a factory will be *long term*. A mortgage over the latter will be good security, which is not the case with computer equipment.

Banks will also want to be sure that the borrower has included all the costs of the purchase in his plan, such as:

(a) installation and testing costs;

(b) cost of any rebuilding; and

(c) staff retraining costs.

Such costs may reduce the profitability of the project and strain the business's cash flow to such an extent that the repayments cannot be met.

Day to day finance

Day to day financing or 'working capital' is one of the most common forms of borrowing. Finance is needed for this purpose because stocks often take a long time to turn into cash: the business has to have them, whether customers buy them or not, but in the meantime the suppliers of the stocks must be paid.

Suppose A Ltd buys some stocks for resale from Z Ltd in month 1 on 30 days credit. It sells the stock to B Ltd at a profit at the beginning of month 2 and at the same time pays Z Ltd. But B Ltd takes 45 days to pay for the stocks. Hence until the middle of month 3 A Ltd has a cash deficit of the amount which it paid its supplier, Z Ltd. This deficit must be financed (the money must come from somewhere) and the most usual source is a bank overdraft.

Terms of a business overdraft are usually set out as follows.

(a) *Repayment:* repayable on demand with review dates set every twelve months or so to decide whether the amount of overdraft allowed needs to be increased.

(b) *Amount:* the account should fluctuate between debit and credit, the debit balance not to exceed a certain level and the average balance to be well within that limit.

(c) *Security:* usually an overdraft is secured by a charge over (a right to possession of) the business's assets.

(d) *Interest:* interest is calculated on the daily balance.

We shall be looking at trade credit and the management of working capital in much more detail in later chapters. However, we have not yet finished with borrowing: there are other ways of borrowing money besides a loan from the bank.

4 OTHER WAYS OF BORROWING

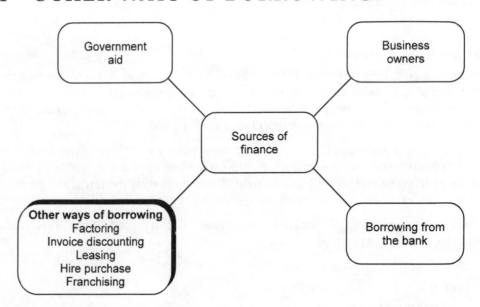

4.1 Factoring

Some businesses might have difficulties in financing the amounts owed by customers (debtors). There are two main reasons for this.

(a) If a business's sales are rising rapidly, its total debtors will rise quickly too. Selling more on credit will put a strain on the company's cash flow. The business, although making profits, might find itself in difficulties because it has too many debtors and not enough cash.

(b) If a business grants long credit to its customers, it might run into cash flow difficulties for much the same reason. Exporting businesses must often allow long periods of credit to foreign buyers, before eventually receiving payment, and their problem of financing debtors adequately can be a critical one.

Factors are organisations that offer their clients a financing service to overcome these problems. They are prepared to advance cash to the client against the security of the client's debtors. The business will assign its debtors to the factor and will typically ask for an advance of funds against the debts which the factor has purchased, usually up to 80% of the value of the debts.

For example, if a business makes credit sales of £100,000 per month, the factor might be willing to advance up to 80% of the invoice value (here £80,000) in return for a commission charge, and interest will be charged on the amount of funds advanced.

The balance of the money will be paid to the business when the customers have paid the factor, or after an agreed period.

This service gives the business immediate cash in place of a debt (which is a promise of cash in the future). If the business needs money to finance operations, borrowing against trade debts is therefore an alternative to asking a bank for an overdraft.

The appeal of factor financing to growing firms is that factors might advance money when a bank is reluctant to consider granting a larger overdraft. Advances from a factor are therefore particularly useful for rapidly growing companies, that need more and more cash to expand their business quickly, by purchasing more stocks and allowing more credit sales than they would otherwise be able to do. However, factoring companies are generally reluctant to assist companies with less than a year's trading behind them, and so which do not have much of a track record in business yet, because of the strong risk that a new company might get into financial difficulties.

4.2 Invoice discounting

Invoice discounting is related to factoring and many factors will provide an invoice discounting service. Invoice discounting is the purchase of a selection of invoices, at a discount. For example, if your business had just redecorated the Town Hall it might have sent the Council an invoice for £5,000. This would be an easy invoice to sell on for cash because the Council are very likely to pay. An invoice for £5,000 sent to 'A Cowboy & Co' would not be so easy to sell for immediate cash!

The invoice discounter does not take over the management of all the business's debtors', and the arrangement is purely for the advance of cash. A business should only want to have some invoices discounted when it has a temporary cash shortage, and so invoice discounting tends to consist of 'one-off deals'. Since the discounter does not control debt administration, and relies on the client to collect the debts for him, it is a more risky operation than factoring and so the discounter might only agree to offer an invoice discounting service to reliable, well-established companies.

Activity 3 [15 minutes]

(a) What are the financial costs of bank loans, factoring and invoice discounting?

(b) What is the financial cost of obtaining finance by issuing shares in a company?

4.3 Leasing

A lease is an agreement between two parties, the lessor and the lessee:

(a) the *lessor* owns an asset, but grants the lessee use of it;

(b) the *lessee* does not own the asset, but uses it, and in return makes payments to the lessor.

Leasing is therefore a form of rental. Leased assets are usually things like plant and machinery, and cars and commercial vehicles, but might also be computers, ships, aeroplanes, oil production equipment, office equipment and so on.

Operating leases are agreements between a lessor and a lessee where the period of the lease is fairly short, less than the useful life of the asset, so that at the end of one lease agreement, the lessor can either:

(a) lease the same equipment to someone else, and obtain a good rental for it; or

(b) sell the equipment at a second-hand value.

With an operating lease the lessee is in effect renting the asset.

Finance leases are lease agreements between the user of the leased asset (the lessee) and a provider of finance (the lessor) for the main part of the asset's expected useful life, if not its entire useful life.

The lessor never has physical possession of the asset, even though he owns it. The lessee is responsible for the upkeep, servicing and maintenance of the asset. The lessor is not involved in this at all.

The lessee effectively owns the asset under a finance lease, although in law the lessor owns it.

What are the attractions of leasing to the supplier of the equipment, the lessee and the lessor?

(a) The supplier of the equipment is paid in full at the beginning. The equipment is sold to the lessor, and apart from obligations under guarantees or warranties, the supplier is free from all further financial concern about the asset.

(b) The lessor invests finance by purchasing assets from suppliers and makes a return out of the lease payments from the lessee. Provided that a lessor can find lessees willing to pay the amounts he wants to make his return, the lessor will make good profits on his deals.

(c) It is natural to want to own an asset instead of 'rent' one, and so the attractions of leasing to the lessee might not seem so obvious. However, under a finance lease, the lessee has use of the asset as though he were the real owner, and the lessor does not interfere at all. Leasing might therefore be attractive to the lessee:

   (i) if the lessee does not have enough cash to pay for the asset, and may be having difficulty obtaining a bank loan to buy it, and so has to rent it in one way or another if he is to have use of the asset at all; or

   (ii) if leasing is cheaper than a bank loan. The cost of payments under a loan might exceed the cost of a lease.

4.4 Hire purchase

Hire purchase (HP) is a form of borrowing whereby an individual or business purchases goods on credit and pays for them by instalments. The HP contract is arranged by the vendor of the goods but is usually between the customer and a finance company. It works like this:

(a) the supplier sells the goods to the finance company; but

(b) delivers the goods to the customer who will eventually purchase them; and

(c) the hire purchase arrangement exists between the finance company and the customer.

The finance company will nearly always insist that the hirer should pay a deposit towards the purchase price, perhaps as low as 15%, or as high as 33%. In contrast, with a finance lease, the lessee does not usually have to make any down-payment.

Goods bought by businesses on hire purchase include company vehicles, plant and machinery, office equipment and farming machinery. Hire purchase arrangements for fleets of motor cars are quite common, and most car manufacturers have a link with a leading finance house for point-of-sale hire purchase credit (for example Austin Rover Cars and Lombard North Central).

Hire purchase is similar to leasing, with the exception that ownership of the goods passes to the hire purchase customer on payment of the final instalment, whereas a lessee never becomes the legal owner of the goods.

The benefits of hire purchase, like leasing, include the following.

(a) A business can obtain assets now and pay for them over a period of time. This avoids putting a strain on the business cash flows.

(b) A business can budget its relevant costs and cash flows accurately with fixed interest rate HP finance.

(c) Hire purchase is fairly simple to arrange, and a useful alternative to borrowing from a bank.

Activity 4 [15 minutes]

Using the above terminology, what sort of arrangements are being made in the following domestic situations?

(a) Jack rents a TV

(b) Jill buys a Golf GTI and agrees to allow the Volkswagen dealer to arrange the finance.

(c) Jack wants his banker to help out until he receives his salary cheque in 3 weeks time.

(d) Jill needs assistance to buy a new flat.

4.5 Franchising

Franchising is a fairly recent development in the UK. It is the means by which a large number of chains have grown very rapidly in the last few years. The franchisor has a successful business (selling hamburgers, pizzas or printing, for example) and instead of establishing branches under its own name it licenses franchisees to use its name, corporate identity and so on. The franchisees actually run the business, employing staff as necessary.

In return for what can be a substantial licence fee, the franchisees receive the following:

(a) they are trained before starting;

(b) their premises are fitted out with the appropriate equipment and decor (the cost of doing this is likely to be loaned to the franchisee by the franchisor);

(c) they must usually buy most or all of their trading stock and other supplies from the franchisor;

(d) they benefit considerably from the marketing and advertising of the franchisor;

(e) they do not have to make pricing or marketing decisions themselves as these are made by the franchisor (at least in outline).

The franchisor is usually willing to put a lot of effort into helping the franchisees because the public perceives the chain as a chain and not as a collection of disparate outlets all using the same name. Thus, if the McDonalds outlet in Macclesfield (a franchise) is up to scratch, then customers will not be deterred from visiting the McDonalds outlet in Pontefract (owned and run by McDonalds plc itself).

The franchisor benefits from the arrangement even where it has no outlets of its own. Because the franchisees are the legal owners of the outlets, the franchisor is freed from the administrative burden of maintaining a branch network and employing large numbers of staff. Its income comes from the licence fees and from collecting an agreed percentage of profits made by the franchisees. This produces a steady stream of cash, less liable to fluctuate and less risky than relying on profits generated by its own branches. The franchisor's cash flow should improve and its need for borrowing decrease.

The franchisee benefits from the 'handholding' of the franchisor, especially when the franchisee has not been self-employed before. He or she is free to concentrate on running the business without having to think about marketing, choosing between suppliers and so on. For all these reasons, franchising has proved attractive to many people made redundant with large redundancy payments, or to people taking early retirement from a first career, with a lump sum from their pension fund to invest.

Activity 5 [15 minutes]

(a) Earlier we said that there are 3 main reasons why a business might borrow money. What are those reasons, and which applies to:

    (i) factoring and invoice discounting;

    (ii) leasing and hire purchase;

    (iii) franchising?

(b) What are the costs, financial and otherwise, of franchising?

Finally in this chapter we turn to 'money for nothing'! You may be getting, say, local authority assistance in financing your studies, because it is seen as a good thing to have an educated population. Similarly, it is in the interests of society as a whole that businesses are given a chance to succeed, so financial support is available.

5 GOVERNMENT AID

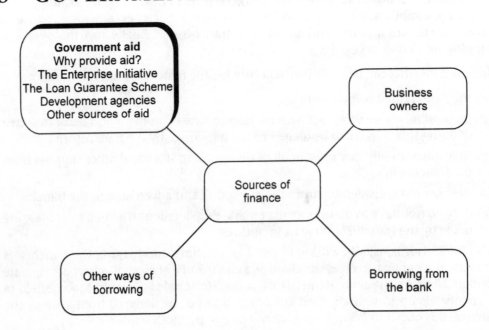

5.1   Why provide aid?

Governments are keen that businesses should start up and prosper because successful businesses provide employment and create wealth for the country.

The UK government has provided finance to companies in cash grants and other forms of direct assistance, as part of its policy of helping to develop the national economy, especially in high technology industries and in areas of high unemployment.

5.2   The Enterprise Initiative

The Enterprise Initiative is a package of measures offered by the Department of Trade and Industry (DTI) to businesses in the UK, including some regional selective grant assistance. Help with consultancy costs has also been provided, but this part of the Initiative is now winding down, to be replaced by a new network of 'Business Links', which are local business advice centres.

Regional Selective Assistance is available for investment projects undertaken by firms in 'Assisted Areas'. The project must be commercially viable, create or safeguard employment, demonstrate a need for assistance and offer a distinct regional and national benefit. The amount of grant will be negotiated as the minimum necessary to ensure the project goes ahead.

The *Regional Enterprise Grants* scheme is specially geared to help small firms employing fewer than 25 in one of the Development Areas to expand and diversify. Regional enterprise grants can help finance viable projects for:

(a) investment - grants of 15% of the cost of fixed assets up to a maximum of £15,000 are available;

(b) innovation - grants of 50% of the agreed project cost up to a maximum grant of £25,000 are available.

5.3   The Loan Guarantee Scheme

The Loan Guarantee Scheme was introduced by the government in 1981. It is intended to help small businesses to get a loan from the bank, when a bank would otherwise be unwilling to lend because the business cannot offer the security that the bank would want.

Under the scheme the bank can lend up to £250,000 without security being given over *personal* assets or a personal guarantee being required of the borrower. However, all available *business* assets must be used as security if required. The government will guarantee the bulk of the loan, while the borrower must pay an annual premium on the guaranteed part of the loan. The scheme is not open to 'local service' businesses such as small retailers.

5.4   Development agencies

The UK government has set up some development agencies (the Scottish and Welsh Development Agencies) which have been given the task of trying to encourage the development of trade and industry in their areas. The strategy of the agencies has been mainly to encourage the start-up and development of small companies, although they will also give help to larger companies.

The assistance that a development agency might give to a firm could include:

(a) free factory accommodation, or factory accommodation at a low rent;

(b) financial assistance, in the form of:

    (i)   an interest relief grant for a bank loan. A company developing its business in an area might obtain a bank loan, and the development agency will agree to compensate the bank for providing the loan at a low rate of interest;

    (ii) direct financial assistance in the form of share capital or loans.

5.5 Other sources of aid

Local authorities are often keen to attract new businesses into their area (or to help existing businesses expand) because of the benefits to the local community of creating extra jobs and therefore increasing spending power to the benefit of all local businesses. The new business may provide a market (or act as a supplier) for other local businesses, which is also beneficial. Grants, loans and advice are therefore likely to be available from the authority or its economic development unit.

Finally, one further source of aid which deserves mention is the *Enterprise Allowance Scheme* whereby people with £1,000 of their own funds to invest in a new venture are given £40 a week for 1 year.

Activity 6 [15 minutes]

In what other ways can governments help businesses (or hinder them) besides providing finance directly?

Think about the impact of government polices on matters such as education, transport, the environment and so on, as well as economic policy.

Chapter roundup

- 'Finance' is money or in broader terms it is a monetary arrangement made in exchange for the ability to do something. The basic sources of money are savings, borrowings, grants and earnings.

- The way in which a business is financed is closely linked with the ownership of the business. The three main forms of business are sole traders, partnerships and companies.

- Banks are the principal source of borrowed money for business purposes. Banks apply principles such as ability to repay and security before they agree to lend.

- Businesses borrow to purchase a business as a whole, to purchase fixed assets or, most commonly, to finance day-to-day trading.

- Other ways of borrowing include factoring and invoice discounting, leasing and HP, and franchising.

- A large variety of government grants are available for businesses that meet certain criteria.

Quick quiz

1   Why do individuals have to do something that generates income?

2   Why do businesses have to do something that generates more?

3   List four sources of business finance.

4   List the three major forms of business ownership

5   In what sense is a limited company limited?

6   What are the owners of a limited company called?

7   What is the difference between 'wholesale' and 'retail' banks?

8   What principles will a bank apply when considering whether to lend money to a business?

9   What is an overdraft used for?

10 What is the difference between factoring and invoice discounting?

11 What are the advantages of leasing and hire purchase?

12 What are the advantages of franchising to a person new to business ownership?

13 What are possible disadvantages of franchising?

14 List four types of Government Aid for businesses.

Answers to quick quiz

1   To provide for ourselves (and possibly for our families).

2   To make profits for their owners.

3   Owners, bank loans, bank overdrafts, hire purchase, factoring, etc.

4   Sole trader, partnership, limited company.

5   The owners cannot lose more than their investment.

6   Shareholders.

7   'Wholesale' banks lend to major businesses, whilst 'retail' banks deal with the public.

8   See Section 3.2

9   To finance fluctuating working capital requirements.

10 See Sections 4.1 and 4.2.

11 See Sections 4.3 and 4.4.

12 See Section 4.5.

13 Lack of complete freedom, cost of franchise, possible disagreement with franchiser.

14 Regional Enterprise Grants, Regional Selective Assistance, Loan Guarantee Scheme, Development Agency accommodation, etc.

Solutions to activities

1   The answer to this activity depends on your local area. You may be suprised at the number of service businesses, and at the number of small, local businesses.

2   (a) Asset

(b) Asset

(c) Liability

(d) None of these (the rent is an expense)

(e) Assets

(f) None of these (the employee's wages are an expense, but businesses do not own people)

(g) Capital

(h) Liability

(i) None of these (it is another expense)

3 (a) The cost of a bank loan is the *interest* paid to the bank. There may also be an *arrangement fee* when the loan is first taken out. (Bank charges are not a cost of borrowing: they are a cost of having a bank account.)

   Factoring and invoice discounting costs are the factors' *commission charge* and *interest* on the funds borrowed.

   (b) *Dividends* usually have to be paid to the shareholders, if only to stop them selling their shares.

4 (a) This is a sort of operating lease

   (b) This is hire purchase

   (c) This is a bank overdraft

   (d) This is a bank loan (a mortgage loan)

5 (a) The three reasons and their application are:

   (i)   to finance working capital (factoring/invoice discounting);

   (ii) to purchase fixed assets (leasing/HP);

   (iii) to buy a business as a whole (franchising).

   (b) There is a *licence fee*, possibly a premium charged on stocks (they may be available more cheaply from other suppliers), and a percentage of profits. The main other cost is the possible dissatisfaction or frustration caused by the lack of overall control of the business.

6 A wide-ranging question!

   Items you could have mentioned as help:

   (a) Low taxes

   (b) Lack of red tape

   (c) A buoyant economy

   (d) Low interest rates

   (e) An educated, skilled workforce

   (f) Good infrastructure - roads, railways, etc

   The reverse of all the above will be a hindrance.

Assignment 1   1½ hours

You should imagine that you have enough money (from a legacy from a relation, a lottery win, etc) to start a business. You should consider the following:

(a) What amount of owner's capital will the business need?

(b) What will it do?

(c) What category would it fall into - manufacturer, trader, service business?

(d) What form of ownership would be suitable - sole trader, partnership, limited company?

(e) What would you have to buy to get it started, and how much would this cost?

(f) Would you need other forms of finance and, if so, what would be the appropriate ones?

You should make a short presentation to your group, outlining your ideas, and the group members should be encouraged to constructively question your ideas.

Clearly, there is no one right answer to this assignment, but the hope is that it will encourage your interest in business and start to raise creative thinking. The ultimate success of the exercise would be if you or your colleagues focused on your future life's work as a result of your input!

Chapter 2

FINANCING LARGE BUSINESSES

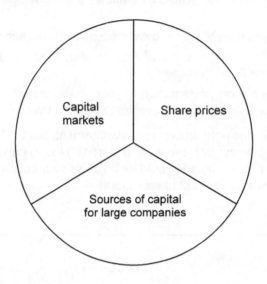

Introduction

When you read about businesses in the pages of a newspaper you will not find much about factoring arrangements or overdraft facilities. Most of what you read will be about events in institutions such as the Stock Exchange - things that go on in financial centres such as the City of London.

This is the world of large company finance in which, because much more finance is needed, there is a good deal more diversity and sophistication in both the range of options available and the number of parties who have an interest. If you work for a larger company it is both useful and important for you to understand that your company's policies and activities are not just the whim of the current managing director. They are, to quite a large extent, influenced by what is and is not acceptable to the City-based providers of finance.

Your objectives

After completing this chapter you should:

(a) be aware of sources of finance for larger businesses;

(b) be able to identify the chief providers of finance for larger businesses;

(c) be able to evaluate alternative methods by which companies may raise finance.

1 CAPITAL MARKETS

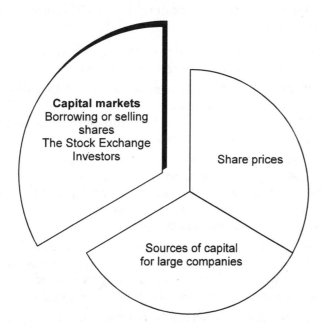

1.1 Borrowing or selling shares

Individuals often need to raise finance; eg to buy a house, a car, a television or furniture. They will in most cases borrow the money needed; their alternative sources will normally be a building society, a bank, a hire purchase or leasing company.

Small businesses often need to borrow, for similar reasons, and their alternatives are similar to those of individuals when they wish to buy business premises, motor lorries, new computer systems, etc.

Larger businesses also often have need for more funds for expansion purposes. However, they have an advantage over the individual and the small businessman. In addition to the various sources of borrowed money, they can often raise the finance they need by selling more shares in their company. So, instead of borrowing (which has to be paid back), they obtain permanent capital (on which the new shareholders will expect dividend income). Most investors (whether they be individuals with some surplus cash, or institutions, such as insurance companies, pension funds, etc.) want to be assured that they can sell their investments at any time (hopefully at a profit, or possibly at a loss).

So most large public limited companies, which have the right to sell their shares to the public and to advertise their shares to the public, wish to be quoted on the London Stock Exchange. The Stock Exchange is in effect a second-hand shop, so that persons becoming shareholders of any plc quoted on the Stock Exchange can always get an up to date valuation of their shares and sell them through Stock Exchange member firms. The function of the Stock Exchange is to bring buyers and sellers together.

The Alternative Investment Market (AIM), which opened in 1995, is a similar 'second-hand shop' for smaller plcs which cannot meet the more stringent requirements needed to obtain a full Stock Exchange listing.

1.2   The Stock Exchange

The London Stock Exchange is an organised capital market based in London which plays an important role in the functioning of the UK economy. It is the main capital market in the UK.

(a) It makes it easier for large firms and the government to raise long term capital, by providing a 'market place' for borrowers and investors to come together.

(b) The Stock Exchange publicises the prices of quoted (or 'listed') securities, which are then reported in daily national newspapers such as the *Financial Times*. Investors can therefore keep an eye on the value of their stocks and shares, and make buying and selling decisions accordingly.

(c) The Stock Exchange tries to enforce certain rules of conduct for its listed firms and for operators in the market, so that investors have the assurance that companies whose shares are traded on the Exchange and traders who operate there are reputable. Confidence in the Stock Exchange will make investors more willing to put their money into stocks and shares.

(d) The index of share prices on the Stock Exchange acts as an indicator of the state of investor confidence in the country's economy. For example, if investors believe that interest rates are too low to curb inflation, they may sell shares and move their funds to other countries, causing a decline in share prices.

The price of shares on a stock market fluctuate up and down.

(a) The price of shares in a particular company might remain unchanged for quite a long time; alternatively, a company's share price might fluctuate continually throughout each day.

(b) The general level of share prices, as measured by share price indices (eg in the UK, by the All-Share Index and the FT-SE 100 or 'Footsie' Index), goes up or down each day.

Activity 1   [15 minutes]

Here are some typical comments from the business pages of a quality newspaper.

> 'Bank note printer De La Rue provided the day's biggest share price upset, tumbling more than 20 per cent ... following a set of interim results that contained the group's second profits warning in 8 months.
>
> In contrast, mobile phones group Vodafone fell 15 to 239p following interim results that disappointed some analysts and a briefing by the company which suggested that the Christmas selling season was proving tough going in the face of keen competition from rival groups.'   *Financial Times*, 21 November 1995

In the light of this, and if possible after glancing through the business pages of a newspaper such as the Times or the Telegraph or the FT, what factors do you think have an influence on share prices?

We have talked about 'investors' on the Stock Exchange. You may own a few shares yourself, but millions and millions of shares change hands on the Stock Exchange every day. Who is it that is doing all this buying and selling?

1.3   Investors

Providers of capital (investors) include private individuals, such as those who buy stocks and shares on the Stock Exchange, and those who invest in National Savings or building societies. However, there are some important groups of *institutional* investors which specialise in lending capital in order to make a return.

(a) *Pension funds*. Pension funds invest the pension contributions of individuals who subscribe to a pension fund, and of organisations with a company pension fund.

(b) *Insurance companies*. Insurance companies invest premiums paid on insurance policies by policy holders. If you think about it, insurance companies, like pension funds, must do something with the premiums they receive, and in practice, they invest the money to earn a return.

(c) *Investment trusts*. The business of investment trust companies is investing in the stocks and shares of other companies and the government. In other words, they trade in investments.

(d) *Unit trusts*. Unit trusts are similar to investment trusts, in the sense that they invest in shares of other companies. A unit trust comprises a 'portfolio' ie a holding of shares in a range of companies, perhaps with all the shares having a special characteristic, such as all shares in property companies or all shares in mining companies. The trust will then create a large number of small units of low nominal value, with each unit representing a stake in the total portfolio. These units are then sold to individual investors and investors will benefit from the income from an increase in value of their units ie their proportion of the portfolio.

(e) *Venture capital*. Venture capital providers are organisations that specialise in raising funds for new business ventures, such as 'management buy-outs' (ie purchases of firms by their management staff). These organisations are therefore providing capital for fairly risky ventures. A venture capital organisation that has operated for many years in the UK is Investors in Industry plc, usually known as '3i'. In recent years, many more venture capital organisations have been set up, for example by large financial institutions such as pension funds.

The capital markets may be summarised in a simplified form in Figure 2.1 below.

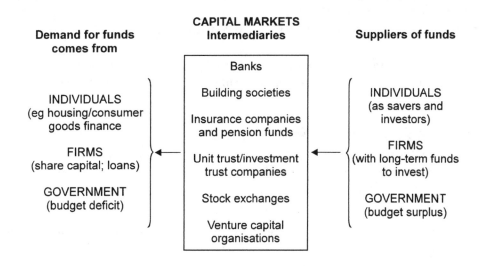

Figure 2.1 The capital markets

The news on the radio or the TV always includes an item telling you that 'the stock market fell today' or 'the stock market reached an all-time high'. While we are on the subject it is worth pausing for a moment to see what this means.

2 SHARE PRICES

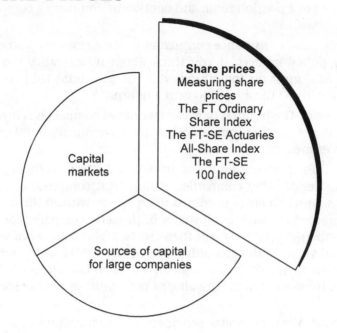

Share prices
Measuring share prices
The FT Ordinary Share Index
The FT-SE Actuaries All-Share Index
The FT-SE 100 Index

Capital markets

Sources of capital for large companies

2.1 Measuring share prices

The Financial Times (FT) publishes various indices which measure the performance of the UK stock market. These include:

(a) the FT Ordinary Share Index;
(b) the FT-Actuaries Indices;
(c) the FT-SE 100 Share Index.

The Financial Times also publishes the FT-Actuaries World Indices, which measure the performance of international stockmarkets. Another newer index is the FT-SE Eurotrack Index for European shares, which is denominated in deutschmarks.

It will be useful to take a brief look at the three UK indices mentioned, since you will often see or hear references to them on the news or in the papers.

2.2 The FT Ordinary Share Index

The Financial Times Ordinary Share Index is recalculated every time there is a movement in the share price of one of its 30 constituent shares and is published 8 times a day, at every hour on the hour from 10 am to 4 pm inclusive and at the close of business for the day.

The primary purpose of the Ordinary Share Index is to act as an indicator of the mood of the market and to provide a guide to the movement of prices in the short term.

The Ordinary Share Index is sometimes criticised on the following grounds.

(a) Each constituent company has the same effect on the index despite any difference in relative size.
(b) Thirty is too small a number of companies to reflect movements in stock market prices accurately.
(c) Because it is based mainly on industrial companies, it is too restrictive.

In considering these points, it must be remembered that the Ordinary Share Index is intended to be an indicator of market sentiment; it is not meant to be an accurate measure of overall market performance (although the layman sometimes thinks it is). Note too that, although the companies do vary in size, they are all big companies.

The index was originally called the FT Industrial Ordinary Share Index, as it was calculated from the share prices of 30 exclusively industrial companies. As a matter of policy, no finance companies or property companies were included since it was felt that these could be influenced by factors other than the state of the market and the 'real' economy. However finance companies have become more and more important in the economy, and the Index does now include shares in such companies. The exclusion of financial companies in the past meant that the FT Ordinary Share Index tended to perform less well than the All-Share Index (see below).

2.3 FT-SE Actuaries All-Share Index

The FT-SE Actuaries indices are compiled jointly by the FT, the Institute of Actuaries and the Faculty of Actuaries. The diagram below shows the composition of the FT-SE Actuaries All-Share Index, with the number of constituent companies in each sector

There are a large number of indices which form a sort of tree (Figure 2.2):

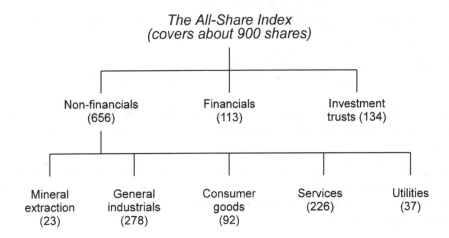

Figure 2.2 FT-SE Actuaries All-Share Index

The All-Share Index is representative of the market as a whole. Not only do the constituent companies cover all the major sectors, such as stores, construction, industrials etc, but together, they also account for around 98% of the total capital of UK listed companies.

2.4 The FT-SE 100 Index

The FT-SE 100 Index (known colloquially as the 'footsie') is based on the average, weighted by the number of the shares in issue, of the prices of the shares of 100 leading companies. (The purpose of weighting is to give due prominence to the stock market value of the larger constituents and not to overstate the significance of the smaller companies.)

Between them, the companies which make up the FT-SE 100 Index account for about 70% of the *value* of all quoted UK companies. As intended, the index covers a very substantial part of the market and is very closely correlated with the All-Share Index.

The FT-SE 100 Index is calculated *once per minute* throughout the trading day.

Activity 2 [15 minutes]

On 21 November 1995 the *Financial Times* had the following market report. Read it and then answer the questions that follow.

'Share prices in London moved up again to all-time highs yesterday, measured by the stock market's main indices, the FT-SE Actuaries All-Share and the FT-SE 100.

There were, however, signs that the market's move to record levels could be running out of steam. Wall Street, one of the prime motivating forces behind the London market's recent rise, briefly penetrated the 5,000 level on the Dow Jones Industrial Average, shortly after the US market opened for trading. But it quickly dropped back to the mid-4980s, and around 2 hours after London closed for business the Dow was still jousting with the 5,000 mark.

The failure of the US index to move decisively through 5,000 was one of a number of worrying signals affecting London. Others included the emergence of yet more profits warnings, notably from Rexam, the paper group, and a decline in international bond markets.

Dealers said London had run into some determined selling pressure when it passed 3,630. "Above that level, we ran into some real selling,"' said one marketmaker.

The FT-SE 100 index finished the day a net 19.6 firmer at an all-time closing high of 3,628.8, after reaching a record intra-day peak of 3,639.5. The FT-SE-A All-Share index ended at a best ever 1,776.87, up 7.47.'

(a) What do you think 'Wall Street' and the 'Dow Jones Industrial Average' mean?

(b) What is a 'profits warning'?

(c) What was the sentiment or mood of the UK stock market on this day?

This brief section is only meant as an introduction. We offer more advice on how to understand the share information given in newspapers in a later chapter.

Having introduced the providers of finance and the markets in which they operate we can now return to the businesses that want to use the finance. We are only concerned with companies now: these options are not available to sole traders and partnerships.

3 SOURCES OF CAPITAL FOR LARGE COMPANIES

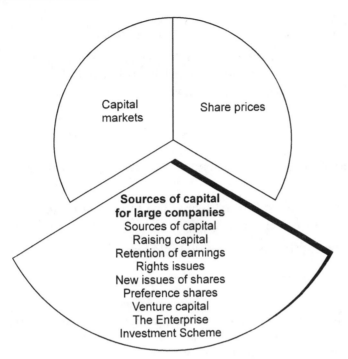

Capital markets

Share prices

Sources of capital for large companies
Sources of capital
Raising capital
Retention of earnings
Rights issues
New issues of shares
Preference shares
Venture capital
The Enterprise
Investment Scheme

3.1 Sources of capital

A company must have capital to carry out its operations. Many companies start in a small way, often as family businesses that operate as a private company, then grow to the point where they become public companies and can invite the public to subscribe for shares. New capital is thus made available which enables the firm to expand its activities and achieve the advantages of large-scale production.

Definitions

A *public company*, or plc, is one that can invite the general public to subscribe for shares. A company has to be fairly large and reasonably well-established for there to be any point in doing this. Examples are Sainsbury, British Airways, Barclays Bank and so on.

A *private company* is prohibited from offering its shares to the general public.

Although nearly all of the biggest and best-known companies are public companies, private companies are far more numerous.

The principal sources of capital for a company are:

(a) *issued share capital*. Share capital is usually in the form of 'ordinary shares' (equity). The ordinary shareholders are the owners of the company;

(b) *retained profits and other reserves*. Retained profits are profits that have been kept within the company, rather than paid out to shareholders as dividends;

(c) *borrowing*

    (i)   from banks (ie bank loans). These were mentioned as a source of credit in the previous chapter.

    (ii) from investors. Investors might purchase 'debt securities' issued by the company. 'Securities' is a general term for any type of investment. Debt securities are 'IOUs', whereby the company promises to repay the debt at a certain date in the future, and until then, pays the investors interest on the debt. Debt capital includes debentures and, for larger companies, eurobonds and commercial paper.

Definitions

Equity means simply the ordinary shares of a company.

Securities is commonly used to mean any sort of investment that can be bought and sold in the financial markets. (Some would object to this definition, but this is how you will find the word used in financial writing.)

Debentures are amounts loaned to a company. Strictly a 'debenture' is a document setting out the terms of a loan but you could buy, say, £10,000 in debentures, this being your portion of a loan of, say, £100m lent collectively by many people. Debentures are usually secured: ie lenders have the right to seize assets if the loan is not repaid.

Bonds are very large fixed interest loans. The term is often used interchangeably with debentures. Commercial paper is just another term for this sort of loan.

Eurobonds are bonds that are bought and sold on an international basis.

Activity 3 [15 minutes]

Spend about five minutes doing this activity as often as you get the opportunity. Skim through the financial pages of a quality newspaper (ideally the 'Companies and Markets' section of the *Financial Times*) and see how many of these terms (or any other new terms you find in this chapter) you can spot.

3.2 Raising capital

If a company wants to raise new capital from sources other than retained profits, it should establish whether it needs long term or short term capital. Short term capital can be obtained either by taking longer to pay suppliers, or by asking the company's bank for a short term loan or bigger overdraft facility.

Raising more long term capital would require the issue of more share capital or more loans. The ability to raise capital by issuing new shares will depend on the status of the company.

A large public limited company is usually in a better position to raise capital than smaller companies, private companies and non-incorporated businesses for the following reasons.

(a) The high standing of such companies makes investors and other creditors more willing to offer finance/credit.

(b) There is a well established 'machinery' for raising capital for plcs quoted on the Stock Exchange. A share issue will be organised for a firm by a merchant bank (known as an issuing house) or similar organisation.

(c) The limited liability of company shareholders usually makes large companies more willing to want to raise capital, in contrast to small company owner-directors, sole traders and partners, who accept greater personal financial risks when they borrow large amounts of capital.

The main source of new *lending* to companies, both long and short term, is the banks. New debenture stock is not often issued by companies to raise new funds because this stock must compete with government loan stock (gilts) to attract investors, and because they are more 'high risk', company debentures must generally offer a higher rate of interest than the interest rate on gilts, which has been very high itself in recent years.

Despite the existence of capital markets, it is not necessarily easy for firms to raise new capital, except by retaining profits. Small firms in particular find it difficult to attract investors, with the banks remaining as the major source of funds for such companies. The capital markets are dominated by institutional investors like pension funds, and these have tended to channel their funds into 'safe' investments such as 'blue chip' stocks and shares which are traded on the Stock Exchange or shares traded on the AIM, as well as government securities.

Factors in the choice of financing method

Several factors will influence the choice of method of raising finance.

(a) *Financial structure.* It is generally considered financially imprudent to have too high a ratio of loan capital to ordinary share capital. A firm in this position ought to seek any extra finance from retained profits or a new issue of ordinary shares.

(b) *The profitability of the company* is obviously important. If the company is making small profits or even losses, it will be unable to raise much or any capital internally. It might also find it difficult to raise new long term funds externally. In such cases, the company might rely heavily on bank lending.

Definition

Profit in simple terms is the excess of income over expenditure. If you buy something for £10 and sell it for £20 you have £10 profit.

In business accounting, profit includes amounts owed by customers and takes into account amounts owed to suppliers. If you buy something with your credit card for £10 and sell it to someone else who gives you an IOU for £20 you have still made a profit of £10 on paper, even though no actual cash has changed hands.

Don't confuse 'profit' with cash.

(c) *The reason for wanting capital.* Capital for financing long term assets should be financed from long term sources, whereas current assets will be financed from a mixture of long term funds and current liabilities.

(d) *A profitable company can raise capital from retained profits*, and most new capital in the UK is currently obtained from this source. However, retaining profits means paying less in dividends and companies must achieve a sound balance between dividends and retained earnings.

(e) When a company wants to take over another, it might be able to pay for the takeover by means of a *share exchange* - issuing more of its own shares and giving these to the shareholders of the target company in exchange for their shares in that company. Companies seeking takeover opportunities commonly use share exchange arrangements in this way to finance their takeovers.

(f) *Interest on loan capital attracts tax relief*, and so there is a good 'cost' reason for seeking to raise long term capital in the form of a loan. However, interest rates on loan capital have been high in the UK for a number of years. Interest rates of gilts have been high, and interest rates on company loan stock would have to be even higher to attract the institutional investors. Rather than compete with the government, companies have tended to borrow from banks, often medium or short term.

(g) International companies have been increasingly attracted in recent years by *borrowing in foreign currency*. Very large companies can borrow long term on the eurobond market.

(h) If *government grants* are available companies will, if feasible, seek to obtain finance from this source, depending on the conditions which must be met for the grant to be obtained.

We will now go on to look at some of the methods of raising finance in more detail, focusing on the implications for the organisation and the advantages and disadvantages of each.

3.3 Retention of earnings

That part of profits which is undistributed (or 'retained') provides a common means of raising funds from shareholders. The funds belong to shareholders and, if not retained, would be distributed as dividends.

Advantages of retained earnings as a form of finance include:

(a) absence of 'brokerage costs' (merchant banks' fees);

(b) simplicity and flexibility;

(c) all gains from investment will still ultimately belong to existing shareholders.

Disadvantages include:

(a) shareholders' expectation of dividends may present a problem;

(b) insufficient earnings may be available.

Activity 4 [15 minutes]

One of the advantages of retained earnings listed above is that 'all gains from investment still ultimately belong to shareholders'. What does this mean?

(Hint. Compare retained earnings with borrowed money.)

3.4 Rights issues

A company which already has a Stock Exchange listing will commonly issue further shares through a rights issue. A rights issue involves the offer of new shares, at a discount below market value, to current shareholders in proportion to their current shareholding.

The shareholder may 'take up' the rights and buy the shares offered at the specified price. Alternatively, he may sell his rights in the markets.

Advantages of a rights issue include the following.

(a) A rights issue is relatively simple and cheap (compared to a new issue of shares).
(b) Shareholders are given some choice.
(c) Large amounts of capital may often be raised.
(d) All gains from any investment will accrue to existing shareholders.

Disadvantages include the following.

(a) A rights issue is not feasible if small amounts of finance are required.

(b) If many shareholders sell their rights, existing shareholders may lose some control over the company.

3.5 New issue of shares

A new issue may be by offer for sale or by a placing.

(a) *Offer for sale*

The company sells shares at a fixed price per share to an issuing house, which sells the shares to the general public at a fixed price through a 'prospectus' (a sort of advertising brochure, but with strict rules about the information that must be given). In an 'offer for sale by tender' the issuing house sets a minimum price and invites bids for the shares at a price of at least that minimum price.

(b) *Placing*

In this case, the issuing house again purchases the shares, and sells them directly to its own clients and not generally to the public. This saves the costs of advertising and producing a prospectus. A placing may be unpopular with existing shareholders if they do not have the right to subscribe, since it involves selling shares at a discount to new shareholders.

Advantages of a new issue include:

(a) suitability for raising large amounts of cash;

(b) avoidance of the need to raise cash from existing shareholders;

(c) reduction of the risk of a future takeover taking place, due to the introduction of new shareholders.

Disadvantages include:

(a) the considerable expenses involved;

(b) difficulty in fixing an issue price, particularly in a volatile market;

(c) unsuitability for small amounts;

(d) dilution of the control of existing shareholders.

3.6 Preference shares

Preference shareholders are entitled to a fixed rate of dividend which is paid before a dividend is paid to ordinary shareholders. (In other words, if there is £100 to distribute and preference shareholders are entitled to £90, ordinary shareholders have to make do with the £10 left over.) Like ordinary dividends, preference dividends can only be paid if there are profits available for distribution. Preference shares do not carry voting rights, so these shareholders do not have a say in the business's activities.

Most ordinary equity shares are *irredeemable*, in that the capital cannot (except in special circumstances involving application to a court to reduce the capital of the company) be repaid to the shareholder. This protects the creditors of the company since it helps to ensure that the company will have sufficient capital to cover any losses. Preference shares are however sometimes issued in *redeemable* form, such that they will be repurchased by the company which issues them at or after a specified date. As with other preference shares, the company may withhold the dividend if profits are insufficient, but in other respects redeemable preference shares are very similar to debentures.

3.7 Venture capital

Venture capital may be available from a number of sources:

(a) clearing bank funds (for example 3i - Investors In Industry);

(b) institutionally-backed funds (for example pension funds);

(c) government-owned funds (for example British Technology Group - BTG);

(d) other funds (for example Innotech; company 'in-house' venture capital units).

Venture capital is capital which is provided for the long term by means of equity investment, sometimes with a loan element as well.

The venture capitalist normally maintains a continuing involvement in the company's business. He is essentially looking for long-term increase in the value of his investment (a capital gain) rather than short-term dividends. Venture capital is often used to finance innovative or 'high-tech' industries, and accordingly the investment carries great risks. If the venture is successful, the venture capitalist may realise his investment through a flotation of the company - the launching of the company on the stock market.

Definitions

A *capital gain* is the increase in value of an investment. If you buy 100 shares in ICI for £700 and sell them for £800 you make a capital gain of £100.

A *flotation* (or 'going public') involves the issue of shares by a new company or a private company for sale to the general public. (So-called 'privatisation' is the same thing really: state-owned businesses are put into the hands of 'private' individuals from the general public.)

3.8   The Enterprise Investment Scheme

The Enterprise Investment Scheme (EIS) which replaced the Business Expansion Scheme is intended to encourage investment in the shares of unquoted companies. When an individual subscribes for eligible shares in a qualifying company, the individual saves income tax at 20% on the amount subscribed up to a limit of £100,000 per individual in one tax year. Capital gains tax reliefs are also available. A limit of £1,000,000 applies per company.

The scheme includes a measure to encourage 'business angels' who introduce finance to small companies by allowing them to become paid directors of the companies they invest in without loss of tax relief.

Activity 5   [15 minutes]

Read the following passage from the *Financial Times* (November 21, 1995) about a company called Cash Converters International (CCI) and answer the questions that follow.

> 'Cash Converters International, the Australia-based retailer, is coming to the Stock Exchange with a value of £23.9m.
>
> Some 34m shares, 34 per cent of the enlarged equity, have been placed at 23.8p, raising £8.1m before expenses. Proceeds will be used to fund expansion which is being concentrated on Europe.
>
> The company has 124 franchised stores, specialising in second-hand goods, in Australia with a further 68 in the UK, France, New Zealand, South Africa and Canada. It is forecasting operating profits of A$1.41m (£670,000) for the 6 months to December 31.
>
> Dealings are expected to start on November 30.'

(a) Suggest 2 ways of classifying the business of CCI.

(b) What is 'equity' and what, in numerical terms, is the 'enlarged equity'?

(c) What does 'placed' mean?

(d) What sort of 'expenses' might there be?

(e) What are 'dealings'?

(f) Why is CCI raising capital?

> ## Chapter roundup
>
> - The Stock Exchange (or for new and small public companies, the Alternative Investment Market) is the main market place for larger businesses. It also enforces rules of conduct and provides a barometer of the country's economy.
> - Individuals invest in the stock market, but the most important participants are the *institutions* such as pension funds, insurance companies and unit trusts.
> - Share prices for the market as a whole are measured by a number of indices, such as the FT Ordinary Share Index, the FT-SE Actuaries All-Share Index and the FT-SE 100.
> - Companies can obtain finance by issuing share capital, by borrowing, by retaining profits or from grants. Various factors, such as financial structure, influence the choice of method of raising finance.
> - Share capital (or equity finance) may be raised by a rights issue, a new issue, by issuing a different type of share such as preference shares, through venture capital providers or through the Enterprise Investment Scheme.

Quick quiz

1 What is the Alternative Investment Market?
2 Give 4 reasons for the importance of the Stock Market.
3 Who are the main providers of capital to the capital markets?
4 Which UK share price index could give you a good idea of the state of the market at, say, 11.42am on a Thursday?
5 What are retained profits?
6 Define the following terms:
   (a) Equity
   (b) Bond
   (c) Securities
   (d) Public company
7 How might a company finance the takeover of another company?
8 What is a rights issue?
9 What is venture capital?
10 What is the intention of the EIS?

Answers to quick quiz

1 See Section 1.1
2 See Section 1.2
3 See Section 1.3
4 The FT-SE 100 (see Section 2.4)
5 Retained profits that have not been paid out to shareholders as dividends
6 (a) to (c)   See Section 3.1
   (d) A company with the right to advertise its shares to the public (see Section 1.1)

7   It may issue more of its shares in exchange for the shares of the company taken over (see Section 3.2).

8   See Section 3.4

9   See Section 3.7

10 See Section 3.8

Answers to activities

1   Share prices respond to:

(a) factors related to the circumstances of individual companies eg news of a company's annual profits, or a proposed takeover bid;

(b) factors related to the circumstances of a particular industry eg increased competition, or new government legislation or regulations for an industry, such as new laws on pollution controls or customer protection measures;

(c) factors related to the circumstances of the national economy eg changes in interest rates, the latest official figures for the balance of trade, or price inflation.

2   (a) Wall Street is the location of the New York Stock Exchange. The Dow Jones Industrial Average is a share price index of 30 shares, the equivalent of the FT Ordinary Share Index (Dow Jones is the publisher of the Wall Street Journal.)

(b) This is an announcement by a company that its profits will be lower than had previously been expected. A profits warning usually results in a drop in a company's share price, because it means that the company is less valuable than was previously thought.

(c) The market reached an all-time high, reflecting a mood of optimism about the future of the economy and business performance. There are some indicators, however, that prices have gone as high as they will for the moment (or that they may begin to fall).

3   This is an on-going exercise. You will probably think that the financial pages are very boring when you first start looking at them. However, it is worth persevering even if you don't understand much at first. With experience, and as you continue reading this book, more and more will become understandable, and you will begin to follow stories from day to day.

4   If money is invested by a company it might make a return of, say, 10%. For example you might buy a machine for £10,000 and use it to make things that you sell for a profit of £1,000 per year. If the money is borrowed this £1,000 is reduced by the interest charge paid to the bank. If retained earnings are used all of the £1,000 is available to be paid out to shareholders.

5   (a) It is a retailer. It is an international organisation based in Australia. It is a franchisor. You may have thought of other classifications.

(b) Equity is another name for ordinary share capital. The 'enlarged equity' must be 100m shares if 34% of it is 34m.

(c) When a company 'places' a new issue of shares it engages an issuing house (probably a merchant bank) which purchases the shares and then sells them directly to its clients. (This is an alternative to offering the newly issued shares to the general public.)

(d) The main expenses will be any fees paid to the merchant bank and to other professionals such as lawyers and accountants.

(e) This means that the shares will start to be bought and sold on the Stock Exchange.

(f) According to the article the purpose is to fund expansion of the business in Europe.

Chapter 3

FINANCE AS A RESOURCE

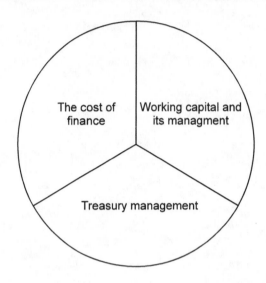

Introduction

You should now have a good idea of where finance comes from so we shall move on to see what a business does with it once it has obtained it.

The essence of management is effective use of *resources*. Resources include things like machines and staff. It is obvious that machines need to be operated properly and maintained if they are going to be used effectively. Likewise people need to be properly instructed and motivated if managers want to get the best out of them.

Money is also a resource, and hopefully personal experience has taught you that there is a need to be careful when using it and that it can be managed effectively.

The need to manage finance arises in business because finance has costs and these should be controlled. We have referred to these costs already in previous chapters and in Section 1 below we expand upon points already made - why a company needs a dividend policy, for example. Then we concentrate upon the day-to-day finance of a business - its working capital - and look in broad terms at how working capital is made up and why it needs to be managed. In the next chapter we go on to look in detail at the management of debtors, stocks and so on.

Your objectives

After completing this chapter you should:

(a) be able to identify the cost of various sources of finance;

(b) be able to explain what is meant by working capital and a business's operating cycle;

(c) understand how a business's working capital requirement can be calculated;

(d) understand and recognise the dangers of over-trading;

(e) be able to describe the functions of a treasury department.

1   THE COST OF FINANCE

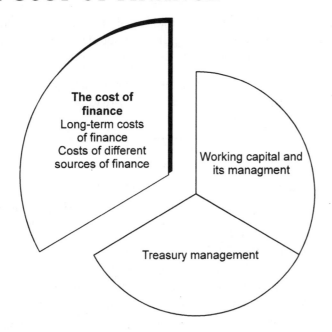

The cost of
finance
Long-term costs
of finance
Costs of different
sources of finance

Working capital and
its managment

Treasury management

1.1   Long-term costs of finance

It is rare for finance to be provided for nothing. Lucky individuals sometimes win large sums in competitions for the price of a postage stamp or a telephone call or a lottery ticket, but businesses do not usually enter competitions of this nature.

Imagine that you spend £1 on a National Lottery ticket and win £9 million. (You possibly imagine this every week in any case!) This will probably be enough to finance the rest of your life. The cost of *obtaining* the finance was £1. But what about the costs of managing such a large sum over the next 50 or more years?

(a) There will be fees to pay to financial consultants, stockbrokers and so on who advise you on how to invest wisely.

(b) There will be fees and commissions to pay to practically any institution you choose to invest the money with.

(c) The winnings are tax-free, but any income generated by investments in the future are not. Even if you have a huge binge and spend £7m in the first week you would still have annual investment income from the remaining £2m of well over £100,000. Your income tax bill would be approximately £40,000 per year! If, in 10 years time, you sell one of your mansions at a profit you would have to pay capital gains tax. Tax is hugely complicated: you would need to pay a tax adviser, too.

For discussion

There are other, non-financial, costs to pay too. The loss of some aspects of your current lifestyle would not be without regret.

Produce a list of things that might change in an individual's life if he or she suddenly had great wealth.

Now see how far this translates into a business context if, say, a small owner-managed company is suddenly transformed into a large plc.

In the two preceding chapters we have already mentioned costs such as interest or dividends that are associated with different methods of obtaining finance. We expand upon this in the next section.

Activity 1 [15 minutes]

Things only get committed to long term memory if you run them through your mind over and over again. A good way of taking the pain out of learning from a book is to use cross-references like the one in the signpost above *proactively*.

Whenever you see such a cross-reference take action! Flick back or forward in the book until you find the passage referred to. Then quickly read or re-read it. This book has a detailed index to help you find topics.

1.2 Costs of different sources of finance

The costs (financial and otherwise) of our 4 basic sources of finance are as follows.

(a) *Share capital* or owners' savings

(i) *Dividends in cash*. If you own say 100 shares in ICI, the company would pay you a dividend of so many pence per share twice a year. If ICI paid a dividend of 20p per share in March and in September the cost of your dividend to the business would be 100 × £0.20 (2 = £40. (If the 100 shares had cost you, say, £800 this is equivalent to an interest rate of £40/£800 = 5%.)

The amount of dividend paid is up to the company's management, within certain legal constraints. However, shareholders usually expect the amount they receive in dividends to *increase* over time and to be reasonably *consistent* from year to year. For some investors dividends are as significant a source of income as a salary is for an employee: for them if a company decides to halve its dividend suddenly it is like telling an employee 'we are going to halve your salary'. The employee would leave as soon as possible, and likewise investors would desert the company. So the company is by no means free to pay whatever dividend it likes.

Dividends also have some quite complicated *tax* implications, both for investors and for companies. These are well beyond the scope of this book.

(ii) *Scrip dividends*. Sometimes, instead of paying out dividends in the form of cash, a company pays them in the form of new shares. These are called scrip dividends.

For example, instead of paying you a £20 dividend ICI might offer you an alternative of 2 new shares in ICI plus £4 in cash. The number of shares would depend on the market value of a share at the time the dividend was decided - in our example we have assumed this was £8.

The advantage is that the company retains far more cash, which it can use to develop the business.

(iii) The cost of providing shareholders or owners with *information* about the performance of the business. This is considerable in the case of a plc: it includes the cost of glossy financial reports, Annual General Meetings at glamorous locations, audit fees and the administrative costs of complying with legal and Stock Exchange requirements for disclosure of information to shareholders.

(iv) If funds are not needed immediately there may be a cost associated with investing them (bank charges, commission, advisers' fees) until they are wanted for use in the operations of the business.

(b) *Borrowed funds*

(i) *Interest* is the main cost. If you take out a loan of £100,000 and pay 10% interest, the cost is £10,000 per year.

The rate of interest may either be fixed or variable. A variable rate is usually the bank 'base rate' (effectively dictated by the government's economic policy) plus an extra amount (a premium) so that the bank makes a profit. For example there may be a base rate of 7% plus a premium of 3% giving the overall rate of 10%. If the base rate rises to 8% the overall rate will rise to 11%.

On the whole businesses prefer fixed rate loans because they then know for certain how much their future costs are going to be.

(ii) There will often be an initial *arrangement fee* to cover the lender's administrative costs on setting up the loan. (Such costs are incurred in checking references, setting up data on a computer system and so on.)

(iii) Factors charge *commission* for advancing funds as well as interest for the period during which a debt remains unpaid.

(iv) Do not forget that the loan itself has to be *repaid*, too. For example a loan of £4,000 over 4 years might have to be repaid at a rate of £250 per quarter.

(v) Financial and non-financial costs arise from the relationship between the borrower and the lender. The lender will require the borrower to provide it with regular *information* about the performance of the business, and this will have a cost as well as creating the uncomfortable feeling of being watched.

The business generally is less in control of its fortunes. If it goes through a bad patch the lender might demand immediate repayment, effectively closing the business down.

Sole traders and partners are often required to put up their personal property as security for a business loan. This puts a good deal of psychological pressure on the borrower and may have damaging effects on their personal life and relationships.

(vi) A useful concept in many circumstances is *opportunity cost*. Instead of paying interest of £10,000 a year the business could do something else with that £10,000 that might help to generate income.

For example, if the company could spend the £10,000 a year on extra advertising this might generate an extra £15,000 of profits. Taking out the loan and paying interest means that the *opportunity* to earn this extra £15,000 is lost. The opportunity cost is £15,000.

As another example, if a loan is secured on the assets of the business, the business has more limited opportunities to do what it likes with its assets, eg sell them.

Definition

The *opportunity cost* of an action is the value of the alternative action which you go without because you do the first action.

Activity 2 [15 minutes]

(a) By taking out a loan of £50,000 a business can buy new machinery which will generate extra profit of £10,000 per year. The interest rate is 10%.

What is the opportunity cost if the business spends £5,000 a year on advertising instead of taking out the loan?

(b) What, if anything, is the opportunity cost of paying a dividend?

(c) *Government grants* may appear to be without cost. However there may well be opportunity costs associated with eligibility for a grant. Being based in a certain region, for example, may deprive a business of certain sales opportunities.

There will also be certain administrative costs to cover *applying* for the grant and (probably) filling in forms on a regular basis to reassure the grant-giving authority that the business is still eligible to receive it.

(d) *Earnings*

(i) A business's sales are only generated by incurring costs such as wages, rent, materials, electricity and so on.

(ii) Businesses have to pay tax on their earnings.

(iii) Dividends are a cost of retained earnings as well as a cost of share capital. If dividends are not paid, shareholders' goodwill will be lost.

(iv) Like capital not needed immediately, retained earnings may be invested in the short term and this will have certain costs.

Activity 3 [15 minutes]

Share capital and retained profits appear to have similar costs. What is the difference between them?

We have mentioned that a certain amount of administration is required to obtain finance in the first place. A good deal more is needed to look after it from day to day when that finance is put to work.

2 WORKING CAPITAL AND ITS MANAGEMENT

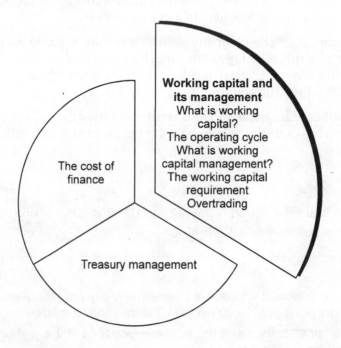

Working capital and its management
What is working capital?
The operating cycle
What is working capital management?
The working capital requirement
Overtrading

The cost of finance

Treasury management

2.1 What is working capital?

The working capital of a business can be defined as its current assets less its current liabilities. Current assets comprise cash, stocks of raw materials, work in progress and finished goods and amounts receivable from debtors. Current liabilities comprise creditors who have to be repaid within 1 year, and may include amounts owed to suppliers of raw materials ('trade creditors'), taxation payable, dividend payments due, short term loans and so on.

Every business needs to be able to maintain day-to-day cash flow. It needs enough to pay wages and salaries as they fall due and enough to pay creditors if it is to keep its workforce and ensure its supplies. Maintaining adequate working capital is not just important in the short term. Sufficient 'liquidity' must be maintained in order to ensure the survival of the business in the long term as well. Even a profitable company may fail if it does not have adequate cash flow to meet its liabilities as they fall due.

Definitions

Current assets are cash, stocks and debtors.

Fixed assets are things, like buildings and machines, that a business intends to keep and use for a long period.

Current liabilities are amounts that must be paid out within 1 year.

Liquid assets are assets that are easily converted into cash. For example Sainsbury's can easily convert packets of washing powder (stock) into cash by selling them. Cash itself is included when measuring the *liquidity* of a business.

A *resource* is a means of doing something. A business's resources are sometimes referred to as the 4 Ms - men, machinery, materials and money. (We should say 'people', not 'men'.)

Cash becomes available and liabilities fall due. Let's consider the pattern of events more formally. All businesses have what is known as an operating cycle.

2.2 The operating cycle

The connection between investment in working capital and cash flow may be illustrated by means of the 'operating cycle'.

The operating cycle may be expressed as a period of time - 40 days, say.

(a) Raw material stocks are obtained from suppliers.

(b) The trade creditors are paid and cash is therefore paid out.

(c) Raw materials are held in stock until they are issued to production (work-in-progress). At this time, additional liabilities (for labour and other expenses) may be incurred.

(d) On completion of production, the finished goods are held in stock until sold, perhaps on credit.

(e) Cash is received when the debt is collected.

(f) The operating cycle is the period between the payment of cash to creditors (cash out) and the receipt of cash from debtors (cash in).

If it takes longer to turn stocks and debtors into cash, or the payment period to creditors shortens:

(a) the operating cycle will lengthen;

(b) the investment in working capital will increase.

A business needs to make decisions about how much stock to hold, how soon to pay creditors, how long to wait until debtors are chased for payment and so on. Let's look at some factors that influence these decisions.

2.3   What is working capital management?

Ensuring that sufficient liquid resources are maintained is a matter of working capital management. This involves achieving a balance between the requirement to minimise the risk of not having enough cash to pay creditors and the requirement to maximise the earnings made by using assets. An excessively conservative approach to working capital management resulting in high levels of cash holdings will harm profits because the opportunity to make a return on the assets tied up as cash will have been missed. For example more stock could have been bought and sold.

The volume of *current assets* required will depend on the nature of the company's business. For example, a manufacturing company may require more stocks than a company in a service industry. As the volume of output by a company increases, the volume of current assets required will also increase.

Even assuming efficient stock holding, debt collection procedures and cash management, there is still a certain degree of choice in the total volume of current assets required to meet output requirements. Policies of low stock-holding levels, tight credit and minimum cash holdings may be contrasted with policies of high stocks (to allow for safety or buffer stocks) easier credit and sizeable cash holdings (for precautionary reasons).

Current liabilities are often a cheap method of finance (suppliers' invoices, or trade creditors, do not usually carry an interest cost) and companies may therefore consider that, in the interest of higher profits, it is worth increasing current liabilities, taking the maximum credit possible from suppliers.

For discussion

Make a list of the different types of business that you and your colleagues work in or know of - banks, supermarkets, toy-makers, building firms or whatever.

How do the different types vary in their need to hold stocks? What are stocks in each case?

The operating cycle and working capital management will be clearer if we look at a numerical example. Take some time over the next passage to make sure that you understand the logic of it and where the numbers are coming from.

2.4   The working capital requirement

Computing the working capital requirement is a matter of calculating the value of current assets less current liabilities, perhaps by taking averages over a 1 year period. First we need to introduce a few new terms.

Definitions

Turnover is just another word for sales.

Raw materials are things that are processed to make the finished product. For example steel is a raw material used to make cars.

Overheads are expenses on things not used directly in the production of the finished item, for example factory rental or the cost of lighting a factory.

Some overheads change depending on how much is produced - for example if the factory is running for longer it will need to be lit for longer. These are called *variable overheads*.

Other overheads do not change no matter how much is produced. For example factory rent has to be paid whether the factory runs for 8 hours or 24 hours a day. These are called *fixed overheads*.

WORKED EXAMPLE: WORKING CAPITAL

The following data relate to Corn Ltd, a manufacturing company.

Turnover for the year	£1,500,000
Costs as percentages of sales	%
Materials	30
Labour	25
Variable overheads (eg lighting)	10
Fixed overheads (eg rent)	15
Selling and distribution costs	5

The operating cycle is as follows, on average.

(a) Debtors take 2.5 months before payment
(b) Raw materials are in stock for 3 months
(c) Work-in-progress represents 2 months worth of half produced goods
(d) Finished goods represents 1 month's production
(e) Credit is taken as follows:

Materials	2 months
Labour	1 week
Variable overheads	1 month
Fixed overheads	1 month
Selling and distribution	0.5 months

Work-in-progress and finished goods are valued at material, labour and variable expense cost. What is Corn Ltd's working capital requirement?

Solution

The working capital requirement of Corn Ltd (assuming the labour force is paid for 50 working weeks a year) can be computed as shown below.

(a) The annual costs incurred will be as follows.

		£
Materials	30% of £1,500,000	450,000
Labour	25% of £1,500,000	375,000
Variable overheads	10% of £1,500,000	150,000
Fixed overheads	15% of £1,500,000	225,000
Selling and distribution	5% of £1,500,000	75,000

(b) The average value of current assets will be as follows.

		£	£
Raw materials	3/12 450,000		112,500
Work-in-progress			
Materials (50% complete)	1/12 450,000	37,500	
Labour (50% complete)	1/12 375,000	31,250	
Variable overheads (50% complete)	1/12 150,000	12,500	
			81,250
Finished goods			
Materials	1/12 450,000	37,500	
Labour	1/12 375,000	31,250	
Variable overheads	1/12 150,000	12,500	
			81,250
Debtors	2.5/12 1,500,000		312,500
			587,500

(c) Average value of current liabilities will be as follows.

Materials	2/12 450,000	75,000	
Labour - 50 weeks	1/50 375,000	7,500	
Variable overheads	1/12 150,000	12,500	
Fixed overheads	1/12 225,000	18,750	
Selling and distribution	0.5/12 75,000	3,125	
			116,875

(d) Working capital required (£(587,500 – 116,875)) =   470,625

Activity 4   [15 minutes]

What would Corn Ltd's working capital requirement be if debtors took only 1 month before payment and finished goods stock were increased to 2 month's production? Do your own calculations then see if you agree with a colleague.

Many businesses fail because they do not have a proper understanding of their working capital requirements, or do not keep proper control over their requirements. This can happen even if, on the face of it, the business is doing very well. Unfortunately it is possible for a business to do too well: this is called over-trading.

2.5   Overtrading

Overtrading happens when a business tries to do too much too quickly with too little long term capital, so that it is trying to support too large a volume of trade with the capital resources at its disposal.

Even if an overtrading business operates at a profit, it could easily run into serious trouble because it is short of money. Such liquidity troubles stem from the fact that it does not have enough capital to provide the cash to pay its debts as they fall due.

Other causes of overtrading are as follows.

(a) When a business repays a loan, it often replaces the old loan with a new one. However a business might repay a loan without replacing it, with the consequence that it has less long term capital to finance its current level of operations.

(b) A business might be profitable, but in a period of inflation, its retained profits might be insufficient to pay for replacement fixed assets and stocks, which now cost more because of inflation. The business would then rely increasingly on credit, and eventually find itself unable to support its current volume of trading with a capital base that has fallen in real terms.

Symptoms of overtrading are as follows.

(a) There is a rapid increase in turnover.

(b) There is a rapid increase in the volume of current assets and possibly also fixed assets. The rate at which stock and debtors are turned into cash might slow down, in which case the rate of increase in stocks and debtors would be even greater than the rate of increase in sales.

(c) There is only a small increase in proprietors' capital (perhaps through retained profits). Most of the increase in assets is financed by credit, especially:

   (i) trade creditors. The payment period to creditors is likely to lengthen;

   (ii) a bank overdraft, which often reaches or even exceeds the limit of the facilities agreed by the bank.

In the next chapter we are going to look in detail at the management of the various components of working capital. We conclude with a few brief words about managing large volumes of cash. The details of treasury management are very complicated - well beyond the scope of this book - but you should know that treasury management exists in large organisations.

3   TREASURY MANAGEMENT

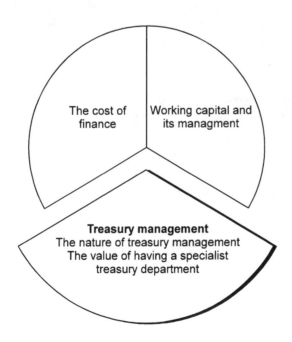

3.1 The nature of treasury management

Large companies rely heavily on the financial and currency markets. These markets are volatile, with interest rates and foreign exchange rates changing continually and by significant amounts. To manage cash and currency efficiently, many large companies have set up a separate treasury department.

A treasury department, even in a very large organisation, is likely to be quite small, with perhaps a staff of 3 to 6 qualified accountants, bankers or corporate treasurers working under the treasurer. In some cases, where the company or organisation handles very large amounts of cash or foreign currency dealings, and often has large cash surpluses, the treasury department might be a little bigger.

3.2 The value of having a specialist treasury department

The following are advantages of having a centralised specialist treasury department.

(a) Centralised management:
   (i) avoids having a mix of cash surpluses and overdrafts in different localised bank accounts;
   (ii) facilitates bulk cash flows, so that lower bank charges can be negotiated.

(b) Larger volumes of cash are available to invest, giving better short term investment opportunities.

(c) Any borrowing can be arranged in bulk, at lower interest rates than for smaller borrowings, and perhaps on the eurocurrency or eurobond markets.

(d) A specialist treasury department will employ experts with knowledge of dealing in forward contracts, futures, options, eurocurrency markets, swaps and so on. (These are all methods of minimising the risk of losses because of interest rate changes or changes in exchange rates.) Localised departments could not have such expertise.

Activity 5 [15 minutes]

(a) ABC plc sells £10,000 worth of goods to a customer in France. The exchange rate is 10 francs to the pound, so ABC sends an invoice for 100,000 francs. One month later the customer pays the invoice. By this time the exchange rate is 11 francs to the pound.

How much does ABC plc receive, in pounds?

(b) ABC plc buys 50,000 French francs worth of materials from a supplier in France and receives an invoice for 50,000 French francs. The exchange rate is 10 francs to the pound.

ABC plc pays the invoice 1 month later. By this time the exchange rate is 9 francs to the pound.

(i) How much would ABC plc have paid out, in pounds, if it had paid the invoice upon receipt?

(ii) How much did ABC plc actually pay, in pounds?

For discussion

In the light of Activity 5, and taking your personal views into account, discuss the pros and cons of European Monetary Union.

Chapter roundup

- Finance cannot be obtained without incurring costs of some description. Besides interest and dividends there are arrangement fees and commissions, the costs of information provision, opportunity costs, and non-financial costs such as loss of control.

- Part of the finance raised is invested in working capital: cash, stocks and debtors less short term creditors. The relationship between the components is reflected in the business's operating cycle.

- Working capital management involves achieving a balance between the risk of having too little cash to pay debts and having too much cash that is not earning profits. Different types of business have different working capital requirements.

- If a business does not control its working capital needs it runs the risk of over-trading not having enough cash to pay debts as they fall due because it is trying to do too much too quickly or with an inadequate capital base.

- Large businesses with substantial cash flows often have a specialised treasury department to manage short and long term investment, foreign currency risks and so on.

Quick quiz

1   What expectations do shareholders have about dividends?
2   What is a scrip dividend?
3   Why do businesses prefer fixed rate loans?
4   What is an opportunity cost?
5   Define working capital.
6   What does 'liquidity' mean?
7   What are the symptoms of overtrading?
8   What are the advantages of having a specialist treasury department?
9   What is the operating cycle?
10 What are fixed assets?

Answers to quick quiz

1   To be paid consistently; to increase over time
2   A dividend paid in the form of additional shares rather than cash
3   They know for certain their future interest costs
4   The value of an alternative action foregone
5   See Section 2.1
6   The degree of ease or difficulty a business has in paying its creditors on time.
7   See Section 2.5
8   See Section 3.2
9   See Section 2.2
10 See Section 2.1

Answers to activities

1 There is no solution, but don't forget that it is a good habit to learn proactively by looking backwards and forwards through anything you are reading.

2 (a) The opportunity cost is the £10,000 extra profit that would be earned if the machinery were bought.

(b) The opportunity cost is the profit that could be earned if the dividend money were invested in business activities.

3 Share capital is money from a source *external* to the business. Retained profits is money generated *within* the business. Both would be repaid to the shareholders if the business were to close down, but only after all creditors had been paid.

4

	£	£
Original working capital requirement		470,625
Original debtors	312,500	
Revised debtors (1/12 × 1,500,000)	125,000	
Decrease		(187,500)
Original finished goods stock (1 month)	81,250	
Revised finished goods stock (2 months)	162,500	
Increase		81,250
Revised working capital requirement		364,375

5 (a) FFr 100,000 ÷11   = £9,090

  (b) (i) FFr 50,000 ÷10   = £5,000

      (ii) FFr 50,000 ÷9   = £5,555

ABC plc has lost out on each foreign exchange transaction. It might equally have gained if the exchange rate movements had been different. Hence the need for treasury management in companies that engage in a great deal of foreign transactions.

Assignment 3   [1½ hours]

There is no new Chapter 3 Assignment!

Instead, a progress check on your Chapter 2 (public company) assignment.

Have you obtained an annual report and accounts yet?

Have you started checking the weekly share price?

Have you spotted any press articles?

If the answer to any of these is 'Not yet', get moving!

Chapter 4

MANAGING DEBTORS, CREDITORS, STOCKS AND CASH

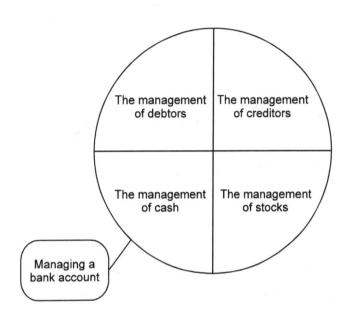

Introduction

In this chapter we are going to look in more detail at the components of working capital and think about the choices available to managers to ensure that working capital is used as effectively as possible.

For example, how much time should customers be allowed before they are expected to pay for their goods? If a supplier offers a discount for payment within the week is it worth taking that discount? You perhaps make decisions of this sort in your personal finances - should you pay off the whole of your credit card bill, say, or just the minimum amount? Should you pay the phone bill as soon as it arrives (and so go overdrawn at the bank) or should you wait for the red final demand (by which time your salary will have been paid into the bank)?

In a business, decisions of this nature can have a major impact on the amount of working capital required.

Your objectives

After completing this chapter you should:

(a) be able to identify factors that influence a business's policies for granting credit and collecting debts;

(b) be able to describe procedures for debt collection and credit control;

(c) understand the use of trade credit as a source of finance;

(d) understand the costs of holding stock and methods to minimise such costs;

(e) recognise the situations in which cash flow problems may arise;

(f) be able to suggest methods of easing cash shortages;

(g) understand the usefulness of cash budgets for monitoring cash flow and be able to prepare a simple cash budget;

(h) be able to describe some services and techniques for managing cash in the bank.

1 THE MANAGEMENT OF DEBTORS

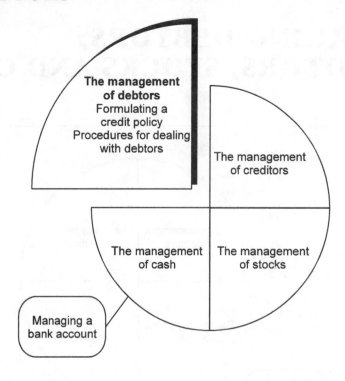

1.1 Formulating a credit policy

Several factors should be considered by management when a policy for managing debtors is formulated. These include:

(a) the administrative costs of debt collection;

(b) the procedures for controlling credit granted to individual customers and for debt collection;

(c) the cost of the additional finance required for any increase in the volume of debtors (or the savings from a reduction in debtors). As we saw in the previous chapter this cost might be for bank overdraft interest, or the cost of long term funds (such as loan stock or equity);

(d) any savings or additional expenses in operating the credit policy (for example the extra work involved in pursuing slow payers);

(e) the ways in which the credit policy could be implemented. For example:

   (i) credit could be eased by giving debtors a longer period in which to settle their accounts. The cost would be the resulting increase in average debtors;

   (ii) a discount could be offered for early payment. The cost would be the amount of the discounts taken;

(f) the effects of easing credit, which might be:

   (i) to encourage a higher proportion of 'bad' debts (debts that are never repaid);

   (ii) an increase in sales volume.

Provided that the extra profit from the increase in sales exceeds the increase in expenses, bad debts, discounts and the finance cost of an increase in working capital, a policy to relax credit terms would be worthwhile.

Definitions

A *bad debt* is a debt that is never repaid. This happens quite a lot in business, unfortunately. For example X Ltd might buy something on credit from your firm but soon afterwards goes out of business owing far more to all its suppliers than there is cash or assets available to repay the debts. The debt to you would never be recovered.

Trade debtors are people who owe you money because they have bought products or services from your business. (Non-trade debtors ('other debtors') are people who owe you money for other reasons: for example you may have earned 70 days interest on a bank deposit but not yet have received the money because it is only paid every 3 months.)

Trade creditors are people you owe money to because you have bought things from them that go into making your product or service. (Other creditors include employees, the tax man, the landlord for rent and so on.)

Activity 1 [15 minutes]

Think about debts that you owe such as your phone bill or electricity bill. How do the companies concerned try to encourage you to pay your debt?

The main areas which ought to be considered in connection with the control of debtors are:

(a) paperwork;

(b) debt collection policy;

(c) discount policy;

(d) credit control;

(e) credit insurance;

We shall have a brief look at each of these areas in turn.

1.2 Procedures for dealing with debtors

Sales paperwork should be dealt with promptly and accurately.

(a) Invoices should be sent out upon or immediately after delivery.

(b) Checks should be carried out to ensure that invoices are accurate.

(c) The investigation of customers' queries and complaints should be carried out promptly.

(d) Monthly statements should be issued promptly so that all items on the statement might then be included in customers' monthly settlements of bills.

The debt collection policy

The overall debt collection policy of the firm should be such that the administrative costs and other costs incurred in debt collection do not exceed the benefits from incurring those costs.

Some extra spending on debt collection procedures might:

(a) reduce bad debt losses;

(b) reduce the average collection period, and therefore the cost of the investment in debtors.

Beyond a certain level of spending, however, additional expenditure on debt collection would not have enough effect on bad debts or on the average collection period to justify the extra administrative costs.

For example, suppose that a company is considering whether its current policy should be discarded in favour of Option 1 or Option 2?

	Current policy	Option 1	Option 2
Annual expenditure on debt collection procedures	£240,000	£300,000	£400,000
Bad debt losses (% of sales)	3%	2%	1%
Average collection period	2 months	1.5 months	1 month

Current sales are £4,800,000 a year, and the cost of obtaining finance for working capital works out at around 15%.

	Current policy £	Option 1 £	Option 2 £
Average debtors (£4,800,000 ÷ 2/12, etc)	800,000	600,000	400,000
Reduction in working capital	-	200,000	400,000
(a) Interest saving (15% of reduction)	-	30,000	60,000
Bad debt losses (sales value)	144,000	96,000	48,000
(b) Reduction in losses	-	48,000	96,000
Benefits of each option (a) + (b)		78,000	156,000
Extra costs of debt collection		60,000	160,000
Benefit/(loss) from option		18,000	(4,000)

Option 1 is preferable to the current policy because the benefits exceed the costs. Option 2 is worse than the current policy.

Activity 2   [15 minutes]

(a) If debtors take an average of 10 days to pay and total sales for a year are £500,000, what is the average amount of debtors?

(b) If the average debtors total is £140,000 and sales for the year total £2,800,000 what is the average collection period (in days)?

Discount policies

A discount may be allowed for early payment of debts. Such an incentive:

(a) affects the average collection period;

(b) affects the volume of demand (and possibly, therefore, indirectly affects bad debt losses).

To see whether the offer of a discount for early payment is financially worthwhile we must compare the cost of the discount with the benefit of a reduced investment in debtors.

For example, based on past experience a company might predict that if a 2% early payment discount is offered, 50% of customers will take advantage of it. If annual sales are £1m the cost of the discount will be 2% (50% (£1m = £10,000. The saving from reduced working capital needs (since debtors are paying up more quickly) might be £12,000. It would therefore be worthwhile to offer the discount.

Credit control

Credit control involves the initial investigation of potential credit customers and the continuing control of outstanding accounts.

The main points to note are as follows.

(a) New customers should give two good references, including one from a bank, before being granted credit.

(b) Creditworthiness can be checked through a credit rating agency such as Dun and Bradstreet.

(c) A new customer's credit limit should be fixed at a low level and only increased if his payment record subsequently warrants it.

(d) For large value customers, a file should be maintained of any available financial information about the customer. This file should be reviewed regularly. Information is available from:

    (i) an analysis of the company's annual report and accounts;

    (ii) Extel cards (sheets of accounting information about public companies in the UK, and also major overseas companies, produced by Extel).

(e) Government bodies such as the Department of Trade and Industry and the Export Credit Guarantee Department will be able to advise on overseas companies.

(f) Press comments may give information about what a company is currently doing (as opposed to the historical results in Extel cards or published accounts which only show what the company has done in the past).

(g) The company could send a member of staff to visit the company concerned, to get a first-hand impression of the company and its prospects. This would be advisable in the case of a prospective major customer.

(h) Aged lists of debts should be produced and reviewed at regular intervals. An 'aged list' shows how long each debt has been outstanding.

(i) The credit limit for an existing customer should be periodically reviewed, but it should only be raised if the customer's credit standing is good.

(j) It is essential to have procedures which ensure that further orders are not accepted from nor goods sent to a customer who is in difficulties. If a customer has exceeded his credit limit, or has not paid debts despite several reminders, or is otherwise known to be in difficulties, sales staff and warehouse staff must be notified immediately (and not, for example, at the end of the week, by which time more goods might have been supplied).

An organisation might devise a credit-rating system for new individual customers that is based on characteristics of the customer (such as whether the customer is a home owner, and the customer's age and occupation). Points would be awarded according to the characteristics of the customer, and the amount of credit that is offered would depend on his or her credit score.

Activity 3 [15 minutes]

Design a credit application form appropriate for the credit customers of a grocery wholesaler.

For discussion

(a) A moral dilemma: if you owed a company £2,000 but you knew it was about to go out of business and that you would not be chased for the debt by the receivers for at least a year, would you pay now or wait? Assume that you have the £2,000 available now.

(b) Large organisations (especially local authorities) are notoriously slow at paying the debts they owe to small suppliers. These organisations know that their small suppliers need them more than they need the supplier. Many failed businesses claim that this is one of the main reasons why they could not survive they could not collect debts owed to them quickly enough to pay their own suppliers.

Suggest what could be done to help small businesses in this respect. Think about things like possible government measures, whether a factoring service would be available to a very small company (see Chapter 1) and what the company could do to help itself.

Credit insurance

Companies might be able to obtain insurance against certain debts going bad through a specialist 'credit insurance' firm. A company cannot insure against all its bad debt losses, but may be able to insure against losses above the normal level.

When a company arranges credit insurance, it must submit specific proposals for credit to the insurance company, stating the name of each customer to which it wants to give credit and the amount of credit it wants to give. The insurance company will accept, amend or refuse these proposals, depending on its assessment of each of these customers.

Credit insurance is normally available for only up to about 75% of a company's potential bad debt loss. The remaining 25% of any bad debt costs are borne by the company itself. This is to ensure that the company does not become slack with its credit control and debt collection procedures, for example by indulging in overtrading and not chasing slow payers hard enough.

Don't forget factoring and invoice discounting as a means of getting early payment from debtors. Go back to Chapter 1 if you need a refresher. We now turn to creditors.

2   THE MANAGEMENT OF CREDITORS

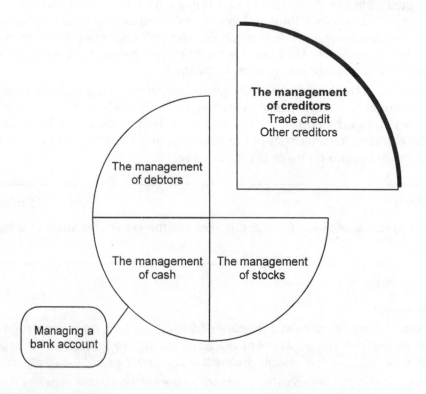

2.1   Trade credit

Taking credit from suppliers is a normal feature of business. Nearly every company has some trade creditors waiting for payment.

The management of trade creditors involves:

(a) attempting to obtain satisfactory credit from suppliers;

(b) attempting to extend credit during periods of cash shortage;

(c) maintaining good relations with regular and important suppliers.

Activity 4   [5 minutes]

What might your firm have to do to obtain credit from a supplier?

(You may like to look back at the section on credit control to give you some ideas.)

Trade credit is a source of short term finance because it helps to keep working capital down. It is usually a cheap source of finance, since suppliers rarely charge interest. However, trade credit *will* have a cost, whenever a company is offered a discount for early payment, but opts instead to take longer credit.

For example, suppose that X Ltd has been offered credit terms from its major supplier of '2/10, net 45'. That is, a cash discount of 2% will be given if payment is made within 10 days of the invoice, and payments *must* be made within 45 days of the invoice.

The company has the choice of paying 98p per £1 on day 10 (to pay before day 10 would be unnecessary), or to invest the 98p for an additional 35 days and eventually pay the supplier £1 per £1. The decision as to whether the discount should be accepted depends on the opportunity cost of investing 98p for 35 days. What should the company do?

Suppose that X Ltd can invest cash to obtain an annual return of 25%, and that there is an invoice from the supplier for £1,000. The two alternatives are as follows.

	Refuse discount £	*Accept discount* £
Payment to supplier	1,000.0	980
Return from investing £980 between day 10 and day 45:		
£980 × 35/365 × 25%	23.5	
Net cost	976.5	980

It is cheaper to refuse the discount because the investment rate of return on cash retained, in this example, exceeds the saving from the discount.

Although a company may delay payment beyond the final due date, thereby obtaining even longer credit from its suppliers, such a policy would be inadvisable (except where an unexpected short-term cash shortage has arisen). Unacceptable delays in payment will worsen the company's credit rating, and additional credit may become difficult to obtain.

So, managing creditors involves many of the same considerations as managing debtors. The important exceptions are mentioned next.

2.2 Other creditors

There is usually less scope for flexibility with other types of short term creditors. Things like rent and tax and dividends have to be paid out in full on certain specific dates. For example:

(a) rent is usually payable on the quarter days 25 March, 24 June, 29 September and 25 December;

(b) corporation tax has to be paid 9 months after the end of a company's accounting year;

(c) employees expect to be paid regularly, usually just before the end of every calendar month;

(d) income tax collected from employees has to be paid over to the Inland Revenue by 19th of every month;

(e) VAT collected by a business has to be paid over every 3 months.

'Management' in such cases is a matter of ensuring that what is due gets paid on time and that the finance is available when needed. This is especially important with tax because the fines for late payment can be very heavy. Because payment dates are known in advance it is possible to plan ahead: this is what *cash budgeting* is all about, and we shall return to this topic later in this chapter.

3   THE MANAGEMENT OF STOCKS

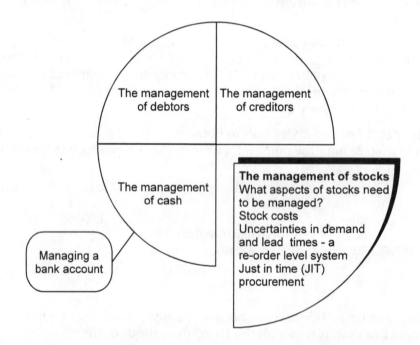

3.1   What aspects of stock need to be managed?

Almost every company carries stocks of some sort, even if they are only stocks of consumables such as stationery. For a manufacturing business, stocks (sometimes called inventories), in the form of raw materials, work in progress and finished goods, may amount to a substantial proportion of the total assets of the business.

Some businesses attempt to control stocks on a scientific basis by balancing the costs of stock shortages against those of stock holding.

The control of stocks from a financial point of view may be analysed into three parts.

(a) The economic order quantity (EOQ) model can be used to decide the optimum order size for stocks which will minimise the costs of ordering stocks plus stockholding costs.

(b) If discounts for bulk purchases are available, it may be cheaper to buy stocks in large order sizes so as to obtain the discounts.

(c) Uncertainty in the demand for stocks and/or the supply lead time may lead a company to decide to hold buffer stocks (thereby increasing its investment in working capital) in order to reduce or eliminate the risk of 'stock-outs' (running out of stock).

Definition

Lead time is the time between starting something and finishing it. Thus supply lead time is the time between placing an order for an item and actually receiving it. Production lead time is the time between starting to make something and completing it.

It may not have occurred to you in the past that it actually costs money for, say, Sainsbury's to have a shelf full of washing powder. Before we look at the EOQ model and so on it will be useful to have a better idea of what the costs of having stock are.

3.2 Stock costs

Stock costs can be conveniently classified into 4 groups.

(a) *Holding costs* comprise the cost of capital tied up, warehousing and handling costs, deterioration, obsolescence, insurance and pilferage.

(b) *Procuring costs* depend on how the stock is obtained but will consist of ordering costs for goods purchased externally, such as clerical costs, telephone charges and delivery costs.

(c) *Shortage costs* may be:

   (i) the loss of a sale and the profit which could have been earned from the sale;

   (ii) the extra cost of having to buy an emergency supply of stocks at a high price;

   (iii) the cost of lost production and sales, where the stock-out brings an entire process to a halt.

(d) *The cost of the stock itself*, the supplier's price or the direct cost per unit of production, will also need to be considered when the supplier offers a discount on orders for purchases in bulk.

Small businesses mainly use trial and error and past experience to decide how much stock to hold, but a more scientific approach is needed when there is a large investment in stock. The EOQ model is one such approach.

3.3 The EOQ formula

The economic order quantity (EOQ) is the optimal ordering quantity for an item of stock which will minimise costs.

The EOQ can be calculated using a mathematical formula, the details of which is beyond the scope of your studies. In its simplest form we assume that:

(a) demand is constant;

(b) the lead time is constant or zero;

(c) purchase costs per unit are constant (ie no bulk discounts).

For example, suppose the demand for a commodity is 40,000 units a year, at a steady rate. It costs £20 to place an order, and 40p to hold a unit for a year. We want to find the order size to minimise stock costs, the number of orders placed each year, and the length of the stock cycle. The EOQ will tell us to order 2,000 units each time, so there will be 40,000/2,000 = 20 orders placed each year. This means that the stock cycle is once every 52÷20 = 2.6 weeks. Total costs will be (20×£20) for ordering, plus £800 a year stock holding costs (2,000/2 = 1,000 units on average held, at 40p a unit).

This approach can be modified to take account of discounts for bulk purchases. So long as you understand the basic principle, however, there is no need for us to go into further detail.

You must have had personal experience of trying to buy an item only to find that the shop has none left. How can this be avoided?

3.4 Uncertainties in demand and lead times: a re-order level system

When the volume of demand is uncertain, or the supply lead time is variable, there are problems in deciding what the re-order level should be. By holding a 'safety stock', a company can reduce the likelihood that stocks run out during the re-order period (due to high demand or a long lead time before the new supply is delivered). The average annual cost of such a safety stock would be:

Quantity of safety stock × Stock holding cost
(in units) per unit per annum

Because stock can be a major investment, and because these days many items tend to be at least partly tailor-made to customer requirements rather than standard models, some new ideas about managing stock have become popular. JIT is the best-known of these ideas.

3.5 Just-in-time (JIT) procurement

In recent years, there have been developments in the inventory policy of some manufacturing companies which have sought to reduce their stocks of raw materials and components to as low a level as possible. This approach differs from other models, such as the EOQ model, which seek to minimise *costs* rather than inventory levels.

Just-in-time procurement and stockless production are terms which describe a policy of obtaining goods from suppliers at the latest possible time (ie when they are needed) and so avoiding the need to carry any materials or components stock.

Reduced stock levels mean that a lower level of investment in working capital will be required.

JIT will not be appropriate in some cases. For example, a restaurant might find it preferable to use the traditional economic order quantity approach for staple non-perishable food stocks but adopt JIT for perishable and 'exotic' items. In a hospital, a stock-out could quite literally be fatal and JIT would be quite unsuitable.

A system of just-in-time procurement depends for its success on a smooth and predictable production flow, and so a JIT policy must also be aimed at improving production systems, eliminating waste (rejects and reworked items), avoiding production bottlenecks and so on. Successful JIT also requires a very close mutually beneficial, working relationship with suppliers.

JIT is often associated with *Total Quality Management,* the basic principle of which is that the cost of preventing mistakes is less than the cost of correcting them once they occur (plus the cost of lost potential for future sales). The aim should therefore be to get things right first time consistently.

For discussion

JIT has complications for a business's suppliers. Not long ago in Japan the main suppliers to a particular industry decided to stop supplying on a JIT basis. Why do you think they might have done this?

4   THE MANAGEMENT OF CASH

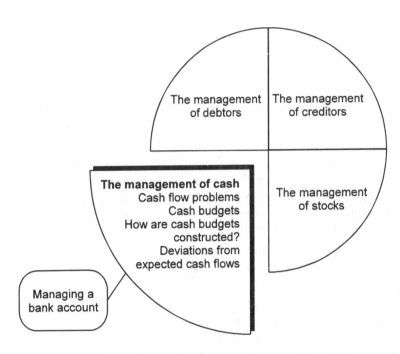

How much cash should a company keep on hand? The more cash which is on hand, the easier it will be for the company to meet its bills as they fall due and to take advantage of discounts. However, holding cash or near equivalents to cash has a cost - the loss of earnings which would otherwise have been obtained by using the funds in another way. The financial manager must try to balance liquidity with profitability.

4.1   Cash flow problems

In the previous chapter, we introduced the operating cycle, which connects investment in working capital with cash flows. Cash flow problems can arise in several ways.

(a) *Making losses.* If a business is continually making losses, it will eventually have cash flow problems.

(b) *Inflation.* In a period of inflation, a business needs ever-increasing amounts of cash just to replace used-up and worn-out assets. A business can be making a profit in accounting terms, but still not be receiving enough cash to buy the replacement assets it needs.

(c) *Growth.* When a business is growing, it needs to acquire more fixed assets, and to support higher amounts of stocks and debtors. These additional assets must be paid for somehow (or financed by creditors).

(d) *Seasonal business.* When a business has seasonal sales, it may have cash flow difficulties at certain times of the year, when cash inflows are low, but cash outflows are high, perhaps because the business is building up its stocks for the next period of high sales.

(e) *One-off items of expenditure.* There might occasionally be a single non-recurring item of expenditure that creates a cash flow problem, such as:

(i) the repayment of loan capital for, say, a 10 year £100,000 loan only repayable in full at the end of 10 years. Businesses often try to finance such loan repayments by borrowing again;

(ii) the purchase of an exceptionally expensive item. For example, a small or medium-sized business might decide to buy a freehold property which then stretches its cash resources for several months or even years.

Methods of easing cash shortages

The steps that are usually taken by a company when a need for cash arises, and when it cannot obtain resources from any other source such as a loan or an increased overdraft, are as follows.

(a) *Postponing capital expenditure*

Some capital expenditure items (ie fixed assets) are more important and urgent than others.

(i) It might be imprudent to postpone expenditure on fixed assets which are needed for the development and growth of the business.

(ii) On the other hand, some capital expenditures are routine and might be postponable without serious consequences. The routine replacement of motor vehicles is an example. If a company's policy is to replace company cars every two years, but the company is facing a cash shortage, it might decide to replace cars every three years.

(b) *Accelerating cash inflows which would otherwise be expected in a later period*

The most obvious way of bringing forward cash inflows would be to press debtors for earlier payment. Often, this policy will result in a loss of goodwill and problems with customers. There will also be very little scope for speeding up payments when the credit period currently allowed to debtors is no more than the norm for the industry. It might be possible to encourage debtors to pay more quickly by offering discounts for earlier payment.

(c) *Reversing past investment decisions by selling assets previously acquired*

Some assets are less crucial to a business than others and so if cash flow problems are severe, the option of selling investments or property might have to be considered.

(d) *Negotiating a reduction in cash outflows*, so as to postpone or even reduce payments

There are several ways in which this could be done.

(i) Longer credit might be taken from suppliers. However, if the credit period allowed is already generous, creditors might be very reluctant to extend credit even further and any such extension of credit would have to be negotiated carefully. There would be a serious risk of having further supplies refused.

(ii) Loan repayments could be rescheduled by agreement with a bank.

(iii) A deferral of the payment of corporation tax could be agreed with the Inland Revenue. Corporation tax is payable 9 months after a company's year end, but it might be possible to arrange a postponement by a few months. When this happens, the Inland Revenue will charge interest on the outstanding amount of tax.

(iv) Dividend payments could be reduced. Dividend payments are discretionary cash outflows, although a company's directors might be constrained by shareholders' expectations, so that they feel obliged to pay dividends even when there is a cash shortage.

None of these things can be done overnight, especially if it is necessary to sell things or hold negotiations. For these measures to be effective the business needs to know in advance when it is likely to be short of cash: it needs to prepare a cash budget.

4.2 Cash budgets

A cash budget is a statement in which estimated future cash receipts and payments are tabulated in such a way as to show the forecast cash balance of a business at defined intervals. For example, in December 1996 an accounts department might wish to estimate the cash position of the business during the three following months, January to March 1997. A cash budget might be drawn up in the following format.

	Jan £	Feb £	Mar £
Estimated cash receipts			
From credit customers	14,000	16,500	17,000
From cash sales	3,000	4,000	4,500
Proceeds on disposal of fixed assets		2,200	
Total cash receipts	17,000	22,700	21,500
Estimated cash payments			
To suppliers of goods	8,000	7,800	10,500
To employees (wages)	3,000	3,500	3,500
Purchase of fixed assets		16,000	
Rent and rates			1,000
Other overheads	1,200	1,200	1,200
Repayment of loan	2,500		
	14,700	28,500	16,200
Net surplus/(deficit) for month	2,300	(5,800)	5,300
Opening cash balance	1,200	3,500	(2,300)
Closing cash balance	3,500	(2,300)	3,000

In the example above (where the figures are purely for illustration) the accounts department has calculated that the cash balance at the beginning of the budget period, 1 January, will be £1,200. Estimates have been made of the cash which is likely to be received by the business (from cash and credit sales, and from a planned disposal of fixed assets in February). Similar estimates have been made of cash due to be paid out by the business (payments to suppliers and employees, payments for rent, rates and other overheads, payment for a planned purchase of fixed assets in February and a loan repayment due in January).

From these estimates it is a simple step to calculate the excess of cash receipts over cash payments in each month. In some months cash payments may exceed cash receipts and there will be a deficit for the month; this occurs during February in the above example because of the large investment in fixed assets in that month.

The last part of the cash budget above shows how the business's estimated cash balance can then be rolled along from month to month. Starting with the opening balance of £1,200 at 1 January a cash surplus of £2,300 is generated in January. This leads to a closing January balance of £3,500 which becomes the opening balance for February. The deficit of £5,800 in February throws the business's cash position into overdraft and the overdrawn balance of £2,300 becomes the opening balance for March. Finally, the healthy cash surplus of £5,300 in March leaves the business with a favourable cash position of £3,000 at the end of the budget period.

The usefulness of cash budgets is that they enable management to make any forward planning decisions that may be needed, such as advising their bank of estimated overdraft requirements or strengthening their credit control procedures to ensure that debtors pay more quickly. In our example, management might well be advised in December 1996 to discuss with the bank the estimated need for an overdraft facility in February 1997.

4.3   How are cash budgets constructed?

Constructing a cash budget in practice is a complex job because a great many forecasts need first to be formulated.

(a) The sales or marketing department might produce estimates of the level of sales.

(b) The credit control department might be able to supply information on how quickly debtors pay and what proportion of debts go bad.

(c) The production or purchasing department might estimate the level of purchases required and the credit period to be taken from suppliers.

(d) Other forecasts would need to be made about the dates and amounts of, for example, purchases and disposals of fixed assets.

An illustration of cash budgeting will give you a better idea of the forecasts that need to be made. Read carefully through the following example and then come back to the initial information and see if you can reproduce the cash budget without looking at the solution. You will probably find this quite hard. Allow at least half an hour.

4.4   Example: cash budget

Peter Blair has worked for some years as a sales representative, but has recently been made redundant. He intends to start up in business on his own account, using £15,000 which he currently has invested with a building society. Peter maintains a bank account showing a small credit balance, and he plans to approach his bank for the necessary additional finance. Peter asks you for advice and provides the following additional information.

(a) Arrangements have been made to purchase fixed assets costing £8,000. These will be paid for at the end of September and are expected to have a five-year life, at the end of which they will possess a nil residual value.

(b) Stocks costing £5,000 will be acquired on 28 September and subsequent monthly purchases will be at a level sufficient to replace forecast sales for the month.

(c) Forecast monthly sales are £3,000 for October, £6,000 for November and December, and £10,500 from January 1997 onwards.

(d) Selling price is fixed at the cost of stock plus 50%.

(e) Two months' credit will be allowed to customers but only 1 month's credit will be received from suppliers of stock.

(f) Running expenses, including rent, are estimated at £1,600 per month.

(g) Blair intends to make monthly cash drawings of £1,000.

Prepare a cash budget for the 6 months October 1996 to 31 March 1997.

Solution

The opening cash balance at 1 October will consist of Peter's initial £15,000 less the £8,000 expended on fixed assets purchased in September, ie the opening balance is £7,000. Cash receipts from credit customers arise two months after the relevant sales.

Payments to suppliers are a little more tricky. We are told that cost of sales is 100/150 × sales. Thus for October cost of sales is 100/15 × £3,000 = £2,000. These goods will be purchased in October but not paid for until November. Similar calculations can be made for later months. The initial stock of £5,000 is purchased in September and consequently paid for in October.

The cash budget can now be constructed.

CASH BUDGET FOR THE SIX MONTHS ENDING 31 MARCH 1997

	Oct £	Nov £	Dec £	Jan £	Feb £	Mar £
Payments						
Suppliers	5,000	2,000	4,000	4,000	7,000	7,000
Running expenses	1,600	1,600	1,600	1,600	1,600	1,600
Drawings	1,000	1,000	1,000	1,000	1,000	1,000
	7,600	4,600	6,600	6,600	9,600	9,600
Receipts						
Debtors	-	-	3,000	6,000	6,000	10,500
Surplus/(shortfall)	(7,600)	(4,600)	(3,600)	(600)	(3,600)	900
Opening balance	7,000	(600)	(5,200)	(8,800)	(9,400)	(13,000)
Closing balance	(600)	(5,200)	(8,800)	(9,400)	(13,000)	(12,100)

4.5 Deviations from expected cash flows

Cash budgets, whether prepared on an annual, monthly, weekly or even a daily basis, can only be estimates of cash flows. Even the best estimates will not be exactly correct, so deviations from the cash budget are inevitable.

This uncertainty about actual cash flows ought to be considered when the cash budget is prepared. It is desirable to prepare additional cash budgets based on different assumptions about sales levels, costs, collection periods, bad debts and so on.

A cash budget model could be constructed, using a PC and a spreadsheet package (which we shall look at in Part B), and the sensitivity of cash flow forecasts to changes in estimates of sales, costs and so on could be analysed.

By planning for different eventualities, management should be able to prepare contingency measures in advance and also appreciate the key factors in the cash budget.

Activity 5   [15 minutes]

If you have access to a computer spreadsheet package and know how to use it, try setting up the cash budget in the example shown above on it.

Then make a second copy of the budget and try making changes to the estimates to see their effect on cash flow.

Businesses do not, of course, have piles of notes and coins in their corporate trouser pockets or purses. Most financial transactions are done by cheque, or only happen on paper at the bank. There are certain aspects of managing a business bank account that you should be aware of.

5   MANAGING A BANK ACCOUNT

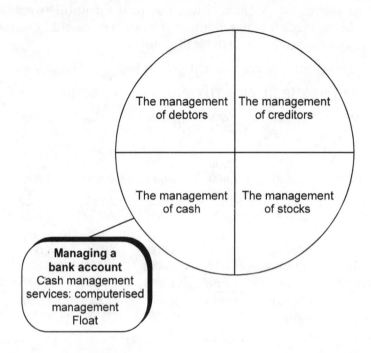

5.1   Cash management services: computerised management

Many banks now offer a cash management service for business customers. A company with many different bank accounts can obtain information about the cash balance in each account through a computer terminal in the company's treasury department linked to the bank's computer. The company can then arrange to move cash from one account to another and so manage its cash position more efficiently and make optimal use of its funds deposited with banks or in various money market investments. A cash management service can be provided to a company with several bank accounts in the UK, or, through an international network of banks, to a multinational company with accounts in different currencies in various countries.

The cash management services provided by the banks comprise 3 basic services.

(a) *Account reporting*

   (i) Information is given about the balances on sterling or currency accounts whether held in the UK or overseas, including details of any uncleared items that have been paid in but not yet added to the account. (As you know it can take several days for a cheque to 'clear'.)

   (ii) Forecast balance reports, which take into account uncleared items and automated entries such as standing orders and direct debits, can be obtained.

   (iii) Reports giving details of individual transactions can be obtained.

(b) *Funds transfer*

   The customer can initiate sterling and currency payments through his terminal. Banks will also give customers with substantial cash 'floats' (see below) the opportunity to get in touch with money market dealers directly and deposit funds in the money markets.

(c) *Decision support services*

   A rates information service, giving information on foreign exchange rates and deposit interest rates, can be used.

5.2   Float

The term 'float' is sometimes used to describe the amount of money tied up between:

(a) the time when a payment is initiated (for example when a debtor sends a cheque in payment, probably by post); and

(b) the time when the funds become available for use in the recipient's bank account.

There are three reasons why there might be a lengthy float.

(a) *Transmission delay*. When payment is sent through the post, it will take a day or longer for the payment to reach the payee.

(b) Delay in banking the payments received (*lodgement delay*). The payee, on receipt of a cheque or cash, might delay putting the cheque or the cash into his bank. The length of this delay will depend on administrative procedures in the payee's organisation.

(c) The time needed for a bank to clear a cheque (*clearance delay*). A payment is not available for use in the payee's bank account until the cheque has been cleared. This will usually take two or three days for cheques payable in the UK. For cheques payable abroad, the delay is much longer.

There are several measures that could be taken to reduce the float.

(a) The payee should ensure that the lodgement delay is kept to a minimum. Cheques received should be presented to the bank on the day of receipt.

(b) The payee might, in some cases, arrange to collect cheques from the payer's premises. This would only be practicable, however, if the payer is local. The payment would have to be large to make the extra effort worthwhile.

(c) The payer might be asked to pay through his own branch of a bank. The payer can give his bank detailed payment instructions, and use the credit clearing system of the Bank Giro. The *Bank Giro* is a means of making credit transfers for customers of other banks and other branches. The payee may include a Bank Giro credit slip on the bottom of his invoice, to help with this method of payment.

(d) *BACS* (Bankers' Automated Clearing Services Ltd) is a banking system which provides for the computerised transfer of funds between banks. In addition, BACS is available to business customers of banks for making payments. The customer must supply a magnetic tape or disk to BACS, which contains details of payments, and payment will be made in two days. BACS is now commonly used by companies for salary payments.

(e) For regular payments *standing orders* or *direct debits* might be used.

(f) *CHAPS* (Clearing House Automated Payments System) is a computerised system for banks to make same-day clearances (that is, immediate payment) between each other. Each member bank of CHAPS can allow its own corporate customers to make immediate transfers of funds through CHAPS. However, there is a large minimum size for payments using CHAPS.

Inefficient cash management

A lengthy float suggests inefficient cash management. But there are other types of delay in receiving payment from debtors, which might also suggest inefficient cash management.

(a) There is the delay created by the length of credit given to customers. There is often a 'normal' credit period for an industry, and companies might be unable to grant less time for payment than this.

(b) There are avoidable delays caused by poor administration (in addition to lodgement delay), such as:

(i) failure to notify the invoicing department that goods have been despatched, so that invoices are not sent promptly;

(ii) cheques from debtors being made out incorrectly, to the wrong company perhaps, because invoices do not contain clear instructions.

For discussion

There are lots of things that people do every day at work that have consequences for working capital - for example 'borrowing' a pen or an envelope for personal use, being impatient with a customer, or failing to pass on a message to a colleague.

Take these and as many other examples as you can think of and trace through their financial consequences to the various components of working capital.

Chapter roundup

- Formulating a policy for managing debtors involves decisions about the administrative resources to be devoted to record-keeping and checking, the credit period allowed to customers, and the procedures for ensuring as far as possible that only customers likely to pay are granted credit in the first place.

- The earlier debtors pay the better. Early payment can be encouraged by good administration and by discount policies. The risk that some debtors will never pay can be partly guarded against by insurance.

- Management of creditors is largely a mirror image of debtors management. Trade creditors are a useful and cheap source of finance, but a successful business needs to ensure that it is *seen* as a good credit risk by its suppliers. Some creditors must be paid on specific dates. This must be remembered and cash must be available.

- Some businesses have a substantial proportion of their total assets tied up in stocks. Financial aspects of stock management consist of keeping the costs of procuring and holding stock to a minimum. The aim of Just-in-Time is to hold as little stock as possible and production systems need to be very efficient to achieve this.

- Cash flow problems arise because of factors such as growth and seasonal fluctuations. Careful management of the other components of working capital helps to avoid such problems. Monitoring cash needs through careful cash budgeting and accurate forecasting is essential.

- Almost all of a business's cash is really a *bank balance* and careful monitoring and management of transactions at the bank will help to reduce bank charges and interest and to take advantage of opportunities to earn interest on deposits.

Quick quiz

1 List five factors that should be considered when formulating a policy for management of debtors.
2 What is a bad debt?
3 What is a collection period?
4 List five credit control procedures.
5 What are three aspects of the management of trade creditors?
6 Is trade credit free?
7 What are the four types of stock cost?
8 What is the difference between the EOQ and the JIT approach to stock management?
9 Why do cash flow problems occur?
10 Write out a skeleton cash budget.
11 How is a cash budget constructed?
12 What is a 'float' and why might it be lengthy?

Answers to quick quiz

1 See Section 1.1
2 A debt that is never repaid
3 The length of time between invoicing of goods or services and the payment of the bill
4 See Section 1.2 - credit control
5 See Section 2.1
6 See Section 2.1
7 See Section 3.2
8 See Section 3.3 and Section 3.5
9 See Section 4.1
10 It should look similar to that in Section 4.2
11 See Section 4.3
12 See Section 5.2

Answers to activities

1 Firstly there is the bill itself: the invoice spells out how much you owe, with the total due shown as the most prominent figure. It gives you some information about how the bill was calculated and what period it covers so that you can check it. Typically you also get an envelope (sometimes even a pre-paid envelope) to make it easy for you physically to send off your payment. The slip you send back has most of the essential details pre-printed so there is minimum writing for you to do and minimum chance of mistakes such as the wrong account number.

Large companies often offer you the chance to pay by direct debit: this actually makes it much easier for the *company* to collect your debt, but there may be an incentive for you, too, such as a small discount.

Other things you might have mentioned include glossy brochures making you 'feel good' about the company's services, and reminder letters (gentle at first but more threatening later) if you forget to pay.

2 (a) $10/365 \times £500,000 = £13,698.63$

(b) Let the average period = x

$$x = \frac{365 \times £140,000}{£2,800,000}$$

$$= 18.25 \text{ days}$$

3 It will probably include the following:

(a) Trading name

(b) Name of owners if sole trader or partnership

(c) Addresses of business and home addresses of owners

(d) Telephone and fax numbers

(e) Banker's name and address

(f) Two trade references

(g) How long in business

(h) Credit limit required.

(I) Request for most recent accounts.

4 You need to look back to this section headed 'credit control' for a full answer. A firm would have to provide good references, maintain a good payment record, allow the supplier to pay a visit, and generally be *known* to be a successful business and a good credit risk.

5 Hopefully, your computer work was successful! You probably found that it was much easier to amend a cash flow when using a computer.

Assignment 4   [1½ hours]

In Chapter 1 we considered the advantages, from the smaller businessman's point of view, of acquiring a franchise rather than starting one's own business 'from scratch'.

Bearing in mind the contents of this chapter, try to evaluate the possible advantages and disadvantages, from the originator's point of view, of offering regional franchises to others rather than setting up a company-owned nationwide network of fast-food restaurants in all the major UK towns and cities.

You should demonstrate your knowledge by writing a report to your long-time friend Chris Corlett, a businessman of limited finances, who operates two local fast food outlets very successfully, and who has invented some new fast food dishes that are the talk of the town.

Chapter 5

ANALYSIS OF COSTS

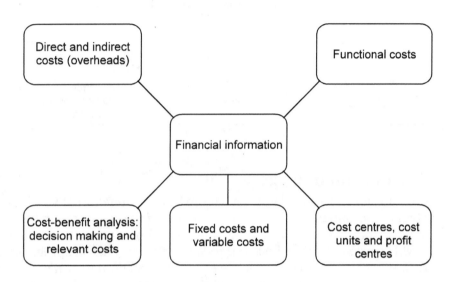

Introduction

The effective management of any resource, including finance, requires good information. Information about finance is derived from an organisation's accounting system. An accounting system records a lot more than simply who owes what to whom. It records the reasons why money was received and, more especially, the reasons why money was paid out. It does this by analysing costs in a variety of ways.

In this chapter we look at the various ways of analysing costs and at how the analyses can be used to help make decisions.

Your objectives

After this chapter you should:

(a) understand the importance of information, and particularly financial information, to the running of a business;

(b) be able to suggest how costs can be classified according to business function;

(c) be able to distinguish between direct costs and overheads;

(d) understand that responsibility for costs is divided between a number of cost centres and profit centres;

(e) know the distinction between fixed and variable costs;

(f) be able to explain what is meant by cost-benefit analysis and relevant costs;

(g) understand the importance of costs in decision making.

1 FINANCIAL INFORMATION

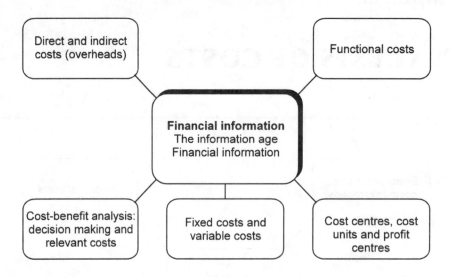

1.1 The information age

To run anything, let alone a business, we have to have information. If you look at a clock it gives you information about what the time is. If the clock rings or beeps the noise gives you the information that it is time to get up. If you turn on the radio someone will give you information about today's traffic or transport problems and the weather. When you get to work you have post (information) to deal with or you carry out the instructions (information) your boss gives you. Modern times have quite rightly been called 'the information age'.

Definition

Information is anything that is communicated.

Information, and the management of information, is the main subject of Part B of this book. For now let's concentrate on financial information.

1.2 Financial information

Since the main objective of a business is to make a profit - to sell things for more than they cost - it follows that the most important kind of *information* used to run the business is information about money: financial information.

Aside from running the business another, more pragmatic, reason for the importance of financial information is that it is the only sort of information covering all of the activities of a business that *must*, by law, be collected. It has to be collected to satisfy the tax man. Companies have to collect it and analyse it to comply with company law, too.

By 'running the business' we mean managing resources such as people or machines or materials. In practice it may be people's *time* that a manager manages, or the type, quantity and quality of materials. But the only *reason* for managing time or quantities is because different amounts of time or quantities of material *cost* more or less money.

Activity 1 [15 minutes]

What financial information do you use in your job, if any? Who decides how you should spend your time and whether you are spending too much or too little time on an aspect of your job? What is the cost to your employer of an hour of your time? Who decides what resources you can have to help you do your job?

The most important sort of information for managing a business, then, is information about costs. To be of real value, though, this information has to be given to the person who is responsible for controlling a particular cost. We shall now look at a variety of ways in which costs can be analysed and so brought to the attention of the individuals responsible for them.

2 FUNCTIONAL COSTS

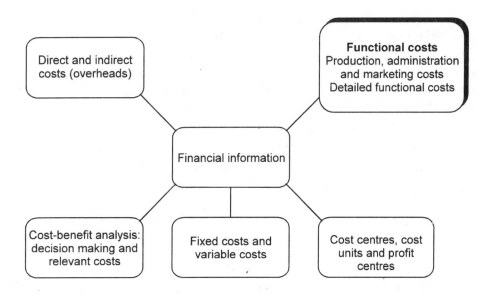

2.1 Production, administration and marketing costs

In a 'traditional' costing system for a manufacturing organisation, costs are classified as follows.

(a) Production or manufacturing costs

(b) Administration costs

(c) Marketing, or selling and distribution costs

Many expenses fall comfortably into one or other of these three broad classifications. Manufacturing costs are associated with the factory, selling and distribution costs with the sales, marketing, warehousing and transport departments and administration costs with general office departments (such as accounting and personnel). Classification in this way is known as classification by function. Other expenses that do not fall fully into one of these classifications might be categorised as 'general overheads' or even listed as a classification on their own (for example, research and development costs).

Activity 2 [15 minutes]

(a) Think of three specific examples of each of the above types of cost in a car manufacturer's business.

(b) Suggest what would be the equivalent of a 'production' cost in a business such as a bank that gives a service as opposed to making things.

2.2   Detailed functional costs

Functional costs include the following.

(a) *Production costs* are the costs which are incurred by the sequence of operations beginning with the supply of raw materials, and ending with the completion of the product ready for warehousing as a finished goods item.

(b) *Administration costs* are the costs of managing an organisation, that is, planning and controlling its operations, but only insofar as such administration costs are not related to the production, sales, distribution or research and development functions.

(c) *Selling costs*, sometimes known as marketing costs, are the costs of creating demand for products and securing firm orders from customers.

(d) *Distribution costs* are the costs of the sequence of operations beginning with the receipt of finished goods from the production department and making them ready for dispatch, transporting them to customers, and ending with the reconditioning for re-use of returned empty containers.

(e) *Research and development costs*

   (i)   Research costs are the costs of searching for new or improved products.

   (ii) Development costs are the costs incurred between the decision to produce a new or improved product and the commencement of full, formal manufacture of the product.

(f) Financing costs are the costs incurred to finance the business such as loan interest.

The cost of, say, a ball-point pen includes the cost of the plastic used to make it and the ink inside it. However the pen's cost also includes things you can't touch or see, such as the cost of processing the order from WH Smith and delivering batches of pens to WH Smith's warehouse. Costs can therefore be analysed as 'direct' or 'indirect'.

3   DIRECT COSTS AND INDIRECT COSTS (OVERHEADS)

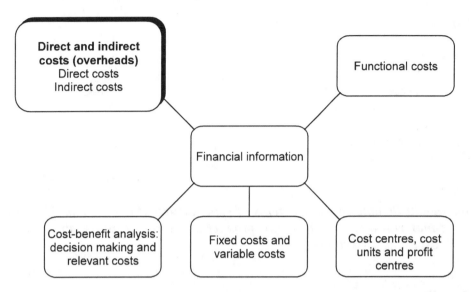

Materials, labour costs and other expenses can be classified as direct costs or as indirect costs.

A direct cost is a cost that can be traced in full to the product, service, or department whose cost is being determined.

(a) Direct materials costs are the costs of materials that are known to have been used in making and selling a product (or even providing a service).

(b) Direct labour costs are the specific costs of the workforce used to make a product or provide a service. Direct labour costs are established by measuring the time taken for a job, or the time taken in 'direct production work'. Traditionally, direct labour costs have been restricted to wage-earning factory workers, but in recent years, with the development of systems for costing services ('service costing'), the costs of some salaried staff might also be treated as a direct labour cost.

(c) Other direct expenses are those expenses that have been incurred in full as a direct consequence of making a product, or providing a service, or running a department (depending on whether a product, a service or a department is being costed).

An indirect cost or overhead is a cost that is incurred in the course of making a product, providing a service or running a department, but which cannot be traced directly and in full to the product, service or department. Examples, respectively, might be supervisors' wages, cleaning materials and buildings insurance.

Total expenditure may therefore be analysed as follows:

Material cost	=	Direct material cost	+	Indirect material cost
+		+		+
Wages	=	Direct wages	+	Indirect wages
+		+		+
Expenses	=	Direct expenses	+	Indirect expenses
Total cost	=	Direct cost	+	Overheads

In costing a small product made by a manufacturing organisation, direct costs are usually restricted to some of the production costs (although it is not uncommon to find a salesman's commission for selling the product as a direct selling cost). Costs are commonly built up as follows.

	£
Production costs:	
Direct materials	A
Direct wages	B
Direct expenses	C
Total direct cost	A+B+C
Production overheads	D
Full factory cost	A+B+C+D
Administration overheads	E
Selling and distribution overheads	F
Full cost of sales	A+B+C+D+E+F

You should be able to specify items of expenditure which are classifiable as direct material cost, direct labour, production overhead and so on. A list of such cost items is given here.

3.1 Direct costs

Direct material costs

All material becoming part of the product (unless used in negligible amounts and having negligible costs) is direct material, the cost of which is charged to the product as part of the prime cost. Material used in negligible amounts and/or having negligible cost can be grouped under indirect materials as part of overhead. Examples of direct material are set out below.

(a) Materials, including component parts, specially purchased for a particular job, order or process.

(b) Materials passing from one operation to another. (For example, if a product is made in two departments, when part-finished work is transferred from Department 1 to Department 2, it becomes finished work of Department 1 and a direct material cost in Department 2).

(c) Primary packing materials like cartons and boxes.

Direct labour costs

All wages paid for labour expended on work on the product itself are direct wages, the cost of which is charged to the product as part of the total direct cost. Some seemingly indirect wages (such as those paid to the foreman) which can be accurately identified with the product, may be considered a direct charge to the product and be included as direct wages.

Examples of groups of labour receiving payment as direct wages are as follows.

(a) Workers engaged in altering the condition or composition of the product (drilling holes, cutting, painting and so on)

(b) Inspectors, analysts and testers *specifically required* for such production

(c) Foremen, chargehands, shop clerks and anyone else whose wages are *specifically identified*

Direct expenses

If any expenses are incurred on a specific product other than direct material cost and direct wages those too are direct expenses, the cost of which is charged to the product as part of the total direct cost. Examples of direct expenses are as follows.

(a) The cost of special designs, drawings or layouts

(b) The hire of tools or equipment for a particular job

(c) Maintenance costs of tools, jigs, fixtures etc.

Direct expenses are also referred to as chargeable expenses.

Activity 3 [15 minutes]

A solicitor charges her clients by the hour for her services. Only hours that can be specifically identified with a particular client are regarded as chargeable.

One Monday she spends half an hour sorting through her post, half an hour on the phone to client A, an hour and a half looking through a contract for client B, two hours studying a new law on property, an hour in a meeting with her partners, and an hour and a half writing letters in reply to the day's post.

How much 'direct' or chargeable time has she spent?

3.2 Indirect costs

Production overheads

All indirect material cost, indirect wages and indirect expenses incurred in the factory from receipt of the order until its completion are included in production (or factory) overhead. Examples are as follows.

(a) Indirect material which cannot be traced in the finished product, such as consumable stores like lubricants or minor items of material used in negligible amounts, or amounts which it is uneconomical to allocate to a particular product, like the cost of glue in box-making.

(b) Indirect wages, meaning all wages not charged directly to a product, which generally include salaries and wages of non-productive personnel in the production department, such as foremen, inspectors, general labourers, maintenance staff, stores staff.

(c) Indirect expenses (other than material and labour) not charged directly to production. The following expenses could be included under this heading.

   (i) Rent, rates and insurance of a factory

   (ii) Depreciation, fuel, power, repairs and maintenance of plant, machinery and factory buildings.

Production overhead is also referred to as factory overhead.

Activity 4 [15 minutes]

Why might it be 'uneconomical' to allocate the cost of glue in box-making to individual boxes?

Administration overheads

These are all indirect material costs, wages and expenses incurred in the direction, control and administration of an organisation. The following are examples.

(a) Depreciation of office machines.

(b) Office salaries, including salaries of administrative directors, secretaries, accountants.

(c) Rent, rates, insurance, lighting, cleaning and heating of general offices, telephone and postal charges, bank charges, legal charges, audit fees, depreciation and repairs of office buildings and machinery.

Definition

Depreciation is a measure of how much a fixed asset wears out until it is completely useless. For example a sales rep's car might last 4 years before it is scrapped. If it originally cost £10,000 it would depreciate by £2,500 per year. All fixed assets except (normally) land and freehold buildings depreciate.

Selling overheads

These are all indirect materials costs, wages and expenses incurred in promoting sales and retaining customers. Examples of selling overhead are set out below.

(a) Printing and stationery, such as catalogues and price lists

(b) Salaries and commission of salesmen, representatives and sales department staff

(c) Advertising and sales promotion; market research

(d) Rent, rates and insurance of sales offices and showrooms; bad debts and collection charges; cash discounts allowed; after sales service

Distribution overheads

These are all indirect materials, costs, wages and expenses incurred in making the packed product ready for despatch and delivering it to the customer. Examples of distribution overhead are as follows.

(a) Cost of packing cases; materials (eg oil, spare parts) used in the upkeep of delivery vehicles; the cost of reconditioning returned packing cases, ready for re-use

(b) Wages of packers, drivers and despatch clerks

(c) Freight and insurance charges; rent, rates, insurance and depreciation of warehouses; depreciation and running expenses of delivery vehicles

You might have decided by now that you understand the distinction between direct costs and overheads, but in practice, there are many 'grey areas' where costs are not obviously direct or indirect, and a reasoned judgement has to be made in classifying them. Attempt the activity below.

Activity 5 [15 minutes]

A direct labour employee's wage in a particular week is made up as follows.

	£
(a) Basic pay for normal hours worked, 36 hours at £4 per hour	144
(b) Pay at the basic rate for overtime, 6 hours at £4 per hour	24
(c) Overtime shift premium, with overtime paid at time-and-a-quarter 1/4 × 6 hours × £4 per hour	6
(d) A plus payment under a group bonus (or 'incentive') scheme - bonus for the month	30
Total gross wages in the week for 42 hours of work	204

Task

Which costs are direct? Are any indirect?

Costs consist of the costs of direct materials, direct labour, direct expenses, production overheads, administration overheads and general overheads. But how do accountants set about recording the actual expenses incurred as any one of these classifications and making individual managers responsible for them?

4 COST CENTRES, COST UNITS AND PROFIT CENTRES

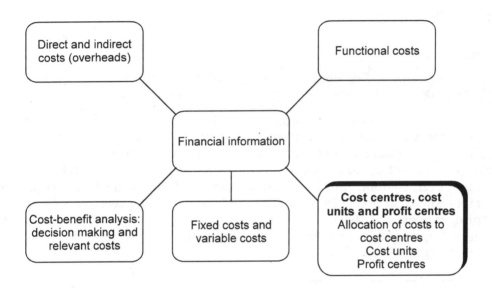

4.1 Allocation of costs to cost centres

To begin with, all costs should be recorded as a direct cost of a *cost centre*. Even 'overhead costs' are directly traceable to an office or an item of expense and there should be an overhead cost centre to cater for these costs.

Definition

A *cost centre* is a location, or a function, or an activity or an item of equipment. Each cost centre acts as a collecting place for certain costs before they are analysed further.

Suitable cost centres might be as follows.

(a) In a production department: the department itself, a machine within the department or group of machines, a foreman's work group, a work bench and so on.

(b) Production 'service' or 'back-up' departments, such as the stores, maintenance, production planning and control departments.

(c) Administration, sales or distribution departments, such as the personnel, accounting or purchasing departments; a sales region or salesman; or a warehouse or distribution unit.

(d) Shared costs (for example rent, rates, electricity or gas bills) may require cost centres of their own, in order to be directly allocated. Shared cost items may be charged to separate, individual cost centres, or they may be grouped into a larger cost centre (for example *factory occupancy* costs, for rents, rates, heating, lighting, building repairs, cleaning and maintenance of a particular factory).

Charging costs to a cost centre simply involves two steps.

(a) Identifying the cost centre for which an item of expenditure is a direct cost

(b) Allocating the cost to the cost centre (usually by means of a *cost code*)

Cost centres are always managed by someone and so they provide a basis for allocating *responsibility* for costs.

Once costs have been traced to cost centres, they can be further analysed in order to establish a cost per 'cost unit'. Alternatively, some items of cost may be charged directly to a cost unit, for example direct materials and direct labour costs.

4.2 Cost units

Definition

A *cost unit* is 'a unit of product or service in relation to which costs are ascertained' (CIMA, *Official Terminology*).

The unit selected must be appropriate to the business and one with which expenditure can be readily associated. Care must be taken in non-manufacturing operations to ensure that the unit is a meaningful measure. For instance in transport the cost per tonne transported may not be particularly useful. The cost per tonne carried from London to Glasgow would probably be greater than the cost per tonne from London to Dover, and it would not be easy to make comparisons for control purposes. If the cost unit was changed to a tonne-mile (the cost of transporting one tonne for one mile) then a comparison between the two journeys would be valid.

Activity 6 [15 minutes]

It is 100 miles from A to B and 200 miles from C to D. It costs £400 for firm X to transport 10 tonnes from A to B and £720 for firm Y to transport 15 tonnes from C to D.

For each firm what is the cost per tonne and the cost per tonne-mile? Which firm would you use in future?

We have seen that a cost centre is where costs are collected. Some organisations, however, work on a profit centre basis.

4.3 Profit centres

Definition

A *profit centre* is accountable for costs and income. It may also be called a business centre, business unit or strategic business unit.

Cost centres only have costs attributed to them. Profit centres, on the other hand, also receive the income associated with those costs. For example, an organisation with two departments each making a different product will allocate the income from each product to the department where each product is made. This ensures that the organisation has some idea as to the relative profitability of each product.

Profit centre managers should normally have control over how income is raised and how costs are incurred. Not infrequently, several cost centres will comprise one profit centre.

A very important distinction in decision making is whether costs are fixed or variable. We encountered this concept briefly in Chapter 3. Here is some more detail.

5 FIXED COSTS AND VARIABLE COSTS

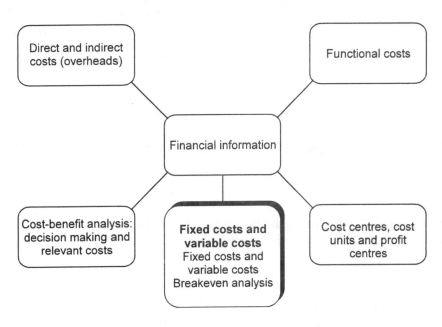

5.1 Fixed costs and variable costs

The distinction between fixed and variable costs lies in whether the amount of costs incurred will rise as the volume of activity increases, or whether the costs will remain the same, regardless of the volume of activity. Some examples are as follows.

(a) Direct material costs will rise as more units of a product are manufactured, and so they are variable costs that vary with the volume of production.

(b) Sales commission is often a fixed percentage of sales turnover, and so is a variable cost that varies with the level of sales (but not with the level of production).

(c) Telephone call charges are likely to increase if the volume of business expands, and so they are a variable overhead cost, varying with the volume of production and sales.

(d) The rental cost of business premises is a constant amount, at least within a stated time period, and so it is a fixed cost that does not vary with the level of activity conducted on the premises.

Costs can be classified as direct costs or overheads, or as fixed or variable costs. These alternative classifications are not mutually exclusive, but are complementary to each other, so that we can identify some direct costs that are fixed costs (although they are commonly variable costs) and some overhead costs that are fixed and others that are variable.

Definitions

Variable cost is that part of cost which varies with the volume of production (or level of activity).

Fixed cost is that part of cost which does not vary with the level of activity or volume of production.

Semi-variable (or *semi-fixed* or *mixed*) *costs* are partly variable and partly fixed.

Activity 7 [15 minutes]

(a) Damien has a mobile telephone. The monthly charge is £20. Calls cost 5p per unit at all times unless more than 500 units are used in a month in which case calls cost 4p per unit. What is the *annual* cost if Damien uses:

    (i) 250 units per month;

    (ii) 600 units per month?

(b) One month Damien uses 405 units, and the next month 502. What will he find when he gets his mobile phone bill?

You have probably heard about businesses trying to 'break even' but do you really know what this means? Cost analysis is crucial to this important concept.

5.2 Breakeven analysis

The distinction between fixed costs and variable costs is very important to decision-making. This can best be illustrated by an example.

Suppose X Ltd makes a single product whose total variable costs per unit are £10. Fixed costs of the business per year are £6,000. The product can be sold for £15.

How can X Ltd decide what is the minimum number of units it will make per year?

Solution

X Ltd needs to make at least enough units to cover the £6,000 of fixed costs.

	£
Selling price per unit	15
Variable costs per unit	10
Contribution to fixed costs	5

X Ltd therefore needs to make at least £6,000/£5 = 1,200 units. At this level of production the company will *break even*: in other words it will not make a loss, although it will not make a profit either.

	£
Sales (1,200 × £15)	18,000
Variable costs (1,200 × £10)	(12,000)
Contribution	6,000
Fixed costs	(6,000)
Profit/loss	0

Activity 8   [15 minutes]

In Year 2 X Ltd is asked to pay its £6,000 of fixed costs in advance. Also, because of a slump in the market, there is no possibility of selling more than 1,000 units in year 2. The managing director of X Ltd says, gloomily 'Well, if we're not even going to break even we may as well close down now'.

Comment on this scenario.

Definition

Contribution (or contribution to fixed costs) is the difference between an item's selling price and its variable costs. In decision making contribution is more important than 'profit', which is sales minus all costs, because some costs have to be paid no matter what decisions are taken. (Activity 8 illustrates this.)

6   COST-BENEFIT ANALYSIS: DECISION MAKING AND RELEVANT COSTS

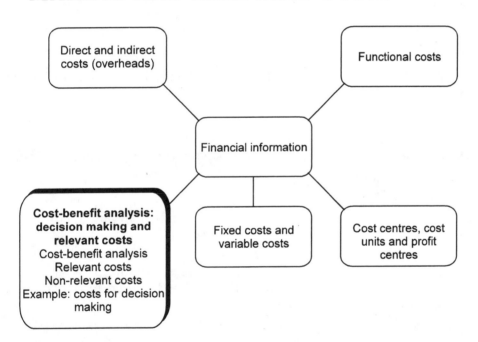

6.1   Cost-benefit analysis

Cost-benefit analysis is a very simple concept that everybody uses all the time. For example, if you were asked to work outside of normal working hours for an extra £1 an hour but this meant that your train ticket would cost an extra £2 it would only be worth doing so if you worked more than two hours.

	£
Cost	2
Benefit from, say, three hours overtime	3
Net benefit	1

This is the basis of all decision-making. If the benefits of doing something are greater than the costs of doing it the decision is to go ahead and do it. If the costs outweigh the benefits the opposite decision is made.

Though it is simple in theory, there are two major problems.

(a) It is often very difficult to identify the costs that are relevant to a decision.

(b) Some costs cannot be expressed in money terms. For example if you were already very tired, you could only work overtime at the 'cost' of getting more tired, but what is this cost?

(c) Benefits can also be very hard to quantify. A benefit of working overtime might be the satisfaction of getting the job done, but what is this worth?

Unfortunately there are no definitive answers to the questions in (b) and (c). Factors that cannot be quantified in financial terms are very often the ones that most heavily influence the final decision, both in personal life and in business.

However, this does not alter the fact that financial information should be collected, analysed and used in any decision. In our example it shows us that if we do decide to work overtime, then we should work more than two hours overtime, and this is very helpful to know.

We shall concentrate on problem (a): identifying the costs that are relevant to a decision.

6.2 Relevant costs

The costs which should be used for decision making are often referred to as *relevant costs*.

Definition

A *relevant cost* is a future cash flow arising as a direct consequence of a decision.

(a) Relevant costs are future costs.

   (i) A decision is about the future; it cannot alter what has been done already. A cost that has been incurred in the past is totally irrelevant to any decision that is being made 'now'.

   (ii) Costs that have been incurred include not only costs that have already been paid, but also costs that are the subject of legally binding contracts, even if payments due under the contract have not yet been made. (These are known as committed costs.)

(b) Relevant costs are cash flows. This means that costs or charges which do not reflect additional cash spending should be ignored for the purpose of decision making. Depreciation is the main example. If you buy a car for £10,000 you might reflect depreciation by deducting £2,500 per annum from your profits for the next four years. But this £2,500 is only a cost on paper. The real cost was the £10,000 that vanished from your bank account on day 1.

(c) A relevant cost is one which arises as a direct consequence of a decision. Thus, only costs which will differ under some or all of the available opportunities should be considered; relevant costs are therefore sometimes referred to as *incremental costs* or *differential costs*. For example, if an employee is expected to have no other work to do during the next week, but will be paid his basic wage (of, say, £100 per week) for attending work and doing nothing, his manager might decide to give him a job which earns only £40 profit. The net gain is £40 and the £100 is irrelevant to the decision because although it is a future cash flow, it will be incurred anyway whether the employee is given work or not.

Definition continued

Relevant costs are therefore future, incremental cash flows. Relevant costs may also be expressed as *opportunity costs* (the benefit forgone by choosing one opportunity instead of the next best alternative). We met this concept in an earlier chapter.

6.3 Non-relevant costs

A number of terms are used to describe costs that are *irrelevant* for decision-making because they are either not future cash flows or they are costs which will be incurred anyway, regardless of the decision that is taken.

Sunk costs

A *sunk cost* is used to describe the cost of an asset which has already been acquired and which can continue to serve its present purpose, but which has no significant realisable value and no income value from any other alternative purpose.

Suppose, for example, a company purchased an item of computer equipment two years ago for £20,000. It has been depreciated down to £7,000 already, but in fact it already has no resale value because of developments in computer technology. The equipment can be used for its existing purpose for at least another year, but the company is considering whether or not to purchase more modern equipment with additional facilities and so scrap the existing equipment now.

In terms of decision making and relevant costs the existing equipment, which initially cost £20,000 but now has a value on paper of £7,000, is a sunk cost. The money has been spent and the asset has no alternative use. 'Writing off' the asset and incurring a 'paper' loss on disposal of £7,000 would be irrelevant to the decision under consideration.

Committed costs

A *committed cost* is a future cash outflow that will be incurred anyway, whatever decision is taken now about alternative opportunities. Committed costs may exist because of contracts already entered into by the organisation, which it cannot get out of.

Notional costs

A *notional cost* or *imputed cost* is a hypothetical accounting cost to reflect something for which no actual cash expense is incurred. Examples common in accounting systems include the following.

(a) Notional rent, such as that charged to the profit centres of an organisation for the use of accommodation which the organisation owns.

(b) Notional interest charges on capital, sometimes made against a profit centre or cost centre.

Fixed and variable costs

Generally you can assume the following.

(a) Variable costs will be relevant costs.

(b) Fixed costs are irrelevant to a decision.

This need not be the case, however, and you should analyse variable and fixed cost data carefully. Do not forget that 'fixed' costs may only be fixed in the short term.

Direct and indirect costs

Direct and indirect costs may be relevant or non-relevant, depending on the situation in question. Direct labour, for example, may be paid regardless of whether or not a particular product is manufactured. On the other hand, additional direct labour may be required and the cost of this would be a relevant cost.

> *The best way to understand relevant costs is to look at numerical examples. The example that follows includes most of the ideas we have encountered in this section. Study it carefully.*

6.4   Example: costs for decision making

O'Reilly Ltd has been approached by a customer who would like a special job to be done for him, and who is willing to pay £22,000 for it. The job would require the following materials.

Material	Total units required	Units already in stock	Book value of units in stock £/unit	Sales value £/unit	Replacement cost £/unit
A	1,000	0	-	-	6
B	1,000	600	2	2.50	5
C	1,000	700	3	2.50	4
D	200	200	4	6.00	9

(a) Material B is used regularly by O'Reilly Ltd, and if units of B are required for this job, they would need to be replaced to meet other production demand.

(b) Materials C and D are in stock as the result of previous over-buying, and they have a restricted use. No other use could be found for material C, but the units of material D could be used in another job as substitute for 300 units of material E, which currently costs £5 per unit (of which the company has no units in stock at the moment).

(c) Book value is the cost of the stock as recorded in the company's accounting system.

(d) Sales value is the amount the stock would fetch if it had to be sold unused.

Calculate the relevant costs of material for deciding whether or not to accept the contract.

Solution

(a) Material A is not yet owned. It would have to be bought in full at the cost of £6 per unit.

(b) *Material B* is used regularly by the company. There are existing stocks (600 units) but if these are used on the contract under review a further 600 units would have to be bought to replace them. Relevant costs are therefore 1,000 units at the replacement cost of £5 per unit.

(c) 1,000 units of *material C* are needed and 700 are already in stock. If used for the contract, a further 300 units must be bought at £4 each. The existing stocks of 700 will not be replaced. However, if they are used for the contract, they could not be sold at £2.50 each. The realisable value of these 700 units is an opportunity cost of sales revenue forgone.

(d) The required units of *Material D* are already in stock and will not be replaced. There is an opportunity cost of using D in the contract because there are alternative opportunities either to sell the existing stocks for £6 per unit (£1,200 in total) or avoid other purchases (of material E), which would cost 300 x £5 = £1,500. Since substitution for E is more beneficial, £1,500 is the opportunity cost.

(e) *Summary of relevant costs*

	£
Material A (1,000 × £6)	6,000
Material B (1,000 × £5)	5,000
Material C (300 × £4) plus (700 × £2.50)	2,950
Material D	1,500
Total	15,450

(f) The *benefit* to be obtained if the contract is accepted is £22,000. This is greater than the materials costs so the job should be taken on. (Note: for clarity, costs of the contract other than materials costs have been ignored.)

For discussion

What non-financial costs and benefits might O'Reilly Ltd also take into consideration when coming to a decision about the job?

Chapter roundup

- Financial information is essential for the management of a business. Most of it is derived from the business's accounting system and its analysis of costs.
- One way of classifying costs is according to function - production, administration, marketing and so on.
- Another classification distinguishes between direct costs and overheads. The idea of direct cost is particularly relevant to manufacturing businesses.
- Responsibility for costs is allocated by charging costs to cost centres and profit centres.
- In decision making the distinction between fixed costs and variable costs becomes very important. Contribution (to fixed costs) is the difference between selling price and variable cost.
- Cost-benefit analysis is simple in theory but difficult in practice because it is hard to identify relevant costs and because other considerations beside money have to be taken into account.

Quick quiz

1 Why is financial information important?

2 What is a production cost and a distribution cost?

3 What are the components of total direct cost?

4 Give two examples of administration overheads.

5 What is the distinction between fixed costs and variable costs?

6 What is contribution?

7 Why is cost-benefit analysis difficult in practice?

8 Why are some costs irrelevant for decision making?

9 If a company accepts a contract it will have to pay a fixed rent of £500 a year for extra office space for the next five years. Is this relevant to the decision as to whether or not to accept the contract?

10 What is a cost unit?

11 What is a profit centre?

12 How would you categorise a telephone bill?

Answers to quick quiz

1 See Section 1.2

2 See Section 2.1

3 See Section 3.1

4 See Section 3.3

5 See Section 5.1

6 See definition in Section 5.2

7 See Section 6.1

8 See Section 6.3

9 Yes; in this case the rental expense arises directly from the decision to accept the contract

10 See Section 4.2

11 See Section 4.3

12 It is a semi-variable cost. The rental part is a fixed cost, but the calls element will fluctuate (although not necessarily in accordance with changes in production or sales levels).

Answers to activities

1 This activity is intended to make you realise that things you do at work have financial implications, even if you personally are not aware of the precise figures involved.

2 (a) Production cost: steel, rubber, assembly line wages.

Administration cost: personnel department salaries, photocopying, office stationery

Marketing, selling, distribution: sales reps' salaries, advertising, car transporting costs.

There are, of course, lots of other possibilities.

(b) The problem is in defining exactly what the service consists of: banking, for example, is actually a collection of several different services. Supplying cash is one such service and cash machine running costs are associated with this. Keeping a record of transactions is another service and there would be associated computer and computer operator costs. The answer is a bit easier if you choose a service like a local bus service or a solicitor.

3
Direct	Hrs	Indirect	Hrs
Client A	0.5	Post	0.5
Client B	1.5	Study	2.0
Letter-writing (?)	1.5	Meeting	1.0
	3.5		3.5

Writing letters can probably be charged to individual clients, unless they were all concerned with the general administration of the practice.

4 The cost would be negligible (far less than 1p) and it would cost far more than this (in terms of time spent on record keeping and calculation) to keep track of the cost.

5 Items (a) and (b) are direct labour costs of the items produced in the 42 hours worked in week 5.

Overtime premium, item (c), is usually regarded as an overhead expense, because it is 'unfair' to charge the items produced in overtime hours with the premium. Why should an item made in overtime be more costly just because, by chance, it was made after the employee normally clocks off for the day?

Group bonus scheme payments (d) are usually overhead costs, because they cannot normally be traced directly to individual products or jobs.

In this example, the direct labour employee costs were £168 in direct costs and £36 in indirect costs, and these costs would be coded differently, to allocate them to different cost units or overhead cost centres.

6

		Firm X		Firm Y
Cost per tonne	(400/10)	£40	(720/15)	£48
Cost per tonne-mile	(£40/100)	£0.40	(£48/200)	£0.24

On a cost per tonne-mile basis, Firm Y could have transported 10 tonnes from A to B for 100 × 10 × £0.24 = £240. This is cheaper than Firm X's cost so Firm Y should be used in future.

7

			£
(a)	(i)	Fixed cost (12 × £20)	240
		Variable cost (12 × 250 × £0.05)	150
			390
	(ii)	Fixed cost, as before	240
		Variable cost (12 × 600 × £0.04)	288
			528

(b) 405 × £0.05 = £20.25

502 × £0.04 = £20.08.

Damien got 97 extra units in month 2 and paid 17p less. Note that fixed costs are not relevant to this calculation: they are the same in both cases.

8 If the company closes down now it will make a loss of £6,000. If it makes as many units as it can sell it will recover 1,000 (£5 = £5,000 as a 'contribution' to fixed costs, so the overall loss will be only £1,000. In the short term, therefore, it is worth continuing in business to minimise the loss.

In the long term (beyond Year 2) it is not worth incurring any more fixed costs unless the market picks up and there is a possibility of at least breaking even.

> ### Assignment 5 [1½ hours]
>
> A new hotel is attempting to plan for its restaurant and bar operations.
>
> In the first year, the hotel expects restaurant sales of £350,000 and bar sales of £250,000.
>
> It is expected that food costs in the restaurant will be 35% of sales, and drink costs 50% of bar sales.
>
> The rental attributed to the restaurant is £40,000 per year and to the bar £30,000 per year.
>
> The restaurant will have a manager at a total cost of £25,000, whilst the bar manager will cost £20,000.
>
> The other staff will all be hourly paid workers at a wage rate of £4 per hour. Wages are expected to cost 25% of restaurant sales and 15% of bar sales.
>
> ### Tasks
>
> (a) Based on the above figures, calculate expected profits for both restaurant and bar for the first year of operation.
>
> (b) Calculate the weekly average number of hours of hourly-paid workers wages payable.
>
> (c) Calculate the break even sales figure for both restaurant and bar.

Chapter 6

BUDGETS

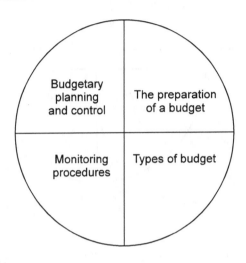

Introduction

You have heard of *the* Budget. To you it is probably just an annual event when the government makes slight changes to the amount of pay you can expect to take home. From the point of view of the government, however, the budget is its *financial plan* for the next year - how much income it expects to have (from taxes) and what it intends to spend that money on (public services and government administration).

A budget in business is a financial plan in exactly the same way. Budgets encourage thinking ahead and help managers to understand how their activities must fit in with the activities of other managers. Budgets also act as a yardstick against which managers can compare their actual performance.

Your objectives

After completing this chapter you should:

(a) be able to explain what a budget is and the variety of uses it has;

(b) know how budgets are prepared;

(c) be able to prepare simple budgets;

(d) understand the value of monitoring actual results against budgets;

(e) be able to prepare simple flexible budgets and calculate variances.

1 BUDGETARY PLANNING AND CONTROL

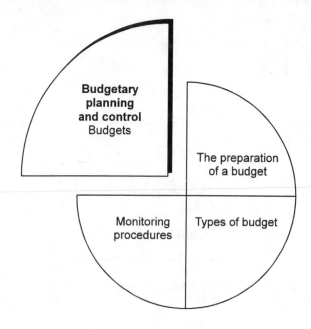

1.1 Budgets

A budget is basically a plan expressed in monetary terms. The plan covers income, expenditure and capital investment (buying fixed assets).

Budgets are an important source of information because they provide a system for ensuring communication, co-ordination and control within an organisation.

The objectives of a budgetary planning and control system are as follows.

(a) *To ensure the achievement of the organisation's objectives*

Objectives for the organisation as a whole, and for individual departments and operations within the organisation, are set. Quantified expressions of these objectives are then drawn up as targets to be achieved within the timescale of the budget plan.

(b) *To compel planning and decision making*

This is probably the most important feature of a budgetary planning and control system. Planning forces management to look ahead, to make decisions, to set out detailed plans for achieving the targets for each department, operation and (ideally) each manager, to anticipate problems and give the organisation purpose and direction. It thus prevents management from relying on spur of the moment or unco-ordinated planning which may be detrimental to the performance of the organisation.

(c) *To communicate ideas and plans*

A formal system is necessary to ensure that each person affected by the plans is aware of what he or she is supposed to be doing. Communication might be one-way, with managers giving orders to subordinates, or there might be a two-way dialogue and exchange of ideas.

(d) *To co-ordinate activities*

The activities of different departments or sub-units of the organisation need to be co-ordinated to ensure maximum integration of effort towards common goals. This concept of co-ordination implies, for example, that the purchasing department should base its budget on production requirements and that the production budget should in turn be based on sales expectations. Although straightforward in concept, co-ordination is remarkably difficult to achieve, and there is often conflict between departmental plans in the budget with the result that the efforts of the various departments are not fully integrated into a combined plan to achieve the company's optimum targets.

(e) *To provide a framework for responsibility*

Budgetary planning and control systems require that managers of cost and profit centres are made responsible for the achievement of budget targets for the operations under their personal control.

(f) *To establish a system of monitoring and control*

A budget is basically a yardstick against which actual performance is measured and assessed. Control over actual performance is provided by the comparisons of actual results against the budget plan. Departures from budget can then be investigated and the reasons for the departures can be divided into controllable and non-controllable factors.

(g) *To motivate employees to improve their performance*

Via a system of feedback of actual results, which lets them know how well or badly they are performing, the interest and commitment of employees can be retained. The identification of controllable reasons for departures from budget gives the managers responsible an incentive for improved future performance.

Two levels of attainment can be set.

(i) A minimum expectations budget

(ii) A desired standards budget which provides some sort of challenge to employees

Despite the simple definition of a budget, its preparation and subsequent use provide the base for a system which should have far reaching implications for the organisation concerned.

For discussion

Does the organisation you work for prepare budgets? If so do you see them and understand them? Do you see a budget for the whole organisation or just for your department? HND students should consider whether budgeting is appropriate for a college.

Budgets can be presented and used in many different ways so it is worth sharing your personal experiences with your colleagues on this course.

Having seen why organisations prepare budgets, we will now turn our attention to the mechanics of budget preparation. Even if you are not personally involved in the preparation process you may well have to work to a budget, so it is helpful to know how the figures might have been calculated. We will consider a typical budget preparation timetable in the next section. In the following section we will go on to consider the actual preparation of various budgets.

2 THE PREPARATION OF A BUDGET

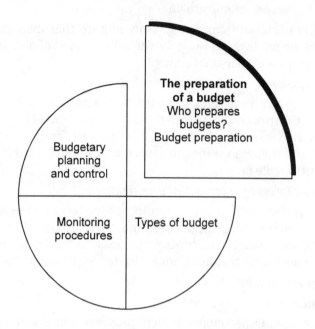

2.1 Who prepares budgets?

Managers responsible for preparing budgets should ideally be the managers whose sections are responsible for carrying out the budget, selling goods and authorising expenditure.

(a) The sales manager should draft the sales budget and selling overhead cost centre budgets.

(b) The purchasing manager should draft the material purchases budget.

(c) The production manager should draft the direct production cost budgets.

(d) Various cost centre managers should prepare the individual production, administration and distribution cost centre budgets for their own cost centre.

Definitions

The *budget period* is the time period to which the budget relates. Except for capital expenditure budgets, the budget period is commonly the accounting year (sub-divided into 12 or 13 control periods).

The co-ordination and administration of budgets is usually the responsibility of a *budget committee* (with the managing director as chairman). The budget committee is serviced by a budget officer who is usually an accountant. Every part of the organisation should be represented on the committee, so there should be a representative from sales, production, marketing and so on.

Let us now look at the steps involved in the preparation of a budget. The procedures will differ from organisation to organisation, but the step-by-step approach described in this chapter is indicative of the steps followed by many organisations.

2.2 Budget preparation

The annual budget is part of a longer term plan, perhaps covering 5 or 10 years. The longer term plan would include a *capital budget* (a fixed assets purchase budget). The company may be aiming at the purchase of, say, a second factory in three years time thus enabling the business to double its production. A key aim of the current year's budget would be to generate some of the cash needed to purchase this factory. A key feature of the budget in three years time would be the doubling of sales when the new factory started to give results.

Not such major fixed asset purchases, such as new tools, or a few new desks and chairs, are often budgeted for by means of a set annual 'allowance' for fixed assets purchase and replacement.

Step 1: identification of the principal budget factor

The first task in the budgetary process is to identify the principal budget factor. This is also known as the key budget factor or limiting budget factor and it is what limits an organisation's activities.

The principal budget factor is usually sales demand: a company is usually restricted from making and selling more of its products because there would be no sales demand for the increased output at a price which would be acceptable/profitable to the company.

However the principal budget factor may alternatively be current machine capacity, distribution and selling resources, the availability of key raw materials or the availability of cash.

Once this factor is defined then the rest of the budget can be prepared. For example, if sales are the principal budget factor then the production manager can only prepare his budget after the sales budget is complete.

Step 2: preparation of a sales budget

This is prepared in units of each product and also in sales value.

Step 3: preparation of a finished goods stock budget

This budget decides the planned increase or decrease in finished stock levels.

Step 4: preparation of a production budget

The production budget is stated in units of each product and is calculated as the sales budget in units plus or minus the budgeted change in finished goods stocks. (Goods may be produced for stock or sold out of stock and therefore planned production and sales volumes are not necessarily the same amount.)

Step 5: preparation of budgets of resources for production

(a) *Materials usage budget.* This budget is prepared for all types of materials, direct and indirect, and is stated in quantities and perhaps cost for each type of material used. It should take into account budgeted losses in production and desired levels of raw materials stocks.

(b) *Machine utilisation budget.* This shows the operating hours required on each machine or group of machines.

(c) *Labour budget* or *wages budget* or *personnel budget.* This budget is prepared for all grades of labour, direct and indirect. For hourly paid staff, the budget will be expressed in hours for each grade of labour and in terms of cost. It should take into account budgeted 'idle time' (when work is not possible, for example because machines have to 'warm up') and expected wage rates.

Step 6: preparation of overhead cost budgets

During the preparation of the sales and production budgets, the managers of the cost centres of the organisation will prepare their draft budgets for the (department) overhead costs. There will be cost centres for each type of overhead.

(a) Production overheads (for example repairs and maintenance, stores, production control, factory supervision and so on)

(b) Administration overheads (for example budgeted costs of the accounting department, personnel department, computer department, corporate planning and so on)

(c) Selling and distribution overheads, or marketing overheads (for example budgeted costs for advertising and sales promotion, perhaps for each product group, budgeted costs of the sales force, distribution cost budgets and so on)

(d) Research and development department overheads

Step 7: co-ordination and review of budgets

Remember that it is unlikely that the above steps will be problem-free. The budgets must be reviewed in relation to one another. Such a review may indicate that some budgets are out of balance with others and need modifying so that they will be compatible with other conditions, constraints and plans. The accountant must identify such inconsistencies and bring them to the attention of the manager concerned. The revision of one budget may lead to the revision of all budgets. This process must continue until the budgeted profit and loss account, balance sheet and cash budget are acceptable.

Step 8: preparation of a master budget

When all the budgets are in harmony with one another they are summarised into a master budget consisting of a budgeted profit and loss account, a balance sheet and cash budget.

Cash budgets were covered in Chapter 4. We shall be going on to look at profit and loss accounts and balance sheets in the next chapter. In the next section we consider sales budgets, production budgets and overhead budgets in a little more detail.

Activity 1 [15 minutes]

In pairs, see if you can define or explain the following terms without reference to the text or glossary.

(a) Raw materials

(b) Finished goods

(c) Distribution

(d) Overhead

(e) Budget

(f) Idle time

(g) Cost centre

(h) Resource

Activity 2 [15 minutes]

A company that manufactures and sells a range of products, with sales potential limited by market share, is considering introducing a system of budgeting.

Task

(a) List (in order of preparation) the various budgets that need to be prepared.

(b) Consider how the work can be co-ordinated in order for the budgeting process to be successful.

3   TYPES OF BUDGET

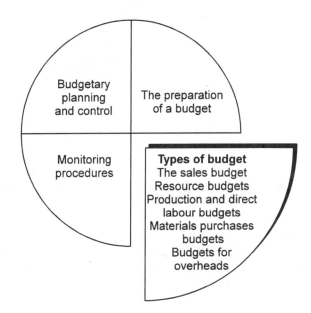

3.1   The sales budget

We have already established that, for many organisations, the principal budget factor is sales volume. The sales budget is therefore often the primary budget from which the majority of the other budgets are derived.

Before the sales budget can be prepared a sales forecast has to be made. A forecast is an estimate of what is likely to occur in the future. The forecast becomes the budget once management have accepted it as the objective or target. Sales forecasting is complex and difficult and involves the consideration of a number of factors.

(a) Past sales patterns

(b) The economic environment

(c) Results of market research

(d) Anticipated advertising during the budget period

(e) Competition

(f) Changing consumer taste

(g) New legislation

(h) Distribution and quality of sales outlets and personnel

On the basis of the sales forecast and the production capacity of the organisation, a sales budget will be prepared. This may be subdivided, possible subdivisions being by product, by sales area, by management responsibility and so on.

Here is an example.

	Units ('000)		Revenue (£'000)	
	North	South	North	South
Product X	2,000	3,200	1,500	2,400
Product Y	1,300	2,500	975	1,875

Activity 3   **[15 minutes]**

Interpret the sales budget shown above. What else could it show to make the information more useful?

Once the sales budget has been agreed, resource budgets can be prepared.

3.2 Resource budgets

If the principal budget factor was production capacity then the production budget would be the first to be prepared.

To assess whether production is the principal budget factor, the production capacity available must be determined. This should take into account the following factors.

(a) Available labour, including idle time, overtime and standard output rates per hour

(b) Availability of raw materials including allowances for losses during production

(c) Maximum machine hours available, including expected idle time and expected output rates per machine hour

The production budget will show the quantities and costs for each product and product group and will tie in with the sales and stock budgets. This co-ordinating process is likely to show any shortfalls or excesses in capacity at various times over the budget period. If there is likely to be a shortfall then decisions need to be made about overtime, subcontracting, machine hire, new sources of raw materials or some other way of increasing output. A significant shortfall means that production capacity is, in fact, the limiting factor.

 Once the production budget has been finalised, the labour, materials and machine budgets can be drawn up. These budgets will be based on budgeted activity levels, existing stock positions and projected labour and material costs. We shall look at two examples.

3.3 Production and direct labour budgets

EXAMPLE: PRODUCTION BUDGETS

Landslide Ltd manufactures two products, A and B, and is preparing its budget for 1997. Both products are made by the same grade of labour, grade Q. The company currently holds 800 units of A and 1,200 units of B in stock, but 250 of these units of B have just been discovered to have deteriorated in quality, and must therefore be scrapped. Budgeted sales of A are 3,000 units and of B are 4,000 units, provided that the company maintains finished goods stocks at a level equal to 3 months' sales.

Grade Q labour was originally expected to produce 1 unit of A in two hours and 1 unit of B in three hours, at an hourly rate of £2.50 per hour. In discussions with trade union negotiators, however, it has been agreed that the hourly wage rate should be raised by 50p per hour, provided that the times to produce A and B are reduced by 20%.

Task

Prepare the production budget and direct labour budget for 1997. (You might like to cover up the solution and try this as an activity.)

Solution

The expected time to produce a unit of A will now be 80% × 2 hours = 1.6 hours, and the time for a unit of B will be 2.4 hours. The hourly wage rate will be £3.

(a) *Production budget*

		Product A			Product B	
		Units	Units		Units	Units
Budgeted sales			3,000		4,000	
Closing stocks	(3/12 of 3,000)	750		(3/12 of 4,000)	1,000	
Opening stocks						
(minus stocks scrapped)		800			950	
(Decrease)/increase in stocks			(50)			50
Production			2,950			4,050

(b) *Direct labour budget*

	Grade Q	Cost
	Hours	£
2,950 units of Product A	4,720	14,160
4,050 units of Product B	9,720	29,160
Total	14,440	43,320

3.4 Material purchases budget

EXAMPLE: MATERIALS BUDGET

Earthquake Ltd manufactures two products, S and T, which use the same raw materials, D and E. 1 unit of S uses 3 litres of D and 4 kilograms of E. 1 unit of T uses 5 litres of D and 2 kilograms of E. A litre of D is expected to cost £3 and a kilogram of E £7.

Budgeted sales for 1996 are 8,000 units of S and 6,000 units of T; finished goods in stock at 1 January 1996 are 1,500 units of S and 300 units of T, and the company plans to hold stocks of 600 units of each product at 31 December 1996.

Stocks of raw material are 6,000 litres of D and 2,800 kilograms of E at 1 January, and the company plans to hold 5,000 litres and 3,500 kilograms respectively at 31 December 1996.

The warehouse and stores managers have suggested that a provision should be made for damages and deterioration of items held in store, as follows.

Product S :	loss of 50 units
Product T :	loss of 100 units
Material D :	loss of 500 litres
Material E :	loss of 200 kilograms

Task

Prepare a material purchases budget for 1996.

Solution

To calculate material purchase requirements, it is first of all necessary to calculate the budgeted production volumes and material usage requirements

(a) *Production budget*

	Product S		Product T	
	Units	Units	Units	Units
Sales		8,000		6,000
Provision for losses		50		100
Closing stock	600		600	
Opening stock	1,500		300	
(Decrease)/increase in stock		(900)		300
Production budget		7,150		6,400

	Material D		Material E	
	Litres	Litres	Kg	Kg
Usage requirements				
To produce 7,150 units of S		21,450		28,600
To produce 6,400 units of T		32,000		12,800
Usage budget		53,450		41,400
Provision for losses		500		200
		53,950		41,600
Closing stock	5,000		3,500	
Opening stock	6,000		2,800	
(Decrease)/increase in stock		(1,000)		700
Materials purchases budget		52,950		42,300
Cost per unit		£3 per litre		£7 per kg
Cost of material purchases		£158,850		£296,100
Total purchases cost		£454,950		

Activity 4 [45 minutes]

JK Limited has recently completed its sales forecasts for the year to 31 December 1996. It expects to sell two products J and K at prices of £135 and £145 each respectively.

Sales demand is expected to be as follows.

    J   10,000 units
    K   6,000 units

Both products use the same raw materials and skilled labour but in different quantities per unit.

	J	K
Material X	10 kgs	6 kgs
Material Y	4 kgs	8 kgs
Skilled labour	6 hours	4 hours

The prices expected during 19X4 for the raw materials are as follows.

Material X	£1.50 per kg
Material Y	£4.00 per kg

The skilled labour rate is expected to be £6.00 per hour.

Stocks of raw materials and finished goods on 1 January 1996 are expected to be as follows.

Material X	400 kgs	@ £1.20 per kg
Material Y	200 kgs	@ £3.00 per kg
J	600 units	@ £70.00 each
K	800 units	@ £60.00 each

All stocks are to be reduced by 15% from their opening levels by the end of 1996 and are valued using the FIFO method.

The company uses absorption costing, and production overhead costs are expected to be as follows.

| Variable | £2.00 per skilled labour hour |
| Fixed | £315,900 per annum |

Task

Prepare for the year to 31 December 1996 the following budgets for JK Limited.

(a) Production budget (in units)

(b) Raw material purchases budget (in units and £)

(c) Production cost budget

Finally we shall give some thought to overhead budgets. If you work for a service company, or in a service department, most of the costs connected with your work are probably overheads.

3.5 Budgets for overheads

Until fairly recently budgeting for overheads was relatively unsophisticated compared with budgeting for direct costs. Typically the figure in the budget for an overhead would simply be last year's figure plus a percentage for inflation. However, noticing a trend for overheads to form a larger and larger proportion of an organisation's total costs (mainly because of technology), academics developed a technique called Activity Based Costing (ABC).

The basic idea of ABC is simple: costs are analysed according to what *causes* them to be incurred. For example the costs of an accounting department are caused by things like the number of customers, the number of suppliers and the number of transactions. Once this is realised overhead budgeting can be far more scientific. For example, if sales are budgeted to increase by 5%, rather than just increasing accounting department costs by 5% it ought to be possible to predict the impact of the extra sales in terms of number of new debtors and number of new transactions. Maybe the plan is simply to sell larger quantities per existing transaction to existing customers, in which case there will be no impact on accounting costs at all.

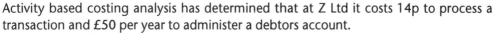

Activity 5 [45 minutes]

Activity based costing analysis has determined that at Z Ltd it costs 14p to process a transaction and £50 per year to administer a debtors account.

Z Ltd have 7,442 credit customers. The total number of transactions with customers was 447,892.

Next year it is expected that 250 new credit customers will buy from Z Ltd and around 30 existing customers will be lost. Transactions are expected to be up to 470,000.

What are the budgeted costs of the accounting department:

(a) if last year's costs are increased by 5%;

(b) if activity based costing is used to make the forecast?

The budgeting process does not stop once the budgets have been agreed. Actual results should be compared on a regular basis with the budgeted results. The frequency with which such comparisons are made depends very much on the organisation's circumstances and the sophistication of its control systems but it should occur at least monthly. Management should receive a report detailing the differences and should investigate the reasons for the differences. If the differences are within the control of management, corrective action should be taken to bring the reasons for the difference under control and to ensure that such inefficiencies do not occur in the future.

The next section describes the techniques that can be used to monitor actual performance by means of budgets.

4   MONITORING PROCEDURES

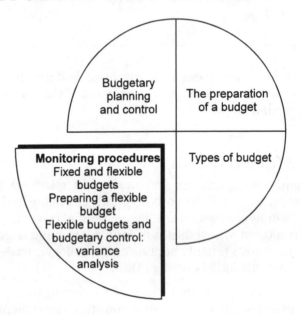

4.1   Fixed and flexible budgets

The master budget prepared before the beginning of the budget period is known as the fixed budget. By the term 'fixed', we do not mean that the budget is kept unchanged. Revisions to a fixed master budget will be made if the situation so demands. The term 'fixed' means the following.

(a) The budget is prepared on the basis of an estimated volume of production and an estimated volume of sales, but no plans are made for the event that actual volumes of production and sales may differ from budgeted volumes.

(b) When actual volumes of production and sales during a control period (month or four weeks) are achieved, a fixed budget is not adjusted (in retrospect) to the new levels of activity.

A flexible budget recognises the existence of fixed, variable and mixed (semi-fixed, semi-variable) costs, and it is designed to change so as to relate to the actual volumes of production and sales in a period. Flexible budgets may be used in one of two ways.

(a) *At the planning stage.* For example, suppose that a company expects to sell 10,000 units of output during the next year. A master budget (the fixed budget) would be prepared on the basis of these expected volumes. However, if the company thinks that output and sales might be as low as 8,000 units or as high as 12,000 units, it may prepare contingency flexible budgets, at volumes of, say 8,000,

9,000, 11,000 and 12,000 units. There are a number of advantages of planning with flexible budgets.

(i)   It is possible to find out well in advance the costs of lay-off pay, idle time and so on if output falls short of budget.

(ii) Management can decide whether it would be possible to find alternative uses for spare capacity if output falls short of budget (could employees be asked to overhaul their own machines for example, instead of paying for an outside contractor?).

(iii) An estimation of the costs of overtime, subcontracting work or extra machine hire if sales volume exceeds the fixed budget estimate can be made and it can be established whether there is a limiting factor which would prevent high volumes of output and sales being achieved.

(b) *Retrospectively.* At the end of each month (control period) or year, flexible budgets can be used to compare actual results achieved with what results should have been under the circumstances. Flexible budgets are an essential factor in budgetary control.

(i)   Management needs to be informed about how good or bad actual performance has been. To provide a measure of performance, there must be a yardstick against which actual performance can be measured.

(ii) Every business is dynamic, and actual volumes of output cannot be expected to conform exactly to the fixed budget. Comparing actual costs directly with the fixed budget costs is meaningless.

(iii) For useful control information, it is necessary to compare actual results at the actual level of activity achieved against the results that should have been achieved at this level of activity. These are shown by the flexible budget.

Let's look at an example of a simple flexible budget.

4.2   Preparing a flexible budget

Suppose that Lodestone Ltd expects production and sales during the next year to be 90% of the company's output capacity, that is, 9,000 units of a single product. Historical records of cost show the following details

Units of output/sales	Cost of sales
9,800	£44,400
7,700	£38,100

The company's management is not certain that the estimate of sales is correct, and has asked for flexible budgets to be prepared at output and sales levels of 8,000 and 10,000 units. The sales price per unit has been fixed at £5.

Task

Prepare appropriate budgets.

Solution

If we assume that within the range 8,000 to 10,000 units of sales, all costs are fixed, variable or mixed (in other words there are no stepped costs, material discounts, overtime premiums, bonus payments etc) the fixed and flexible budgets would be based on the estimate of fixed and variable cost.

	£
Total cost of 9,800 units	44,400
Total cost of 7,700 units	38,100
Variable cost of 2,100 units	6,300

The variable cost per unit is £6,300/2,100 = £3.

	£
Total cost of 9,800 units	44,400
Variable cost of 9,800 units (9,800 × £3)	29,400
Fixed costs (all levels of output and sales)	15,000

The fixed budgets and flexible budgets might now be prepared as follows.

	Flexible budget 8,000 units	Master budget 9,000 units	Flexible budget 10,000 units
	£	£	£
Sales (× £5)	40,000	45,000	50,000
Variable costs (× £3)	24,000	27,000	30,000
Fixed costs	15,000	15,000	15,000
Profit	1,000	3,000	5,000

The above illustrates the use of flexible budgets at the planning stage. Let's now see how they can be used retrospectively for monitoring purposes.

4.3 Flexible budgets and budgetary control: variance analysis

The most important method of budgetary control is variance analysis, which in this context involves the comparison of actual results achieved during a control period (a month, or 4 weeks) with a flexible budget. The differences between actual results and expected results are called *variances* and these are used to provide a guideline for control action by individual managers.

Definition

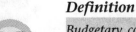

Budgetary control is the practice of establishing budgets which identify areas of responsibility for individual managers (for example production managers, purchasing managers and so on) and of regularly comparing actual results against expected results.

Note that individual managers are held responsible for investigating differences between budgeted and actual results, and are then expected to take corrective action or amend the plan in the light of actual events.

The wrong approach to budgetary control is to compare actual results against a fixed budget. Consider the following example.

Sidewinder Limited manufactures a single product. Budgeted results and actual results for June 1996 are shown below.

	Budget	Actual results	Variance
Production (units)	2,000	3,000	1,000
	£	£	£
Direct materials	6,000	8,500	2,500
Direct labour	4,000	4,500	500
Maintenance	1,000	1,400	400
Depreciation	2,000	2,200	200
Rent and rates	1,500	1,600	100
Other costs	3,600	5,000	1,400
Total costs	18,100	23,200	5,100

In this example, the variances are not nearly as meaningful as they could be. Costs were higher than budget because the volume of output was higher; variable costs would be expected to increase above the budgeted costs in the fixed budget. There is no information to help decide whether any action is needed for any aspect of costs or revenue. For control purposes, it is therefore necessary to know the answers to questions such as: were actual costs higher than they should have been to produce 3,000 units?

A better approach to budgetary control is as follows.

(a) Identify fixed and variable costs.
(b) Produce a flexible budget using marginal costing techniques.

In the example of Sidewinder Ltd, let us suppose that we have the following estimates of cost behaviour.

(a) Direct materials and maintenance costs are variable.

(b) Although basic wages are a fixed cost, direct labour is regarded as variable in order to measure efficiency/productivity.

(c) Rent and rates and depreciation are fixed costs.

(d) Other costs consist of fixed costs of £1,600 plus a variable cost of £1 per unit made and sold.

The budgetary control (variance) analysis should be as follows.

	Fixed budget (a)	Flexible budget (b)	Actual results (c)	Budget variance (b) - (c)
Production (units)	2,000	3,000	3,000	
	£	£	£	£
Variable costs				
Direct materials	6,000	9,000	8,500	500 (F)
Direct labour	4,000	6,000	4,500	1,500 (F)
Maintenance	1,000	1,500	1,400	100 (F)
Semi-variable costs				
Other costs	3,600	4,600	5,000	400 (A)
Fixed costs				
Depreciation	2,000	2,000	2,200	200 (A)
Rent and rates	1,500	1,500	1,600	100 (A)
Total costs	18,100	24,600	23,200	1,400 (F)

Note. (F) denotes a favourable variance (where less than expected was spent) and (A) an adverse or unfavourable variance (where more than expected was spent).

Activity 6 [15 minutes]

(a) How are the following figures in the flexible budget above calculated?

(i) Direct materials

(ii) Other costs

(b) What is depreciation and why is it the same in both the fixed and the flexible budget? Comment also on the actual depreciation figure.

We can analyse the above as follows.

(a) In producing 3,000 units the expected costs should have been, not the fixed budget costs of £18,100, but the flexible budget costs of £24,600. Instead, actual costs were £23,200 ie £1,400 less than we should have expected. The reason for the improvement is that, given output of 3,000 units, costs were lower than expected.

(b) Variable costs should have been greater than the £11,000 in the fixed budget because the company produced 3,000 units instead of 2,000 units. Costs should have increased by ½ (6,000 + 4,000 + 1,000) = £5,500, which was budgeted as the variable cost of 1,000 units. This is the difference between the fixed and flexible budgets. Semi-variable costs should have risen by £1,000 for the increased production. (We do not take fixed costs into account since they remain unchanged as activity levels change.)

(c) A full variance analysis statement would be as follows.

	£		£
Fixed budget costs			18,100
Budgeted difference due to increased production level			
(£5,500 + £1,000)			6,500
Flexible budget costs			24,600
Variances			
Direct materials cost	500	(F)	
Direct labour cost	1,500	(F)	
Maintenance cost	100	(F)	
Other costs	400	(A)	
Depreciation	200	(A)	
Rent and rates	100	(A)	
			1,400 (F)
Actual costs			23,200

Such a statement could be prepared by the accountant and then circulated to senior management and/or operational management in a periodically-prepared budgetary control report. Operational management may then be asked to investigate the reasons for large variances so that they can decide whether any corrective action is necessary.

Table 6.1 shows a variety of common variances that can be calculated and suggests possible reasons why they might have occurred.

Brief summary of the meanings of variences

Variance	Favourable	Adverse
Material price	Unforeseen discounts received. Greater care taken in purchasing Change in material standard	Price increase Careless purchasing Change in material standard
Material usage	Material used of higher quality than standard / less wastage More efficient use made of material Errors in allocating material to jobs	Defective material Excessive waste Theft Stricter quality control Errors in allocating material to jobs
Labour rate	Use of apprentices or other workers at a rate of pay lower than standard	Wage rate increase Excessive overtime, with over-time premium charged to (direct) labour costs
Idle time		Machine breakdown Non-availability of material Illness or injury to worker
Labour efficiency	Output produced more quickly than expected, that is actual output in excess of standard output set for same number of hours because of worker motivation, better quality of equipment or materials Errors in allocating time to jobs	Lost time in excess of standard allowed Output lower than standard set because of deliberate restriction, lack of training, or substantial materials used Errors in allocating time to jobs
Fixed overhead price	Savings in costs incurred More economical use of services	Increase in cost of services used Excessive use of services Change in type of service used

Activity 7 [15 minutes]

One month an unfavourable variance of £10,000 arises because a company uses hundreds of kilograms more materials than was expected.

Who is responsible for this variance?

One way of monitoring performance, then, is to compare actual results with what was originally planned. Another way is to compare actual results with results achieved in the past and with results achieved by other businesses. To do this we need to understand a business's annual 'financial accounts'. these are the subject of the next two chapters in this book, the last chapters in the Managing Finance part.

Chapter roundup

- The objectives of a budgetary planning and control system are as follows.
    - To ensure the achievement of the organisation's objectives
    - To compel planning
    - To communicate ideas and plans
    - To co-ordinate activities
    - To provide a framework for responsibility accounting
    - To establish a system of control
    - To motivate employees to improve their performance
- A budget is a quantified plan of action for a forthcoming accounting period.
- Managers responsible for preparing budgets should ideally be the managers responsible for carrying out the budget.
- The budget committee is the co-ordinating body in the preparation and administration of budgets.
- The principal budget factor should be identified at the beginning of the budgetary process, and the budget for this is prepared before all the others.
- Once prepared, the resource budgets must be reviewed to ensure they are consistent with one another.
- The master budget consists of a budgeted profit and loss account, balance sheet and cash budget.
- The budgeting process does not end for the current period once the budget period has begun: budgeting should be seen as a continuous and dynamic process.
- Budgets can be used as a yardstick against which actual results can be compared. If done regularly this is an effective way of monitoring the success of the business. Ideally, flexible budgets should be used.

Quick quiz

1   What are the objectives of a system of budgetary planning and control?
2   What is meant by the term *principal budget factor?*
3   What are the steps in the preparation of a budget?
4   What factors need to be considered when forecasting sales?
5   When might production capacity be the principal budget factor?
6   What is the basic idea of ABC?
7   How can budgets be used to make decisions?
8   What is a variance?
9   What documents comprise the master budget?
10 What do you understand by 'flexible budgets'?

Answers to quick quiz

1   See Section 1.1
2   See Section 2.2, step 1
3   See Section 2.2
4   See Section 3.1
5   When demand exceeds the factory's current ability to manufacture, for reasons such as shortage of raw materials, skilled labour or machine capacity.
6   See Section 3.5
7   See Section 4.3
8   See Section 4.3
9   See Section 2.2, step 8
10 See Section 4.1

Answers to activities

1   (a) Raw materials are things like steel and rubber that a business does work on to make finished products.

    (b) Finished goods are manufactured items that are ready to sell.

    (c) Distribution is the function of a business that sees to it that the finished stock is in a place where the customer can buy it, or is delivered directly to the customer's premises.

    (d) An overhead is a cost which is incurred in the course of making a product, delivering a service, or running a department, but which cannot be traced directly to the product, service or department.

    (e) A budget is a plan expressed in money.

    (f) Idle time is time when workers are at work and being paid but are unable to get on with their job, perhaps because they are waiting for other workers to finish their job or because a machine breaks down.

    (g) A cost centre is a location, a function, an activity or an item of equipment.

    (h) A resource is something that is used in the operations of a business - people, materials, machines, time, space (land and buildings), finance and information.

2   (a) The sequence of budget preparation will be roughly as follows.

        (i)   Sales budget. (The market share limits demand and so sales are the principal budget factor. All other activities will depend upon this forecast.)

        (ii) Finished goods stock budget (in units)

        (iii) Production budget (in units)

        (iv) Production resources budgets (materials, machine hours, labour)

(v) Overhead budgets for production, administration, selling and distribution, research and development and so on

Other budgets required will be the capital expenditure budget, the working capital budget (debtors and creditors) and, very importantly, the cash budget.

(b) Procedures for preparing budgets can be contained in a budget manual which shows which budgets must be prepared when and by whom, what each functional budget should contain and detailed directions on how to prepare budgets including, for example, expected price increases, rates of interest, rates of depreciation and so on.

The formulation of budgets can be co-ordinated by a budget committee comprising the senior executives of the departments responsible for carrying out the budgets: sales, production, purchasing, personnel and so on.

The budgeting process may also be assisted by the use of a spreadsheet/computer budgeting package.

3   The budget shows that 2 million units of product X will be sold in the north and 1.3 million of product Y, while 3.2 million units of product X will be sold in the south and 2.5 million of product Y. It also shows the income that will be received in each case.

The budget could helpfully show totals as follows.

	Units ('000)			Revenue (£'000)		
	North	South	Total	North	South	Total
Product X	2,000	3,200	5,200	1,500	2,400	3,900
Product Y	1,300	2,500	3,800	975	1,875	2,850
	3,300	5,700	9,000	2,475	4,275	6,750

It would also be useful to show the selling price per unit. (In fact it is 75p for both products in both regions.)

4   (a) *Production budget*

		J	K
		Units	Units
Opening stock		(600)	(800)
Closing stock (85%)		510	680
Sales		10,000	6,000
		9,910	5,880

(b) *Raw materials purchases budget*

		X	Y
		kg	kg
Opening stock		(400)	(200)
Production (per (a))			
J (10 kg/4 kg)		99,100	39,640
K (6 kg/8 kg)		35,280	47,040
		133,980	86,480
Closing stock		340	170
		134,320	86,650
Cost per kg		£1.50	£4.00
Purchase cost		£201,480	£346,600

(c) *Production cost budget*

	£
Materials	
Opening stock (400 kg × £1.20) + (200 kg × £3)	1,080
Purchases £(201,480 + 346,600)	548,080
	549,160
Closing stock (340 kg × £1.50) + (170 kg × £4)	(1,190)
	547,970
Skilled labour (W1)	497,880
Variable overhead (W2)	165,960
Fixed overhead	315,900
	1,527,710

Workings

1 *Labour hours budget*

	J	K
Units produced per (a)	9,910	5,880
Hours per unit	6	4
Total hours	59,460	23,520

(59,460 + 23,520) = 82,980 hours × £6 = £497,880

2 *Variable overheads*

82,980 hours (W1) × £2 = £165,960

5 (a)

	£
Credit customers' costs (7,442 × £50)	372,100
Transaction costs (447,892 × £0.14)	62,705
	434,805
Increase by 5%	£456,545

(b)

	£
Credit customers' costs ((7,442 + 250 – 30) × £50)	383,100
Transaction costs (470,000 × £0.14)	65,800
	448,900

6 This activity is to encourage you to study and work through the figures for yourself.

(a) (i) Direct materials are a variable cost. If 3,000 units are produced instead of 2,000 the cost may be expected to be:

(£6,000 × 3,000)/2,000 = £9,000

(ii) Other costs are part variable and part fixed. The fixed part should not be expected to change.

	£
Fixed cost	1,600
Variable cost × 3,000 × £1)	3,000
	4,600

(b) Depreciation is a measure of how much a fixed asset has worn out during a period. It is stated in the information given to be a fixed cost. The actual results suggest that it may not be, or that new information has come to light that means that the original estimate was 'wrong' (though depreciation is only ever an estimate).

7 The variance might have been caused by the department that uses the materials if they did so wastefully. Alternatively the *purchasing* department may have bought poor quality materials to try to save money, meaning that more materials were wasted. This is an example of how the price of something might affect its usage - the so-called interdependence of variances. Another possibility is that the original estimate was wrong in the first place - whoever prepared the budget would then be responsible.

(*Note.* If you answered along the lines that the extra kilograms might have been used because the production department made more units than expected you are wrong. Remember that the budget should be flexed to allow for this before any variances are calculated.)

Assignment 6 [2 hours]

At the start of your course, your Chapter 1 assignment was to consider some of the aspects of a business you would like to start if you came into some money.

Using your additional newly acquired financial knowledge, progress your business planning further by preparing budgets for sales, materials purchase, overheads and cash flow by month for the first 6 months of your business.

You would probably find it to your advantage to do this work on a computer, if one is available.

There is, of course, no right answer to this assignment, but you are encouraged to swap answers with one of your colleagues, and each constructively criticise the content, presentation and business logic of each others' finished product. Alternatively, your tutor may wish to review your work.

Chapter 7

FINANCIAL PERFORMANCE

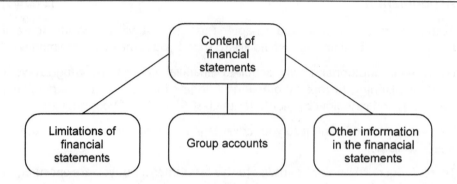

Introduction

During Part A of this book we have traced the history of a business from the initial raising of money to finance it, through various aspects of the management of the business and its money until this point, where we come to the end result. The results of a business's activities are presented in financial terms in the form of what are commonly called the 'accounts'.

In this context 'accounts' means two statements a balance sheet and a profit and loss account - and perhaps a third, showing cash flow.

This chapter describes these statements and illustrates the format in which they are usually presented. In the next chapter we shall see how the statements can be interpreted to give an idea of how well a business is performing.

Your objectives

After completing this chapter you should:

(a) understand how a balance sheet and profit and loss account fit together, and know what they look like;

(b) understand why cash flow statements are prepared and know what sort of information they contain;

(c) be aware of the range of information contained in the notes to published accounts;

(d) be aware of some of the peculiarities of group accounts;

(e) be able to list the limitations of financial statements;

(f) understand the meaning of an auditor's report.

1 CONTENT OF FINANCIAL STATEMENTS

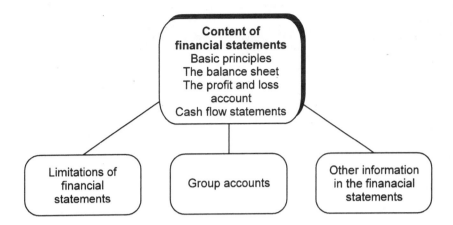

1.1 Basic principles

Businesses produce statements of their financial results for a number of reasons:

(a) in the case of companies, to comply with the law (Companies Act 1985);

(b) to inform the people who are interested in the company about its situation (the shareholders, employees, bank, Inland Revenue, trade contacts, financial markets etc); and

(c) to help management in managing the company.

A business's 'accounts' - more properly called 'financial statements' - can be confusing documents when you first encounter them. For the completely uninitiated we begin by setting out some basics.

The principles of a balance sheet and a profit and loss account are very simple. Suppose you decide on Wednesday to invest £100 of your savings in a business venture. This is represented in a balance sheet as follows.

BALANCE SHEET WEDNESDAY

	£
Net assets	
Cash at the bank	100
Capital	
Owner's capital	100

It 'balances' because net assets are equal to capital: they are both £100. Balance sheets *always* balance.

On Thursday you buy an item for £50 and some paint for £5. Later you sell the painted item for £70. You are very pleased with yourself and so you pay yourself £5 to have a drink. You also buy another £50 item and another £5 of paint.

This time we can draw up both a balance sheet and a profit and loss account. Note how the balance sheet has changed and how the profit not squandered on drink turns into *retained* profit.

PROFIT AND LOSS ACCOUNT THURSDAY

	£	£
Sales		70
Cost of sales	55	
Drawings or wages	5	
		(60)
Profit		10

Figures in brackets are negative.

BALANCE SHEET THURSDAY

	£
Net assets	
Stock	55
Cash at the bank	55
	110
Capital	
Owner's capital	100
Retained profit	10
	110

A full balance sheet and profit and loss account prepared by a company is no more complicated than this in principle, it just covers a longer period (typically one year) and shows more detail.

Activity 1 [15 minutes]

(a) If all the transactions had been done on credit the net assets would include debtors and creditors. Can you draw up the balance sheet?

(b) (i) What is the value of the business if it stops trading on Thursday?

(ii) What is the value of the business if it carries on trading in exactly the same way (not on credit) for another four days but does not buy any stock on the last day?

(c) Why are there two lots of £110?

We shall now consider the basic structure and contents of detailed financial statements. These can be looked at in four stages: the balance sheet, the profit and loss account, the cash flow statement and the notes to the accounts.

1.2 The balance sheet

A balance sheet is a statement of the assets, liabilities and capital of a business at a given moment in time. It is like a 'snapshot' photograph, since it captures on paper a still image, frozen at a single moment in time, of something which is dynamic and continually changing. Sometimes it is called the 'position statement', because it shows the financial position of a business at a given moment. A balance sheet is prepared to show the assets, liabilities and capital as at the end of the accounting period to which the financial accounts relate.

Balance sheets are nearly always presented in the format shown below, but because each business is different there can be some variations in classifications and presentation. However, one of the main aims of interpretation of financial statements is consistency between one company and the next and between one accounting period and the next.

A LIMITED
BALANCE SHEET AS AT 31 MARCH 1996

	Cost £	Depreciation £	Net Book Value £
Fixed assets			
Land and buildings	10,000	4,000	6,000
Plant and machinery	10,000	6,000	4,000
Vehicles	4,000	2,000	1,000
	24,000	13,000	11,000
Current assets			
Stock	2,900		
Debtors	8,600		
Cash in hand	2,500		
		14,000	
Creditors: amounts falling due in less than one year			
Bank overdraft	(1,500)		
Trade creditors	(2,000)		
Other creditors	(3,000)		
		(7,000)	
Net current assets			7,000
			18,000
Creditors: amounts falling due in more than one year			
Bank loan			(3,000)
			15,000
Capital and reserves			
Share capital			5,000
Profit and loss account			10,000
			15,000

Activity 2 [15 minutes]

(a) There are two deliberate mistakes in the balance sheet figures shown above. See if you can find them.

(b) What is 'net book value'?

(c) Why do you think the 'profit and loss account' is shown as a single figure in the balance sheet?

1.3 The profit and loss account

A profit and loss account is a record of income generated and expenditure incurred over a given period. The period chosen will depend on the purpose for which the statement is produced. The profit and loss account which forms part of the 'published' annual accounts of a limited company will usually be made up for the period of a year, commencing from the date of the previous year's accounts. On the other hand, management might want to keep a closer eye on a company's profitability by making up a quarterly or monthly profit and loss account. These are known as management accounts.

Definition

Published accounts are not published in the sense that you can go and buy a copy in a bookshop or a newsagents. 'Published' means that they are available for consultation by the general public. You have to pay a small fee to a government body called Companies House to see them. *All* companies have to publish their accounts in this way.

Large public companies are usually happy to send out copies of their financial statements to anybody that asks.

Many businesses try to distinguish between a gross profit earned on trading activities, and a net profit after deducting all non-trading costs and adding any non-trading income. They do this by preparing a statement called the trading, profit and loss account.

(a) In the first part of the statement (the trading account) revenue from selling goods is compared with direct costs of acquiring or producing the goods sold, to arrive at a *gross profit* figure.

(b) In the second part of the statement (the profit and loss account), deductions and additions are made from gross profit to arrive at a *net profit* figure. The deductions are in respect of costs not directly linked with trading: indirect costs (or overheads). Similarly, the additions are in respect of income not directly linked with trading, and are usually called non-trading income.

Here is an example of a 'detailed' trading and profit and loss account.

B LIMITED TRADING AND PROFIT AND LOSS ACCOUNT
FOR THE YEAR ENDED 30 SEPTEMBER 1996

	£	£
Sales		33,340
Cost of sales		
Opening stock	890	
Purchases	18,995	
	19,885	
Closing stock	775	
		19,110
Gross profit		14,230
Less expenses		
Bank charges	120	
Rent	2,400	
Postage and stationery	65	
Profit on sale of plant	(315)	
Wages	1,930	
Motor expenses	1,155	
Electricity	585	
Business rates	2,700	
Depreciation	2,069	
		10,709
Profit before taxation		3,521
Corporation tax		810
Profit after taxation		2,711
Dividend		700
Retained profit for the year		2,011

This level of detail would be useful for the company's own use and may be required by the Inland Revenue. However, there is less information in a profit and loss account in the format normally used for *publication*. This is because the Companies Act only requires a limited amount of information to be disclosed.

C LIMITED
PROFIT AND LOSS ACCOUNT FOR THE YEAR ENDED 31 MARCH 1996

	£	£
Turnover		20,000
Cost of sales		(9,000)
Gross profit		11,000
Administration expenses	3,000	
Distribution costs	2,000	
		5,000
Profit on ordinary activities before taxation		6,000
Exceptional gain		1,000
		7,000
Tax on profit on ordinary activities		1,750
Profit for the financial year		5,250
Dividend proposed		1,250
Retained profit for the financial year		4,000

The required format for the profit and loss account has recently changed but most of the changes relate to larger companies. These aspects are discussed briefly later in this chapter.

The 'exceptional' gain might be receipt of insurance proceeds, or profit on disposal of part of the business or any other item which wouldn't be expected in the normal run of trading. (An exceptional loss can also arise.) Just like other profits, there is likely to be a tax charge on these gains, and this is included in the tax charge on ordinary activities.

'Ordinary activities' are precisely that - the things that the company usually does. Some accounts used to show 'extraordinary items', ie 'one-off' items but regulations have made these extremely rare.

The balance sheet and the profit and loss account are the main financial statements. However you may remember that we pointed out the distinction between profits and cash in an earlier chapter - profit takes account of money owed to you and money you owe to others, and it reflects 'notional' expenses like depreciation, so it is not the same as cash in the bank. An apparently profitable company can be in great difficulties in reality because it is short of cash. Where many investors are involved it is important to have a fuller picture of the state of the company.

1.4 Cash flow statements

A cash flow statement explains differences between profit and cash and also shows where a business gets its capital from and what uses it puts the capital to. Only large companies are *required* to produce a cash flow statement, though smaller companies can do so if they wish.

We will not describe the preparation of a cash flow statement in detail. However, you should certainly be aware of what the statement looks like because you may encounter them in practice. Here is the standard format, together with the accompanying notes that companies have to produce.

Study the cash flow statement and then do the activity that follows.

Definition

An *intangible fixed asset* is a fixed asset that does not have a physical existence. It cannot be 'touched'. A good example is a trade mark. 'Coca-Cola' is a trade mark. It is an asset because it helps the Coca-Cola company to make profits - people buy things with the trade mark Cola-Cola in preference to other types of cola.

XYZ LIMITED
CASH FLOW STATEMENT FOR THE YEAR ENDED 31 MARCH 1996

	£	£
Net cash inflow from operating activities		6,889
Returns on investments and servicing of finance	3,011	
Interest paid	(12)	
Dividends paid	(2,417)	
Net cash inflow from returns on investments and servicing of finance		582
Taxation		
Corporation tax paid		(2,922)
Investing activities		
Payments to acquire intangible fixed assets	(71)	
Payments to acquire tangible fixed assets	(1,496)	
Receipts from sales of tangible fixed assets	42	
Net cash outflow from investing activities		(1,525)
Net cash inflow before financing		3,024
Financing		
Issue of ordinary capital	211	
Repurchase of debenture loan	(149)	
Expenses paid in connection with share issues	(5)	
Net cash inflow from financing		57
Increase in cash and cash equivalents		3,081

NOTES TO THE CASH FLOW STATEMENT

1 *Reconciliation of operating profit to net cash inflow from operating activities*

	£
Operating profit	6,022
Depreciation charges	893
Loss on sale of tangible fixed assets	6
Increase in stocks	(194)
Increase in debtors	(72)
Increase in creditors	234
Net cash inflow from operating activities	6,889

2 *Analysis of changes in cash and cash equivalents during the year*

	£
Balance at 1 April 1995	21,373
Net cash inflow	3,081
Balance at 31 March 1996	24,454

3 *Analysis of the balances of cash and cash equivalents as shown in the balance sheet*

	1996 £	1995 £	Change in year £
Cash at bank and in hand	529	681	(152)
Short-term investments	23,936	20,700	3,236
Bank overdrafts	(11)	(8)	(3)
	24,454	21,373	3,081

4   *Analysis of changes in finance during the year*

	Share Capital £	Debenture loan £
Balance at 1 April 1995	27,411	156
Cash inflow/(outflow) from financing	211	(149)
Profit on repurchase of debenture loan for less than its book value		(7)
Balance at 31 March 1996	27,622	-

Note that companies are encouraged, but not required, to provide further information on the make-up of 'net cash inflow from operating activities' as shown below.

	£
Operating activities	
Cash received from customers	79,006
Cash payments to suppliers	(43,690)
Cash paid to and on behalf of employees	(22,574)
Other cash payments	(4,938)
Net cash inflow from continuing operating activities	7,804
Net cash outflow in respect of discontinued activities and reorganisation costs	(915)
Net cash inflow from operating activities	6,889

Activity 3   [45 minutes]

The cash flow statement and its notes contain many reminders of topics you have encountered earlier in this book. See if you can answer the following questions.

(a) How has the company raised capital during the year?

(b) Does the company have a larger amount of borrowed money than of shareholders' capital?

(c) Note 1 shows changes in the components of working capital. What might be the reasons for an increase in debtors and for an increase in creditors?

(d) What is a debenture loan?

(e) Is depreciation included anywhere in the cash flow statement or notes? Where, if so, or why not, if not?

(f) What cash has to be paid 'on behalf of' employees?

If you get hold of a company's financial statements you will probably find it difficult to locate the three main statements at first. An annual 'Report and Accounts' contains a wealth of other information about the company, which we shall look at now.

2   OTHER INFORMATION IN THE FINANCIAL STATEMENTS

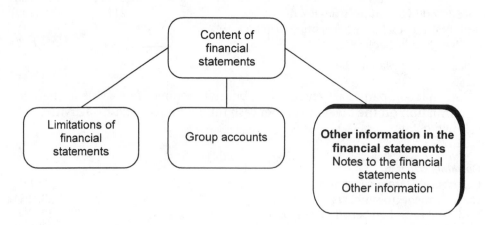

2.1   Notes to the financial statements

As the example of a cash flow statement shows, the *notes* to financial statements give supplementary information which can be useful:

(a) in analysing figures in the accounts; and

(b) in providing information not otherwise available from the accounts.

An example of the extra detail to be found in the notes is the stocks note. In the notes in A Ltd's accounts, the stocks note might look like this.

	1996 £	1995 £
Stocks and work in progress		
Raw materials and consumables	500	1,200
Work in progress	800	1,100
Finished goods and goods for resale	1,600	1,700
	2,900	4,000

Note that in published accounts the requirement is to show not only the current year's figures but also the previous year's. The previous year's figures are known as the *comparatives* because they allow users of the financial statements to see how much better or worse the company has done this year compared with last year.

Other figures in the accounts analysed in more detail are as follows.

(a) Fixed assets (tangible, intangible, investments)

(b) Debtors

(c) Creditors (current and long term)

(d) Interest payable

(e) Tax on profits

(f) Extraordinary items (now very rare)

(g) Dividends payable

For example, long term creditors are analysed by the date the loan has to be repaid as well as by type of creditor. Here is an example.

Loans

	1996 £	1995 £
Wholly repayable within five years	100,000	100,000
Not wholly repayable within five years		
Bank loan at 15% per annum, repayable in instalments of £10,000 from 1 January 1997	60,000	60,000
US dollar loan at 14% per annum, wholly repayable on 31 December 2005	120,000	-
	280,000	160,000
Amounts repayable after five years		
other than by instalments	120,000	-
Amounts repayable by instalments		
Within five years	150,000	140,000
After five years	10,000	20,000
	280,000	160,000
Included in current liabilities	30,000	-
	250,000	160,000

The US dollar loan is secured by a fixed charge on the freehold property, and the bank loans are secured by a floating charge on the assets of the company.

Information not given elsewhere in the financial statements includes:

(a) directors' pay and rewards;

(b) average number of employees;

(c) details of transactions with directors.

This is useful information (although probably out of date by the time you get hold of the accounts) because it gives a fuller picture of the company's activities than that given by the accounts.

Definition

A *director* of a company is a person who takes part in making decisions and managing a company's affairs. Private companies *must* have at least one director and public companies must have at least *two*. Directors have to be re-elected by the shareholders at regular intervals. Appointment as a director carries many duties. The law is complex, but in broad terms directors must be honest and not seek personal advantage and must also show reasonable competence in managing the company.

For discussion

There has been a lot of fuss in the press recently about directors' pay. What are your views on the senior managers of large companies receiving very large salaries?

Besides the notes (which are required by law), large company annual reports usually have pictures of the directors, or of staff members at work, or of the company's buildings and machines, perhaps some charts, graphs and diagrams, and commentaries by leading figures in the company saying how well it is doing. Is any of this useful, or is it just hype?

2.2 Other information

Sometimes you can get useful information from other statements in the accounts. For example, all financial statements must include a *directors' report* which is supposed to include, amongst other things, a fair review of the business for the year and an indication of future developments. As you would expect, however, the directors are rarely overwhelmingly frank about problems in the business nor are they likely, except where things are obviously going badly wrong, to be gloomy in their forecasts.

Another drawback is that (except for the directors' report) the other information sent out with the accounts is not independently verified by auditors (see below) and therefore there is less likelihood of objectivity in the *chairman's* report or in a glossy brochure looking at the company's activities in detail (so long as they are photogenic) than in the accounts.

Most well-known companies are actually groups made up of a number of smaller companies. There are certain peculiarities about group accounts that you should know about.

3   GROUP ACCOUNTS

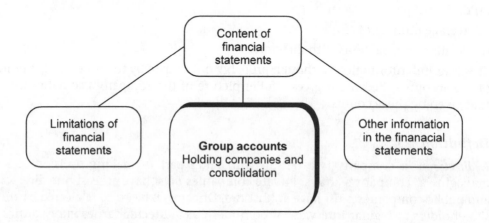

3.1 Holding companies and consolidation

When one company (a holding company) owns or controls a majority of the shares in another company or controls another business (has 'Associates' or 'Subsidiaries'), it is required by law to prepare 'consolidated' accounts (or group accounts) which effectively show the assets, liabilities, income and expenses of the group as if it were one company instead of two or more legally separate entities.

For example, Unilever plc is a holding company that owns shares in numerous subsidiaries.

Unilever's accounts only show Unilever plc's results - you cannot see how well, say, Birds Eye Walls did, unless you apply to Companies House.

The basic method of consolidation simply to add the accounts together but there are refinements, such as allowing for *minority interests*. These are the holders of the other shares in a subsidiary which is not 100% owned by the holding company; as shareholders they are entitled to a share of net assets if the subsidiary closes down. In consolidated accounts, they are treated as providers of long term funds to the group, just like long term creditors.

The purpose of consolidated accounts is to recognise that when a company controls other businesses, it could simply absorb their operations into its own, perhaps by setting up different divisions or branches. If it chooses to keep them as separate entities, then its own accounts would be misleading if it simply recorded its own trading results, assets and liabilities. There would be a single entry in the balance sheet for its subsidiaries, shown as investments, possibly at cost, and a single entry in the profit and loss account for dividends received from subsidiaries. This would not reflect the economic realities of the situation.

Group accounts always include the holding company's own balance sheet but need not include its own profit and loss account, although its profit then has to be disclosed separately. Details of subsidiaries will be given in a note and there will probably be some analysis, also by way of note, showing the group's turnover, profit and net assets broken down by geographical market and by class of business. This will help you to sort out which businesses engage in which activities and how profitable and significant each is.

Large (generally group) companies have to use a layered format for the profit and loss account to highlight a number of important components of financial performance:

(a) results of continuing operations (including the results of acquisitions), that is of those operations which continue during the financial year;

(b) results of discontinued operations that those which have been sold or closed down during the financial year;

(c) profits or losses on the sale or termination of an operation, costs of a fundamental reorganisation or restructuring and profit or losses on the disposal of fixed assets.

Definitions

Here are some terms you may find in published group accounts.

A *holding company* is a company which controls another, its subsidiary, by holding the majority of its shares. The term *parent company* is sometimes used instead.

A *subsidiary* is a company under the control of another company, its holding company or 'parent'.

An *associated company* is one in which a holding company has a very large interest, although it does not control it.

A *minority interest* is the shares held in a subsidiary by people other than the holding company. For example a holding company may own 95% of the shares and another person or company may own the other 5%.

Share premium is the amount paid for a new share in excess of the share's 'nominal value'. For example when the water industry was privatised shares had a nominal value of £1 but buyers had to pay a total of £2.40 to acquire them (spread over about a year and a half). The extra £1.40 is the share premium.

Goodwill is the amount paid to buy a business in excess of the value of its assets. For instance if you bought a newsagent's shop and its stock for £100,000 this might consist of £80,000 for the building and its contents and £20,000 because the newsagents was in a good location - by a station, say. The extra £20,000 is called goodwill.

We have already suggested that there are some drawbacks to using the information found in financial statements. Let's think about this in a bit more detail, and see how far we can trust the accounts we see.

4 LIMITATIONS OF FINANCIAL STATEMENTS

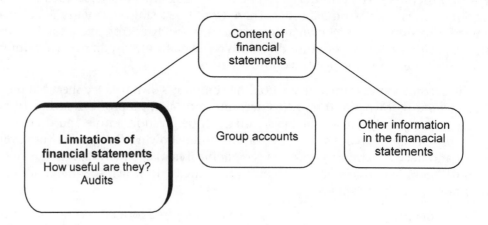

4.1 How useful are they?

Two very important drawbacks of financial statements are mentioned above.

(a) They are often out of date by the time you receive them.

(b) They are not audited in full, but only as far as required by statute.

To these we can add several other limitations.

(a) Accounts can only show the performance and standing of a business in financial terms - they cannot place a value on the staff or customer base, nor assess the business's competition.

(b) Accounts are a record of the past, not a predictor of the future.

(c) Although the Companies Acts and accounting standards are very detailed, they sometimes leave room for choice of accounting treatment and they do not cover every type of financial transaction encountered in business.

(d) The audit is not a guarantee that the accounts are 'correct'.

4.2 Audits

A recent opinion poll looked at the public's expectations of audits. It revealed an astonishing gap between the real purpose of audits and the public's perception of their purpose. Most people apparently believe that auditors set out to detect fraud and that an audit report guarantees the financial soundness of the company or even that the balance sheet shows the current value of the company. None of these is true.

Auditors are required by law to confirm that the financial statements give a 'true and fair' view of the company's position as at the balance sheet date. 'True and fair' is not defined in law, but it is generally assumed that as long as the accounts are materially correct and overall do not present a misleading picture, then the auditor can give a 'clean' audit report. To find out whether there are significant errors in the accounts, auditors test samples of transactions - rarely is every item checked as this would be impractical and very expensive. Even the errors which are found are not necessarily corrected, if they do not alter the basic picture of the company's health shown by the original financial statements.

In an effort to reduce the gap between what the public expects and what the auditor actually does (the 'expectations gap'), the Auditing Practices Board recently produced a new standard on the audit report. The following paragraphs are based on that standard.

Here is an example of an audit report that would be found in the accounts if the auditors are happy with them.

EXAMPLE: AUDIT REPORT

AUDITORS' REPORT TO THE SHAREHOLDERS OF XYZ PLC

We have audited the financial statements on pages ... to ... which have been prepared under the historical cost convention* (as modified by the revaluation of certain fixed assets) and the accounting policies set out on page ....

Respective responsibilities of directors and auditors

As described on page ... the company's directors are responsible for the preparation of financial statements. It is our responsibility to form an independent opinion, based on our audit, on those statements and to report our opinion to you.

Basis of opinion

We conducted our audit in accordance with Auditing Standards issued by the Auditing Practices Board. An audit includes examination, on a test basis, of evidence relevant to the amounts and disclosures in the financial statements. It also includes an assessment of the significant estimates and judgements made by the directors in the preparation of the financial statements, and of whether the accounting policies are appropriate to the company's circumstances, consistently applied and adequately disclosed.

We planned and performed our audit so as to obtain all the information and explanations which we considered necessary in order to provide us with sufficient evidence to give reasonable assurance that the financial statements are free from material misstatement, whether caused by fraud or other irregularity or error. In forming our opinion we also evaluated the overall adequacy of the presentation of information in the financial statements.

Opinion

In our opinion the financial statements give a true and fair view of the state of the company's affairs as at 31 December 19.. and of its profit for the year then ended and have been properly prepared in accordance with the Companies Act 1985.

Registered auditors   *Address*

Date

* A reference to the convention draws attention to the fact that the values reflected in the financial statements are not current but historical and, where appropriate, to the fact that there is a mixture of past and recent values. Buildings bought fifty years ago, for instance, may well be included in the accounts at their present day values to show their real worth rather than their worth in the 1940s.

The auditors must distinguish between their responsibilities and those of the directors. To this end, a statement of directors' responsibilities should be included. This states that directors must:

(a) prepare financial statements for each financial year which give a true and fair view of the state of affairs of the company and of the profit or loss of the company for that period;

(b) select suitable accounting policies and then apply them consistently;

(c) make judgements and estimates that are reasonable and prudent;

(d) state whether applicable accounting standards have been followed, subject to any material departures disclosed and explained in the financial statements (large companies only);

(e) prepare the financial statements on the basis that the company will continue in business when this is inappropriate;

(f) keep proper accounting records which disclose with reasonable accuracy at any time the financial position of the company and enable them to ensure that the financial statements comply with company law;

(g) safeguard the assets of the company and hence take reasonable steps for the prevention and detection of fraud and other irregularities.

Activity 4 [15 minutes]

(a) Who is the auditors' report shown on the previous page prepared for?

(b) The report refers to 'significant estimates and judgements'. What sort of things do you think these might relate to? *(Clue.* Look at the balance sheet shown earlier.)

(c) What are the auditors reasonably sure about?

(d) Why is the auditors' opinion more credible than that of the directors responsible for actually preparing the financial statements?

In spite of these reservations it is possible to carry out a very through check of a company's health if we know how to interpret the information provided in financial statements. In the next chapter we shall see how this is done.

Chapter roundup

- Financial statements comprise:
  (a) balance sheet;
  (b) profit and loss account;
  (c) cash flow statement;

  An annual report and accounts will also contain notes to the financial statements, directors' and auditors' reports and usually a chairman's report.

- The balance sheet shows the business's financial position as at the balance sheet date whereas the profit and loss account shows its trading results, overheads, interest, tax and dividends for the year. The cash flow statement reconciles the trading profit to operational cash flows and shows other movements in cash for capital transactions etc.

- Larger companies generally produce group accounts.

- The principal limitations of financial statements are that:
  (a) they are usually out of date by the time you receive them;
  (b) they can only tell you about the past of the company and its financial affairs;
  (c) there is sometimes confusion because of a company's chosen accounting policy.

Quick quiz

1 Why do businesses produce financial statements?
2 Distinguish between a balance sheet and a profit and loss account.
3 What is the difference between gross and net profit?
4 What are the main *headings* in a cash flow statement.
5 Give 4 examples of information disclosed in the notes to the financial statements or elsewhere in the accounts.
6 What is a holding company?
7 What is the purpose of consolidated accounts?
8 What is an auditor required to do?

Answers to quick quiz

1 See Section 1.1
2 See Section 1.2 and Section 1.3
3 See Section 1.3
4 See Section 1.4
5 See Section 2.1
6 See Section 3.1
7 See Section 3.1
8 See Section 4.2

Answers to activities

1 (a)

Net assets	£	£
Stock	55	
Debtors	70	
Cash	95	
		220
Creditors		(110)
		110
Capital		
Owner's capital		100
Retained profit		10
		110

(b) (i) The value is the amount that will be received when the assets are disposed of. If the stock can be sold for the same amount as it was bought for this will be:

	£
Cash	55
Stock	55
	110

It is unlikely that the stock can be sold for as much as was paid for it (any buyer could simply go to the original supplier instead). The value is thus between £55 and £110.

(ii) The business will make £10 profit per day. The value is therefore as follows.

	£
Original capital	100
Retained profit	50
	150

There is no stock so this will all be in cash.

Note that this is a simplified example. There are many other matters to take into account when selling a real business.

(c) There are *not* two lots of £110. A balance sheet shows two different ways of looking at the same £110, one in terms of the *assets* making up the £110 and the other in terms of who *owns* the £110.

2 (a) The depreciation figure for vehicles should be £3,000, not £2,000. One of the figures for creditors falling due in less than one year should be increased by £500 (it could be any one of the three amounts shown).

(b) 'Book value' is the amount at which an asset or liability is valued 'on paper' ie in the business's accounting system. *Net book value* is the purchase price of the asset minus amounts charged to date for depreciation.

(c) This is the value of all the profits that the company has made and not paid out in dividends in the past (it really means 'retained profits). When the business starts it will be nil. Every year the profit made by the company (as shown in its profit and loss account) will be added to the retained profits figure shown in the balance sheet.

If you do not understand this, go back to Section 1.1 and work through it again.

3 (a) It has issued some ordinary share capital.

(b) No. The 'interest paid' figure is tiny compared with the 'dividends paid' figure.

(c) (i) Increase in debtors: debtors are paying more slowly or there are more of them or they are buying more.

(ii) Increase in creditors: larger amounts are being bought, a longer time is waited before paying them or there are more of them.

(d) A debenture loan is a long term loan. A debenture is the name of the document setting out the terms of the loan.

(e) Depreciation is now shown because it is not a flow of cash.

(f) A company collects employees' income tax and national insurance through the PAYE system and pays it over to the Inland Revenue. Pension contributions may be included here, too.

4 (a) The company's shareholders (not its managers).

(b) Estimates would include such things as the current values of fixed assets and stocks; judgements would include matters such as whether some long-outstanding debts would ever be repaid.

(c) That the financial statements are free from material misstatement. In other words, that there are no mistakes that would alter a user's view of the performance of the company.

(d) Because the auditors are independent of the management of the company. The directors have a vested interest in making it look as though the company is doing well, because this would suggest that they are doing their jobs well.

Assignment 7 [1½ hours]

Return to the Annual Report and Accounts of 'your' Company.

You should now have a far greater understanding of the contents of the report and accounts than when you first reviewed them.

Your task is to prepare a short written summary of the results shown by your company, incorporating the following:

(a) Audit report. Is the report of your auditors very similar to that shown in Section 4.2, or have the auditors any qualifications or reservations in their opinion paragraph?

(b) Did your company make a profit or a loss? Did it do better or worse than the previous year? (Look at the Profit and Loss Account.)

(c) Has the company greater or fewer net assets than it had a year ago? (Look at the Balance Sheet.)

(d) Does your company have cash in the bank or does it owe its bankers? Is the cash situation better or worse than a year ago? What are the main causes of the cash movement? (Look at the Cash Flow Statement.)

Chapter 8

EVALUATING FINANCIAL PERFORMANCE

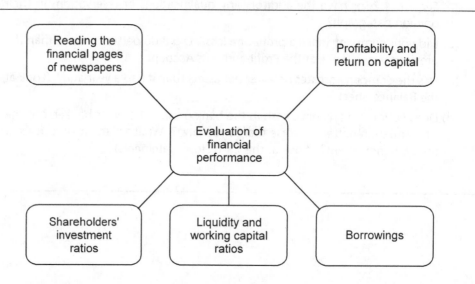

Introduction

This chapter completes Part A of this book and our coverage of Section 1 of Core Module Four.

In this chapter we revisit a great many of the topics that have been covered so far in this book, so you should find it a very useful memory jogger. If you cannot remember the meaning of some of the terms used this will show you that you need to go back and revise.

Having looked at the basic contents of a business's financial statements we are now going to consider how that information can be used. This is important whichever side of the fence you are on: if you are providing capital for companies as an investor you ought to take the trouble to check that those companies are performing well. If you are a manager of financial resources within a company you need to take into account how the results you achieve will be interpreted by others.

Your objectives

After completing this chapter you should:

(a) understand the principles of interpretation of financial information, especially the importance of comparisons;

(b) realise that non-financial information is needed to supplement financial information;

(c) know how to calculate and interpret profitability ratios, especially ROCE and its components;

(d) be able to analyse a company's borrowings in terms of gearing and interest cover;

(e) be able to calculate liquidity and working capital ratios and comment on their significance;

(f) be able to calculate simple shareholders' ratios and be aware of their significance;

(g) understand the share price information published in newspapers.

132

1 EVALUATION OF FINANCIAL PERFORMANCE

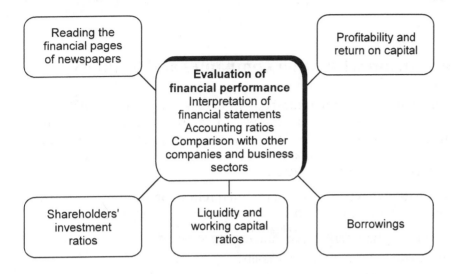

1.1 Interpretation of financial statements

As we have seen, the profit and loss account, the balance sheet and the cash flow statement are all sources of useful information about the condition of a business. But we need to know more about how to analyse and interpret them if they are to be truly useful. In this chapter we will examine the various additional figures which can be calculated from accounts and discuss what they can (and cannot) tell us about the business.

There are a few rules to bear in mind when using any method of interpretation.

(a) Always be aware of the context in which the business operates - manufacturing, service and finance companies will show very different results.

(b) Compare like with like. Try to eradicate unusual items like major write-offs or changes in policy which distort the comparison and disguise underlying trends.

(c) Findings should always be double-checked. Do not base your interpretation on the result of one fact only (such as a major decline in sales).

(d) To interpret effectively, the statements of more than one accounting period should be analysed to give an idea of the trend.

You can gain an initial overall impression of a business just by looking at the figures: is it a multi-million pound business, does it have lots of fixed assets, does it owe large amounts of money, and so on.

However a more sophisticated approach than this has been developed. This is ratio analysis, which involves comparing one figure against another to produce a ratio, and assessing whether the ratio indicates a weakness or strength in the company's affairs.

1.2 Accounting ratios

Broadly speaking, accounting ratios can be grouped into four categories: profitability and return; borrowings; liquidity and working capital; and shareholders' investment ratios.

Within each heading we will identify a number of standard measures or ratios that are normally calculated and generally accepted as meaningful indicators. However each individual business must be considered separately: a ratio that is meaningful for a manufacturing company may be completely meaningless for a financial institution.

1.3 Comparison with other companies and business sectors

The key to obtaining meaningful information from ratio analysis is *comparison*. This may involve comparing ratios over time within the same business to establish whether things are improving or declining, and comparing ratios between similar businesses to see whether the company you are analysing is better or worse than average within its specific business sector.

Ratio analysis on its own is not sufficient for interpreting company accounts. There are other items of information which should be looked at, for example:

(a) comments in the Chairman's report and directors' report;

(b) the age and nature of the company's assets;

(c) current and future developments in the company's markets, at home and overseas, recent acquisitions or disposals of a subsidiary by the company.

For discussion

Read through the following extract from an article in the Financial Times *(1.12.95). How much of the information is of the sort that can be derived from financial statements and how much concerns the company's markets and competition?*

'BPB advances as plasterboard market grows

BPB Industries, Europe's biggest plasterboard manufacturer, increased pre-tax profits almost 4 % to £78.9m in the 6 months to the end of September.

The increase would have been 13% but for a £7.5m exceptional loss on the sale of the group's Wireline mineral exploration business.

BPB, which supplies about half of the European market, said demand for plasterboard had risen in spite of sluggish housing and construction markets. Operating profits increased from £76.6m to £86.6m.

Plasterboard profits in France and Germany were largely flat and down narrowly in the UK.

An increase in European plasterboard volumes of 5.5 % more than offset the slight fall in the UK.

Sales volumes worldwide rose 3.5 %. Prices held steady in the main European markets but operating margins were trimmed by about half a percentage point reflecting increased raw material prices, principally paper.

Mr Jean-Pierre Cuny, BPB's chief executive, said continuing expansion of the European market justified the group's decision to invest £50m in a plant in Berlin capable of producing 50m sq m of plasterboard a year.

There has been concern about overcapacity in the German market which might cause a resurgence of the European price war that several years ago damaged BPB and its main competitors, Lafarge of France and Knuaf of Germany.

Mr Cuny said yesterday that cuts in capacity and imports meant the net gain to supply would be only 10m sq m.

Total building material profits rose by 9.5 % to £76.4m (£69.8m). Paper and packaging profits rose by half to £10.2m (£6.8m).

Group turnover increased 15 % to £720.2m (£625m).'

Note. Get your tutor to explain any terms you don't understand. Most of the unfamiliar ones will be explained in the course of this chapter.

We shall remind you of the need to compare with other companies and take account of market conditions wherever appropriate in this chapter.

To illustrate the calculation of many of the ratios we will use the following balance sheet and P & L account figures, with further information from the notes to the accounts.

FURLONG PLC PROFIT AND LOSS ACCOUNT
FOR THE YEAR ENDED 31 DECEMBER 1995

	Notes	1995 £	1994 £
Turnover	1	3,095,576	1,909,051
Operating profit	1	359,501	244,229
Interest	2	17,371	19,127
Profit on ordinary activities before taxation		342,130	225,102
Taxation on ordinary activities		74,200	31,272
Profit on ordinary activities after taxation		267,930	193,830
Dividend		41,000	16,800
Retained profit for the year		226,930	177,030
Earnings per share		12.8p	9.3p

FURLONG PLC BALANCE SHEET
AS AT 31 DECEMBER 1995

	Notes	1995 £	1994 £
Fixed assets			
Tangible fixed assets		802,180	656,071
Current assets			
Stocks and work in progress		64,422	86,550
Debtors	3	1,002,701	853,441
Cash at bank and in hand		1,327	68,363
		1,068,450	1,008,354
Creditors: amounts falling due within one year	4	881,731	912,456
Net current assets		186,719	95,898
Total assets less current liabilities		988,899	751,969
Creditors: amounts falling due after more than one year			
10% first mortgage debenture stock 2001/2006		(100,000)	(100,000)
Provision for liabilities and charges			
Deferred taxation		(20,000)	(10,000)
		868,899	641,969
Capital and reserves			
Called up share capital	5	210,000	210,000
Share premium account		48,178	48,178
Profit and loss account		610,721	383,791
		868,899	641,969

NOTES TO THE ACCOUNTS

			1995	1994
1		*Turnover and profit*		
			£	£
	(i)	Turnover	3,095,576	1,909,051
		Cost of sales	2,402,609	1,441,950
		Gross profit	692,967	467,101
		Administration expenses	333,466	222,872
		Operating profit	359,501	244,229
	(ii)	Operating profit is stated after charging:		
		Depreciation	151,107	120,147
		Auditors' remuneration	6,500	5,000
		Leasing charges	47,636	46,336
		Directors' emoluments	94,945	66,675
2		*Interest*		
		Payable on bank overdrafts and other loans	8,115	11,909
		Payable on debenture stock	10,000	10,000
			18,115	21,909
		Receivable on short term deposits	744	2,782
		Net payable	17,371	19,127
3		*Debtors*		
		Amounts falling due within one year		
		Trade debtors	884,559	760,252
		Prepayments and accrued income	89,822	45,729
		Advance corporation tax recoverable	7,200	-
			981,581	805,981
		Amounts falling due after more than one year		
		Advance corporation tax recoverable	9,000	7,200
		Trade debtors	12,120	40,260
			21,120	47,460
		Total debtors	1,002,701	853,441
4		*Creditors: amounts falling due within one year*		
		Trade creditors	627,018	545,340
		Accruals and deferred income	81,279	280,464
		Corporation tax	108,000	37,200
		Other taxes and social security costs	44,434	32,652
		Dividend	21,000	16,800
			881,731	912,456
5		*Called up share capital*		
		Authorised ordinary shares of 10p each	1,000,000	1,000,000
		Issued and fully paid ordinary shares of 10p each	210,000	210,000

2 PROFITABILITY AND RETURN ON CAPITAL

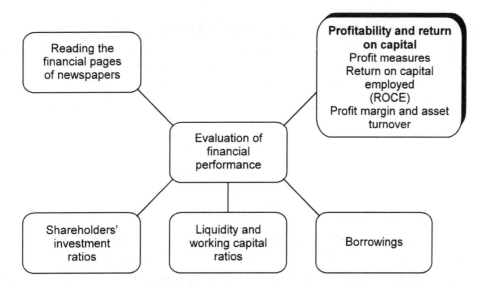

2.1 Profit measures

In our example, the company made a profit in both 1995 and 1994, and there was an increase in profit on ordinary activities between one year and the next:

(a) of 52% before taxation;

(b) of 38% after taxation.

Activity 1 [15 minutes]

How are these figures calculated?

Profit on ordinary activities *before* taxation is generally thought to be a better figure to use than profit after taxation, because there might be unusual variations in the tax charge from year to year which would not affect the profitability of the company's operations over the long term.

Another profit figure that should be looked at is profit before interest and tax (PBIT). This is the amount of profit which the company earned before having to pay interest to the providers of loan capital (the amount it could have earned if it had its own capital and did not have to pay interest). By providers of loan capital, we usually mean longer-term loan capital, such as debentures and medium-term bank loans, which will be shown in the balance sheet as 'creditors: amounts falling due after more than one year'. .

	1995	1994
	£	£
Profit on ordinary activities before tax	342,130	225,102
Interest payable (Note 2)	18,115	21,909
PBIT	360,245	247,011

PBIT shows a 46% growth between 1994 and 1995

Activity 2 [15 minutes]

(a) The figure shown for 'Interest' in the profit and loss account for 1995 is £17,371. Why have we used a different figure in the calculation above?

(b) Is 46% growth a good performance?

Ten pounds is a good profit if you only invest £20. It is not so good if you invest £20,000. We shall look at how this can be taken into account.

2.2 Return on capital employed (ROCE)

It is impossible to assess profits or profit growth properly without relating them to the amount of finance (capital) that was employed in making the profits. The most important profitability ratio is therefore return on capital employed (ROCE), which states the profit as a percentage of the amount of capital employed.

$$ROCE = \frac{\text{Profit on ordinary activities before interest and taxation}}{\text{Capital employed}}$$

Capital employed = Shareholders' funds plus creditors: amounts falling due after more than one year

In our example, capital employed is calculated as follows

1995: £(868,899 + 100,000 + 20,000) = £988,899
1994: £(641,969 + 100,000 + 10,000) = £751,969

These total figures are the total assets less current liabilities figures for 1995 and 1994 in the balance sheet.

		1995	1994
ROCE	=	$\frac{360,245}{988,899}$	$\frac{247,011}{751,969}$
	=	36.4%	32.8%

What does a company's ROCE tell us? What should we be looking for? There are 3 comparisons that can be made.

(a) The change in ROCE from one year to the next can be examined. In this example, there has been an improvement in ROCE from its 1994 level.

(b) The ROCE being earned by other companies, if this information is available, can be compared with the ROCE of this company.

(c) A comparison of the ROCE with current market borrowing rates may be made.

   (i) What would be the cost of extra borrowing to the company if it needed more loans, and is it earning a ROCE that suggests it could make profits to make such borrowing worthwhile?

   (ii) Is the company making a ROCE which suggests that it is getting value for money from its current borrowing?

In this example, if we suppose that current market interest rates, say, for mediumterm borrowing from banks, is around 10%, then the company's actual ROCE of 36% in 1995 might seem high.

However there is always a chance that the company's fixed assets, especially property, are undervalued in its balance sheet, and so the capital employed figure might be unrealistically low, making ROCE unrealistically high. If the company had earned a ROCE of, say only 6%, then its return would have been below current borrowing rates and so disappointingly low.

Activity 3 [15 minutes]

Why does ROCE become unrealistically high if capital employed is unrealistically low?

We often sub-analyse ROCE, to find out more about why the ROCE is high or low, or better or worse than last year.

2.3   Profit margin and asset turnover

There are two factors that contribute towards a return on capital employed, both related to sales (or 'turnover').

(a) *Profit margin*. A company might make a high or low profit margin on its sales. For example, a company that makes a profit of 25p per £1 of sales is making a bigger return on its sales than another company making a profit of only 10p per £1 of sales.

(b) *Asset turnover*. Asset turnover is a measure of how well the assets of a business are being used to generate sales. For example, if two companies each have capital employed of £100,000 and Company A makes sales of £400,000 per annum whereas Company B makes sales of only £200,000 per annum, Company A is making a higher turnover from the same amount of assets (twice as much asset turnover as Company B) and this will help A to make a higher return on capital employed than B. Asset turnover is expressed as 'x times' so that assets generate x times their value in annual turnover. Here, Company A's asset turnover is four times and B's is two times.

Profit margin and asset turnover together explain the ROCE. The relationship between the three ratios can be shown mathematically.

Profit margin × Asset turnover = ROCE

$$\frac{PBIT}{Sales} \times \frac{Sales}{Capital\ employed} = \frac{PBIT}{Capital\ employed}$$

In our example:

		Profit margin		*Asset turnover*		*ROCE*
(a)	1995	$\frac{360,245}{3,095,576}$	×	$\frac{3,095,576}{988,899}$	=	$\frac{360,245}{988,899}$
		11.64%	×	3.13 times	=	36.4%
(b)	1994	$\frac{247,011}{1,909,051}$	×	$\frac{1,909,051}{751,969}$	=	$\frac{247,011}{751,969}$
		12.94%	×	2.54 times	=	32.8%

In this example, the company's improvement in ROCE between 1994 and 1995 is attributable to a higher asset turnover. Indeed the profit margin has fallen a little, but the higher asset turnover has more than compensated for this.

It is also worth commenting on the change in sales turnover from one year to the next. You may already have noticed that Furlong plc achieved sales growth of over 60% from £1.9 million to £3.1 million between 1994 and 1995. This looks like very strong growth, and this is certainly one of the most significant items in the P & L account and balance sheet.

For discussion

(a) *Why do we say it 'looks like' very strong growth, not that it is very strong growth?*

(b) *Employees' skills and personalities are not 'assets' in a financial sense, but they contribute to sales. Is 'asset turnover' a good name for what is really being measured?*

Is asset turnover more meaningful in some types of business than others?

Activity 4 [1 hour]

Calculate ROCE, profit margin and asset turnover for the following two companies. Compare and comment on the ratios you calculate.

Company A		Company B	
Sales	£1,000,000	Sales	£4,000,000
Capital employed	£1,000,000	Capital employed	£1,000,000
PBIT	£200,000	PBIT	£200,000

Gross profit margin and net profit margin

Depending on the format of the P & L account, you may be able to calculate the gross profit margin as well as the net profit margin. Looking at the two together can be quite informative.

For example, suppose that a company has the following summarised profit and loss accounts for two consecutive years.

	Year 1 £	Year 2 £
Turnover	70,000	100,000
Cost of sales	42,000	55,000
Gross profit	28,000	45,000
Other costs	21,000	35,000
Net profit	7,000	10,000

Although the net profit margin is the same for both years at 10%, the gross profit margin is not.

In Year 1 it is: $\dfrac{28,000}{70,000}$ = 40%

and in Year 2 it is: $\dfrac{45,000}{100,000}$ = 45%

The improved gross profit margin has not led to an improvement in the net profit margin. This is because other costs as a percentage of sales have risen from 30% in Year 1 to 35% in Year 2.

If capital could be obtained for nothing profits would be higher because businesses would not have to pay the costs of finance, notably interest. We shall now go on to see how the impact of borrowing capital can be measured using the accounting figures.

3 BORROWINGS

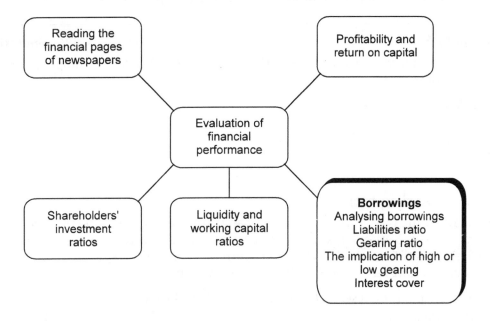

3.1 Analysing borrowings

Borrowing ratios are concerned with how much the Company owes in relation to is size, whether its liabilities are getting larger or smaller, and whether its burden of liabilities seems heavy or light.

(a) When a company has high liabilities banks and other potential lenders may be unwilling to advance further funds.

(b) When a company is earning only a modest profit before interest and tax, and has large-scale borrowings, there will be very little profit left for share-holders after interest changes have been paid. And if interest rates were to rise, the company might find that the interest charges on overdrafts and loans might exceed its net profit before interest and taxes (PBIT). This might lead to the collapse and liquidation of the company.

3.2 Liabilities ratio

The debt ratio is the ratio of a company's total liabilities to its total assets.

(a) Assets consist of fixed assets at their balance sheet value, plus current assets.

(b) Liabilities consist of all creditors, whether amounts falling due within one year or after more than one year.

There is no absolute guide to the maximum safe liability ratio, but as a very general guide, you might regard 50% as a safe limit. In practice, many companies operate successfully with a higher ratio than this, but 50% is nonetheless a helpful benchmark. In addition, if the ratio is over 50% and getting worse, the company's position will be worth looking at more carefully.

In the case of Furlong plc the liabilities ratio is as follows.

	1995	1994
Total debts	(881,731 + 100,000)	(912,456 + 100,000)
Total assets	(802,180 + 1,068,450)	(656,071 + 1,008,354)
	= 52%	= 61%

In this case, the liabilities ratio is quite high, mainly because of the large amount of current liabilities. However, the ratio has fallen from 61% to 52% between 1994 and 1995, and so the company appears to be improving its position.

Activity 5 [30 minutes]

A company approaches a bank asking for a loan of £100,000. The company has a liabilities ratio of 100%.

Should the bank make the loan?

Give reasons for your answer.

3.3 Gearing ratio

Capital gearing is concerned with a company's long term capital structure. We can think of a company as consisting of fixed assets and net current assets (ie working capital, which is current assets minus current liabilities). These assets must be financed by long term capital of the company, which is either:

(a) share capital and reserves (shareholders' funds) which can be divided into:

    (i) ordinary shares plus reserves; and

    (ii) preference shares; or

(b) long term loan capital: 'creditors: amounts falling due after more than one year'.

Preference share capital is not a liability. However, like loan capital, preference share capital has a *prior claim* over profits before interest and tax, ahead of ordinary shareholders. Preference dividends must be paid out of profits before ordinary shareholders are entitled to an ordinary dividend, and so we refer to preference share capital and loan capital as 'prior charge capital'.

> *If you cannot remember what preference shares are, go back to Chapter 2.*

The *capital gearing ratio* is a measure of the proportion of a company's capital that is prior charge capital. It is measured as:

$$\frac{\text{prior charge capital}}{\text{total capital}}$$

(a) Prior charge capital is capital carrying a right to a fixed return. It will include preference shares and debentures.

(b) Total capital is ordinary share capital and reserves plus prior charge capital plus any long term liabilities or provisions. (It is the same as 'total assets less current liabilities', a figure which you will find given to you in the balance sheet.)

As with the liabilities ratio, there is no absolute limit to what a gearing ratio ought to be. A company with a gearing ratio of more than 50% is said to be high-geared (whereas low gearing means a gearing ratio of less than 50%). Many companies are high geared, but if a high geared company is becoming increasingly high geared, it is likely to have difficulty in the future when it wants to borrow even more, unless it can also boost its shareholders' capital, either with retained profits or by a new share issue.

A similar ratio to the gearing ratio is the *debt/equity ratio*, which is the ratio of:

$$\frac{\text{prior charge capital}}{\text{ordinary share capital and reserves}}$$

This gives us the same sort of information as the gearing ratio, and a ratio of 100% or more would indicate high gearing.

In the example of Furlong plc, we find that the company, although having a high liabilities ratio because of its current liabilities, has a low gearing ratio. It has no preference share capital and its only long term debt is the 10% debenture stock.

	1995	1994
Gearing ratio	$\dfrac{100,000}{988,899}$	$\dfrac{100,000}{751,969}$
	= 10%	= 13%
Debt/equity ratio	$\dfrac{100,000}{868,899}$	$\dfrac{100,000}{641,969}$
	= 12%	= 16%

A company's gearing is something you often see mentioned in the financial section of the newspapers. It can have a big impact on the way a business is perceived by potential providers of finance. Let's see why this is so.

3.4 The implications of high or low gearing

The problem of a highly geared company is that it has a disproportionally large amount of liabilities and / or preference shares compared with its equity capital (or ordinary shares). Most liabilities give rise to interest payments, and all preference shares give rise to preference dividends, so that a large amount of PBIT is paid in interest and dividends before arriving at a residue available for distribution to the holders of equity.

On the other hand, in any year when a company makes a very large PBIT the providers of loan capital and preference share capital will still only get their fixed amount. The residue may be huge, and the profits remaining after loan interest and the fixed preference dividends will all belong to the ordinary shareholders.

Gearing compares two items on the balance sheet. We can also look at the impact of borrowing from the point of view of the figures in the profit and loss account.

3.5 Interest cover

The interest cover ratio shows whether a company is earning enough profits before interest and tax to pay its interest costs comfortably, or whether its interest costs are high in relation to the size of its profits, so that a fall in PBIT would then have a significant effect on profits available for ordinary shareholders.

$$\text{Interest cover} = \frac{\text{Profit before interest and tax}}{\text{Interest charges (less receipts)}}$$

An interest cover of two times or less would be low, and should really exceed three times before the company's interest costs can be considered within acceptable limits.

Note. Although preference share capital is included as prior charge capital for the gearing ratio, it is usual to exclude preference dividends from 'interest' charges. We also look at all interest payments, even interest charges on short term liabilities, and so interest cover and gearing do not quite look at the same thing.

Activity 6 [15 minutes]

Returning to the example of Furlong plc at the beginning of this chapter, what is the company's interest cover?

One of the worst things about interest is that it has to be paid when it is due. It is therefore highly desirable that the cash should be available at the right time, whatever profits are being earned. As you know from earlier chapters this is a matter of good working capital management.

4   LIQUIDITY AND WORKING CAPITAL RATIOS

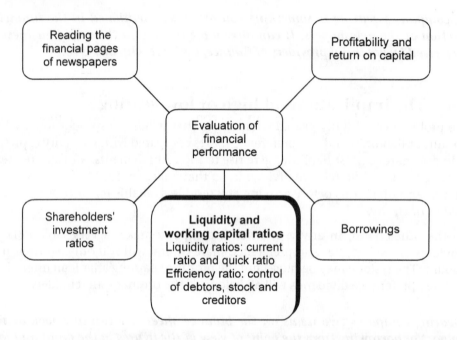

4.1   Liquidity ratios: current ratio and quick ratio

The 'standard' test of liquidity is the current ratio. It can be obtained from the balance sheet, and is the ratio of:

$$\frac{\text{current assets}}{\text{current liabilities}}$$

The idea behind this is that a company should have enough current assets that give a promise of 'cash to come' to meet its future commitments to pay off its current liabilities.

Companies are not able to convert all their current assets into cash very quickly. In particular, some manufacturing companies might hold large quantities of raw material stocks, which must be used in production to create finished goods stocks. Finished goods stocks might be warehoused for a long time, or sold on lengthy credit. In such businesses, where stock turnover is slow, most stocks are not very 'liquid' assets, because the cash cycle is so long. For these reasons, we calculate an additional liquidity ratio, known as the quick ratio or acid test ratio.

The quick ratio, or acid test ratio is:

$$\frac{\text{current assets less stocks}}{\text{current liabilities}}$$

This ratio should ideally be at least one for companies with a slow stock turnover. For companies with a fast stock turnover, a quick ratio can be comfortably less than one without suggesting that the company should be in cash flow trouble.

Both the current ratio and the quick ratio offer an indication of the company's liquidity position, but the absolute figures should not be interpreted too literally. It is often theorised that an acceptable current ratio is 1.5 and an acceptable quick ratio is 0.8, but these should only be used as a guide. Different businesses operate in very different ways. Budgens (the supermarket group) for example had (as at 30 April 1993) a current ratio of 0.52 and a quick ratio of 0.17. Budgens has low debtors (people do not buy groceries on credit), low cash (good cash management), medium stocks (high stocks but quick turnover, particularly in view of perishability) and very high creditors (Budgens buys its supplies of groceries on credit).

Compare the Budgens ratios with the Tomkins group which had a current ratio of 1.44 and a quick ratio of 1.03 (as at 1 May 1993). Tomkins is a manufacturing and retail organisation and operates with liquidity ratios closer to the standard.

What is important is the *trend* of these ratios. From this, one can easily ascertain whether liquidity is improving or deteriorating. If Budgens has traded for the last 10 years (very successfully) with current ratios of 0.52 and quick ratios of 0.17 then it should be supposed that the company can continue in business with those levels of liquidity. If in the following year the current ratio were to fall to 0.38 and the quick ratio to 0.09, then further investigation into the liquidity situation would be appropriate. It is the relative position that is far more important than the absolute figures.

Don't forget the other side of the coin either. A current ratio and a quick ratio can get bigger than they need to be. A company that has large volumes of stocks and debtors might be over-investing in working capital, and so tying up more funds in the business than it needs to. This would suggest poor management of debtors or stocks or creditors by the company.

4.2 Efficiency ratios: control of debtors, stock and creditors

A rough measure of the average length of time it takes for a company's debtors to pay what they owe is the 'debtor days' ratio, or average debtors' payment period.

The estimated average debtors' payment period is calculated as:

$$\frac{\text{trade debtors}}{\text{sales}} \times 365 \text{ days}$$

The figure for sales should be taken as the turnover figure in the P & L account. The trade debtors are not the total figure for debtors in the balance sheet, which includes prepayments and non-trade debtors. The trade debtors figure will be itemised in an analysis of the debtors total, in a note to the accounts.

Sales are usually made on 'normal credit terms' of payment within 30 days. Debtor days significantly in excess of this might be representative of poor management of funds of a business. However, some companies must allow generous credit terms to win customers. Exporting companies in particular may have to carry large amounts of debtors, and so their average collection period might be well in excess of 30 days.

The trend of the collection period (debtor days) over time is probably the best guide. If debtor days are increasing year on year, this is indicative of a poorly managed credit control function (and potentially therefore a poorly managed company).

Debtor days: examples

The debtor days of Budgens and Tomkins were as follows. (*Note:* 'K' following a number denotes 'thousands').

	1993 Trade debtors/ turnover		Debtor days (× 365)	1993 Trade debtors/ turnover		Debtor days (× 365)
Budgens	$\dfrac{£5,016K}{£284,986K}$	=	6.4 days	$\dfrac{£3,977K}{£290,668K}$	=	5.0 days
Tomkins	$\dfrac{£458.3m}{£2,059.5m}$	=	81.2 days	$\dfrac{£272.4m}{£1,274.2m}$	=	78.0 days

The differences in debtor days reflect the differences between the types of business. Budgen's has hardly any trade debtors at all, whereas the manufacturing company has far more. The debtor days are fairly constant from the previous year for both companies.

Stock turnover period

Another ratio worth calculating is the stock turnover period, or stock days. This is another estimated figure, obtainable from published accounts, which indicates the average number of days that items of stock are held for. As with the average debt collection period, however, it is only an approximate estimated figure, but one which should be reliable enough for comparing changes year on year.

Stock turnover is calculated as:

$$\frac{\text{stock}}{\text{cost of sales}} \times 365 \text{ days}$$

It is another measure of how vigorously a business is trading. A lengthening stock turnover period from one year to the next indicates:

(a) a slowdown in trading; or

(b) a build-up in stock levels, perhaps suggesting that the investment in stocks is becoming excessive.

If we add together the stock days and the debtor days, this should give us an indication of how soon stock is convertible into cash. Both debtor days and stock days therefore give us a further indication of the company's liquidity.

Creditors' turnover

Creditors' turnover is ideally calculated by the formula:

$$\frac{\text{Trade creditors}}{\text{Purchases}} \times 365 \text{ days}$$

However, it is rare to find purchases disclosed in published accounts and so cost of sales serves as an approximation. The creditors' turnover ratio often helps to assess a company's liquidity; an increase in creditor days is often a sign of lack of long term finance or poor management of current assets, resulting in the use of extended credit from suppliers, increased bank overdraft and so on.

Activity 7 [15 minutes]

Calculate liquidity and working capital ratios from the following accounts of the BET Group, a business which provides service support (cleaning etc) to customers worldwide.

	1993 £'m	1992 £'m
Turnover	2,176.2	2,344.8
Cost of sales	1,659.0	1,731.5
Gross profit	517.2	613.3

	1993 £'m	1992 £'m
Current assets		
Stocks	42.7	78.0
Debtors (note 1)	378.9	431.4
Short-term deposits and cash	205.2	145.0
	626.8	654.4
Creditors: amounts falling due within one year		
Loans and overdrafts	32.4	81.1
Corporation taxes	67.8	76.7
Dividend	11.7	17.2
Creditors (note 2)	487.2	467.2
	599.1	642.2
Net current assets	27.7	12.2

Notes

1	Trade debtors	295.2	335.5
2	Trade creditors	190.8	188.1

There are also ratios which help equity shareholders and other investors to assess the value and quality of an investment in the ordinary shares of a company. We shall look at five of these: earnings per share, dividend per share, dividend cover, P/E ratio and dividend yield.

5 SHAREHOLDERS' INVESTMENT RATIOS

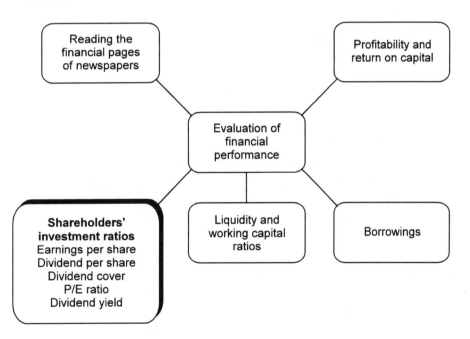

5.1 Earnings per share

It is possible to calculate the return on each ordinary share in the year. This is the earnings per share (EPS). Earnings are profits after tax, preference dividends and 'extraordinary items' (separately disclosed, large and very unusual items), which can either be paid out as a dividend to ordinary shareholders or retained in the business.

Suppose that Draught Ltd reports the following figures:

PROFIT AND LOSS ACCOUNT FOR 1996 (EXTRACT)

	£
Profit before interest and tax	120,000
Interest	(20,000)
Profit before tax	100,000
Taxation	(40,000)
Profit after tax	60,000
Preference dividend	(1,000)
Profit available for ordinary shareholders (= earnings)	59,000
Ordinary dividend	(49,000)
Retained profits	10,000

The company has 80,000 ordinary shares and 20,000 preference shares.

Calculate earnings per share for Draught Ltd in 1996.

Solution

$$\text{EPS is} \quad \frac{£59,000}{80,000} \quad = 73.75 \text{ pence per share}$$

In practice there are usually further complications in calculating the EPS, but these are well beyond the scope of this book.

5.2   Dividend per share

The dividend per share in pence is self-explanatory, and clearly an item of some interest to shareholders.

5.3   Dividend cover

Dividend cover is a ratio of:

$$\frac{\text{Earnings per share}}{\text{Net dividend per (ordinary) share}}$$

It shows what proportion of profit has been paid (or proposed) as a dividend and what proportion will be retained in the business to finance future growth. A dividend cover of two times would indicate that the company had paid 50% of its profits as dividends, and retained 50% in the business to help to finance future operations. Retained profits are an important source of funds for most companies, and so the dividend cover can in some cases be quite high.

A significant change in the dividend cover from one year to the next would be worth looking at closely. For example, if a company's dividend cover were to fall sharply between one year and the next, it could be that its profits had fallen, but the directors wished to pay at least the same amount of dividends as in the previous year, so as to keep shareholder expectations satisfied.

5.4   P/E ratio

The P/E ratio is the ratio of a company's current share price to the earnings per share.

A high P/E ratio indicates strong shareholder confidence in the company and its future, and a lower P/E ratio indicates lower confidence.

The P/E ratio of one company can be compared with the P/E ratios:

(a) of specific companies in the same business sector;

(b) of other companies generally;

(c) on average, for the business sector as a whole.

5.5 Dividend yield

Dividend yield is the return a shareholder is currently expecting on the shares of a company. It is calculated as:

$$\frac{\text{Dividend on the share for the year } (before\ tax)}{\text{Current market value of the share}} \times 100\%$$

The company will pay tax to the Inland Revenue on the shareholders' behalf. So, in this instance, if the relevant tax rate is 20%, the total cost to the company of each dividend is as follows.

	Pence	%
Cash paid to shareholder	40	80
Basic rate tax to Inland Revenue	10	20
Total	50	100

So, if a company pays a net dividend of 40p (giving a gross dividend of 50p) and the market price of its shares is 500p per share, the dividend yield is (50p ÷ 500p) × 100 = 10%. An investor can compare this with the return available on other investments, such as interest rates available from banks and building societies.

Shareholders look for both dividend yield and capital growth. Obviously, dividend yield is therefore an important aspect of a share's performance.

Activity 8 [15 minutes]

The following information is taken from the Profit and Loss Accounts of two companies:

	Company P		Company Q	
	£m	£m	£m	£m
Profit on ordinary activities after tax		41.1		5.6
Dividends				
Preference	0.5		-	
Ordinary	20.6		5.4	
		21.1		5.4
Retained profits		20.0		0.2

In addition, we have been advised of the following:

	Company P	Company Q
Number of ordinary shares	200m	50m
Market price per share	285p	154p
Relevant tax rate	20%	20%

Calculate the dividend yield and dividend cover of the two companies.

---

6 READING THE FINANCIAL PAGES OF NEWSPAPERS

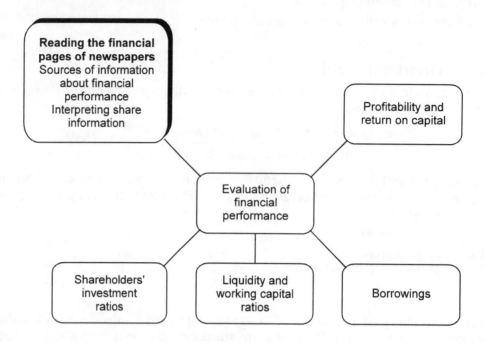

6.1 Sources of information about financial performance

All quality newspapers (such as *The Guardian*, *The Independent*, *Daily Telegraph*, *The Times* and, above all, the *Financial Times*) have detailed information and comment each day in their financial pages on:

(a) the activities in the City of London (especially the Stock Exchange);

(b) the financial results of large companies;

(c) announcements by large companies and financial institutions of important plans, such as proposed takeovers and mergers, sales of parts of a business, expansion into new activities or geographical markets and so on;

(d) UK and overseas government policies on interest and exchange rates, industrial strategy, privatisation plans and so on;

(e) longer term developments in the business world, such as changes in management theories or consumer tastes.

When you first try to read the financial pages, they can seem very dull and difficult to understand, especially as they are full of jargon. However, if you persevere, you will gradually find that you become familiar with the jargon and you will come to realise that the financial pages can be very helpful in developing your understanding of the financial marketplace.

There are also useful general programmes on financial matters on radio and television (such as *Money Box* and *The Financial World Tonight* on BBC Radio 4 and *The Money Programme* on BBC 2).

We will close Part A of this book by looking at how to interpret the share price information given in the newspapers.

6.2 Interpreting share information

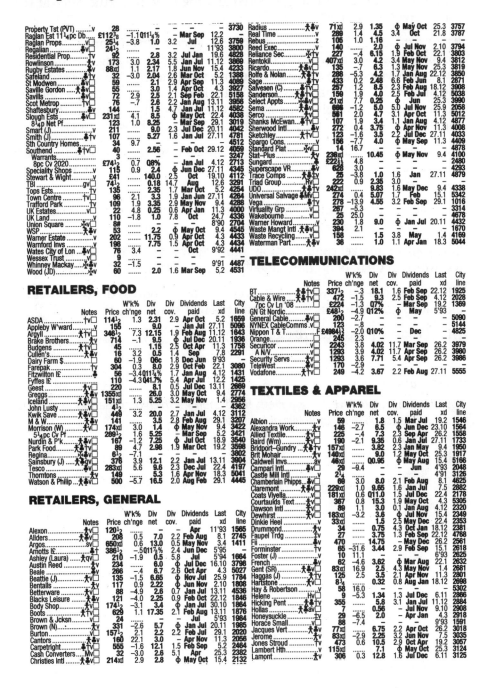

Figure 8.1 Share price information from the *Financial Times*

The above table and notes are extracts from the *Financial Times* London Share Service on 13 May 1996.

All newspapers show which shares are *most actively bought and sold*. The *Financial Times* does this by putting a white square in the notes column. Prices for such shares are published continuously on the Stock Exchange Automated Quotation System (SEAQ) and appear on dealers' computer screens.

The price shown is the *middle market price* in pence at the close of trading on the previous working day. This price is midway between the buying and selling prices at which marketmakers and brokers will deal. The difference between buying and selling prices represents the profit to the marketmakers. Just like any other business, they aim to sell their stocks (of shares) for more than they paid for them.

You will sometimes see two prices quoted, the *bid* price (the price which you would get if you sold the share to someone) and the *offer* price (the price at which you could buy the share).

If 'xd' (standing for *ex-dividend*) appears after a closing price, it means that a company is about to pay a dividend but that anyone buying the shares before the dividend payment is made will not receive the dividend. This is because companies pay dividends to all shareholders on the share register at a stated time before the payment is due. This gives them time to deal with all the administration without constantly having to change the names on the list of those to receive payment.

The column headed '+ or -' shows the changes from the last closing price in pence (or in fractions of one pound sterling for the few shares whose prices is quoted in pounds rather than pence).

The columns headed 'high' and 'low' show the highest and lowest closing prices in the current calendar year.

'Mkt Cap' or 'market capitalisation' shows how much the company's share capital was worth in total, in millions of pounds, at the closing price given.

'Yld Gr's' stands for gross yield, in other words the (gross) dividend yield. This is a measure of the return on an investment in that share.

P/E, of course, stands for P/E ratio.

For discussion

You have £8,000 to invest in Retailers, food *shares. Which of those shares listed above will you buy? Select no more than five different shares.*

Chapter roundup

- Ratios provide information through comparison:
  - trends in a company's ratios from one year to the next, indicating an improving or worsening position;
  - in some cases, against a 'norm' or 'standard' for the industry or market;
  - in some cases, against the ratios of other companies, although differences between one company and another should often be expected.
- This lengthy chapter has gone into quite a lot of detail about basic ratio analysis. The ratios you should be able to calculate and/or comment on are as follows.
  - *Profitability ratios*
    - return on capital employed
    - net profit as a percentage of sales
    - asset turnover ratio
    - gross profit as a percentage of sales
  - *Liability and gearing ratios*
    - liability ratio
    - gearing ratio
    - interest cover
  - *Liquidity and working capital ratios*
    - current ratio
    - quick ratio (acid test ratio)
    - debtor days (average debt collection period)
    - average stock turnover period
  - *Ordinary shareholders' investment ratios*
    - earnings per share
    - dividend cover
    - P/E ratio
    - dividend yield

This chapter concludes Part A of this book. Do not move on before reviewing what you have read thoroughly. Spend at least one hour flicking through the previous chapters, noting key points and re-reading passages you found difficult or have forgotten about.

Quick quiz

1 What rules should be born in mind when using any method of interpretation, and why are comparisons so important?
2 What is the usual formula for ROCE?
3 ROCE can be calculated as the product of two other ratios. What are they?
4 Define the 'liability ratio'.
5 Give two formulae for evaluating gearing.
6 In a period when profits are fluctuating, what effect does a company's level of gearing have on the profits available for ordinary shareholders?
7 Explain 'interest cover'

8   What are the formulae for:

   (a)   the current ratio;

   (b)   the quick ratio;

   (c)   the debtors payment period;

   (d)   the stock turnover period?

9   What is earnings per share?

10 What is the formula for dividend cover?

11 What do you understand by P/E ratio?

Answers to quick quiz

1   See Section 1.1

2   $\dfrac{\text{Profit on ordinary activities before interest and taxation}}{\text{Capital employed}}$ (see Section 2.2)

3   Profit margin and asset turnover (see Section 2.3)

4   Total liabilities as a percentage of total assets (see Section 3.2)

5   Capital gearing ratio $\dfrac{\text{prior charge capital}}{\text{total capital}}$

   Debt / equity ratio $\dfrac{\text{prior charge capital}}{\text{ordinary share capital plus reserves}}$

6   See Section 3.4

7   A comparison of net interest expense with profits before interest, to show whether the level of interest expense is comfortable.

8   (a) $\dfrac{\text{current assets}}{\text{current liabilities}}$

   (b) $\dfrac{\text{current assets less stocks}}{\text{current liabilities}}$

   (c) $\dfrac{\text{trade debtors}}{\text{sales}}$ x 365 days

   (d) $\dfrac{\text{stocks}}{\text{cost of sales}}$ x 365 days

9   $\dfrac{\text{Profits after tax, preference dividends and extraordinary items}}{\text{Number of ordinary shares}}$

10 $\dfrac{\text{Earnings per share}}{\text{Net dividend per ordinary share}}$

11 The price to earnings ratio is the ratio of the company's current ordinary share price to the earnings per share, with a high P/E showing market confidence in the share.

Answers to activities

1   A percentage increase is calculated as follows.

   $\dfrac{\text{New figure – old figure}}{\text{Old figure}}$

   (a) $= \dfrac{£342,130 - £225,102}{£225,102} = 52\%$

   (b) $= \dfrac{£267,930 - £193,830}{£193,830} = 38\%$

2   (a) We have used the figure for interest payable, as shown in Note 2 of the accounts. The interest received is not included because receiving interest is not considered

to be part of the normal operating activities of the company - it just so happens that the company has cash surpluses to invest at different times. Interest received *should* be considered, however, when interpreting the financial management of the company.

(b) It is better than a fall in the PBIT, of course, but it is difficult to say whether it is a good performance without further information. Competitors may have achieved 100% growth. Last year may have been an unusually bad one.

3 The lower the figure you are dividing by, the higher the result will be. For example:

$$10/5 = 2 \qquad\qquad 10/1 = 10$$

If managers or companies want to look good in ROCE terms, therefore, it is in their interests not to increase capital employed by buying new assets.

4 These figures would give the following ratios.

Company A

$$\text{ROCE} = \frac{£200,000}{£1,000,000} = 20\%$$

$$\text{Profit margin} = \frac{£200,000}{£1,000,000} = 20\%$$

$$\text{Asset turnover} = \frac{£1,000,000}{£1,000,000} = 1$$

Company B

$$\text{ROCE} = \frac{£200,000}{£1,000,000} = 20\%$$

$$\text{Profit margin} = \frac{£200,000}{£1,000,000} = 5\%$$

$$\text{Asset turnover} = \frac{£4,000,000}{£1,000,000} = 4$$

The companies have the same ROCE, but it is arrived at in a very different fashion. Company A operates with a low asset turnover and a comparatively high profit margin whereas Company B carries out much more business, but on a lower profit margin. Company A could be operating at the luxury end of the market, whilst Company B is operating at the popular end of the market (Mercedes v Ford).

5 Your instant response may have been 'No', but a bank would be more open-minded, at least at first. What would the money be used for? If it is used to buy assets the debt ratio will still be 100%. If the assets in question consist of fantastic new machines that will generate huge profits the bank might be very interested to help. Look back at Chapter 1 for other matters that a bank would consider.

6 Interest payments should be taken gross, from the note to the accounts, and not net of interest receipts as shown in the P & L account.

	1995	1994
PBIT	£360,245	£247,011
Interest payable	£18,115	£21,909
	= 20 times	= 11 times

Furlong plc has more than sufficient interest cover. In view of the company's low gearing, this is not too surprising and so we finally obtain a picture of Furlong plc as a company that does not seem to have a debt problem, in spite of its high (although declining) debt ratio.

7

	1993	1992
Current ratio	$\frac{£626.8}{£599.1} = 1.05$	$\frac{£654.4}{£642.2} = 1.02$
Quick ratio	$\frac{£584.1}{£599.1} = 0.97$	$\frac{£576.4}{£642.2} = 0.90$
Debtors' payment period	$\frac{£295.2}{£2,176.2} \times 365 = 49.5$ days	$\frac{£335.2}{£2,344.8} \times 365 = 52.2$ days
Stock turnover period	$\frac{£42.7}{£1,659.0} \times 365 = 9.4$ days	$\frac{£78.0}{£1,731.5} \times 365 = 16.4$ days

155

Creditors' turnover $\dfrac{£190.8}{£1,659.0} \times 365 = 42.0$ days $\qquad \dfrac{£188.1}{£1,731.5} \times 365 = 39.6$ days

BET Group is a service company and hence it would be expected to have very low stock and a very short stock turnover period. The similarity of debtors' and creditors' turnover periods means that the group is passing on most of the delay in receiving payment to its suppliers.

BET's current ratio is a little lower than average but its quick ratio is better than average and very little less than the current ratio. This suggests that stock levels are strictly controlled, which is reinforced by the low stock turnover period. It would seem that working capital is tightly managed, to avoid the poor liquidity which could be caused by a high debtors' turnover period and comparatively high creditors.

8

	Company P £m	Company Q £m
Profit on ordinary activities after tax	41.1	5.6
Preference dividend	0.5	0
Earnings	40.6	5.6
Number of shares	200m	50m
EPS	20.3p	11.2p
Ordinary dividend per share	10.3p	10.8p
Dividend cover	20.3	11.2
	10.3	10.8
	= 1.97 times	= 1.04 times

Dividend yield $\qquad \dfrac{10.3 \times (100/80) \times 100\%}{285} \qquad \dfrac{10.8 \times (100/80) \times 100\%}{154}$

$$= 4.5\% \qquad\qquad\qquad = 8.8\%$$

Assignment 8 [1½ hours]

The following profit and loss accounts for the years ended 31 December 1994 and 1995 and balance sheets at the end of those years are for Manx Clothiers Ltd, a retailer of clothing for the whole family. Betty and Brian Baines are the only directors of the company and the only shareholders.

MANX CLOTHIERS LIMITED
PROFIT AND LOSS: ACCOUNT YEAR ENDED 31 DECEMBER

		1995		1994
	£	£	£	£
Sales		600,000		750,000
Less cost of goods sold		360,000		420,000
Gross profit		240,000		330,000
Less: Expenses				
Wages	68,000		63,000	
Rent and rates	52,000		50,000	
Light and heat	16,000		13,000	
Directors remuneration	30,000		50,000	
Advertising	16,000		23,000	
Other	24,000		22,000	
		206,000		221,000
Net profit		34,000		109,000
Add retained earnings b/fwd		152,000		63,000
		186,000		172,000
Less proposed dividend		40,000		20,000
		146,000		152,000

BALANCE SHEETS AS AT 31 DECEMBER

		1995		1994
	£	£	£	£
Fixed assets (net)		110,000		80,000
Current assets				
Stock	140,000		110,000	
Bank and cash	-		40,000	
	140,000		150,000	
Creditors: amounts due within 1 year				
Bank overdraft	6,000		-	
Trade creditors	48,000		48,000	
Proposed dividend	40,000		20,000	
	94,000		68,000	
Net current assets		46,000		82,000
		156,000		162,000
Financed by				
Share capital		10,000		10,000
Retained profits		146,000		152,000
		156,000		162,000

Your tasks are to examine the amounts, calculate relevant ratios and comment on possible reasons for the apparent deterioration of the business during 1995.

MANAGING INFORMATION

Chapter 9

EVALUATING INFORMATION

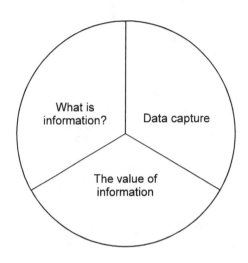

Introduction

As the BTEC Guidelines for the Core Module Four point out, finance and information 'are interrelated in that the effective management of any resources, including financial, requires good information on which to base decision making'.

In this chapter we introduce you to some basic ideas about information which are relevant throughout Part B of this book - especially the qualities of good information.

We begin to consider the *value and costs of benefits of information*, but the importance of information will only become fully apparent when we consider an organisation's information needs in the next chapter.

Your objectives

After completing this chapter you should:

(a) know what information is and how to distinguish data and information;

(b) know the qualities of good information such as accuracy, relevance and completeness;

(c) be able to describe how data is captured and stored by an organisation;

(d) be able to explain how data is processed;

(e) understand the difficulty of placing a value on information.

1 WHAT IS INFORMATION?

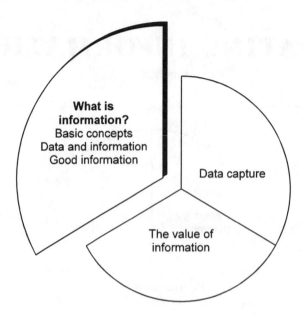

1.1 Basic concepts

Information is anything that is communicated. You can communicate with someone else using any of the 5 senses, but hearing and sight (talking, reading and drawing pictures) are the most sophisticated methods.

Business information consists of words, numbers and graphics (pictures, charts, graphs).

Let's examine the qualities and characteristics of information itself.

1.2 Data and information

In normal everyday speech the terms data and information are used interchangeably, and we will use them interchangeably in this book. However, strictly speaking the terms have distinct meanings.

Definitions

Data is the raw material for data processing. Data relates to facts, events, and transactions and so forth.

Information is data that has been processed in such a way as to be meaningful to the person who receives it.

An example might make things clear. Many companies providing a product or service like to research consumer opinion, and employ market research organisations to do so. A typical market research survey employs researchers who request a sample of the public to answer a number of questions relating to the product. Several hundred questionnaires may be completed. The questionnaires are input to a system. Once every questionnaire has been input, a number of processing operations are performed on the data. A report which summarises the results and discusses their significance is sent to the company that commissioned the survey. The processing operations carried out to obtain the results include:

(a) classifying;

(b) sorting;

(c) calculating; and

(d) summarising

Individually, a completed questionnaire would not tell the company very much, only the views of one consumer. In this case, the individual questionnaires are data. Once they have been processed, and analysed, the resulting report is information: the company will use it to inform its decisions regarding the product. If the report revealed that consumers disliked the product, the company would scrap or alter it.

The quality of source data affects the value of information. Information is worthless if the source data is flawed. If the researchers filled in questionnaires themselves, inventing the answers, then the conclusions drawn from the processed data would be wrong, and poor decisions would be made.

For discussion

Distinguish between data and information in your own job. Are things that you regard as data in your job regarded as information by a colleague in their job?

Different levels of management take different types of decision and often require different types of information. However, the information provided to them can be good or bad, and in fact information which is good information at one level can be poor information at another. We shall now go on to describe the factors which are important for the successful conversion of data to information.

1.3 Good information

The qualities of good information are as follows.

(a) It should be *relevant* for its purpose.

(b) It should be *complete* for its purpose.

(c) It should be sufficiently *accurate* for its purpose.

(d) It should be *clear* to the user.

(e) The user should have *confidence* in it.

(f) It should be *communicated* to the right person.

(g) It should not be excessive its *volume* should be manageable.

(h) It should be *timely* in other words communicated at the most appropriate time.

(i) It should be communicated by an appropriate *channel* of communication.

(j) It should be provided at a *cost* which is less than the value of the benefits it provides.

Activity 1   **[15 minutes]**

Your personal information system might include an address book. The address might include an entry such as the following.

Dave & Liz
14 Broughton Road
Macclesfield   01462 123456

Is this good information? Give reasons for your answers

Relevance

Information must be relevant to the purpose for which a manager wants to use it. In practice, far too many reports fail to 'keep to the point' and contain purposeless, irritating paragraphs which only serve to annoy the managers reading them. The consequences of irrelevant data are that managers might be confused by the data and might waste time.

Completeness

An information user should have all the information he needs to do his job properly. If there are *omissions* and he does not have a complete picture of the situation, he might well make bad decisions. Suppose that the debt collection section of a company is informed that a customer owes £10,000 and the debt is now four months old and overdue. The debt collection section therefore decides to write a strongly-worded letter to the customer asking for immediate payment. Now suppose that an important piece of information had been kept from the debt collection section, for example that the debt had already been paid or that the customer had negotiated special credit terms of six months. In these circumstances, sending a strongly-worded demand for payment would be a mistake and likely to create bad will that might harm the prospects of future sales to the customer.

Accuracy

Information should obviously be accurate because using incorrect information could have serious and damaging consequences. However, information should only be accurate enough for its purpose and there is no need to go into unnecessary detail for pointless accuracy.

(a) Supervisors and office workers might need information that is accurate to the nearest penny, second or kilogram. For example, a cashier will check the company's records to the bank statement to the exact penny, and purchase department staff will pay creditors exactly what they are owed. Much financial accounting information for day-to-day transactions must indicate amounts to the exact penny.

(b) More senior managers might be satisfied with revenues and costs rounded to the nearest £100 or £1,000, since greater detail would serve no purpose. For example, in budgeting, revenue and cost figures are often rounded to the nearest £1,000 because trying to be more exact would usually only give a false impression of accuracy when the figure is no more than an estimate.

(c) Top managers in a medium-sized to large organisation might be satisfied with figures to the nearest £10,000, or even £100,000 or £1 million. Estimates to the nearest pound at this level of decision-making would be so inappropriate that they would seem ridiculous and so, oddly enough, perhaps undermine the manager's confidence in the accuracy of estimates.

Clarity

Information must be clear to the user. If the user does not understand it properly he cannot use it properly. Lack of clarity is one of the causes of a breakdown in communication, which is referred to in information system theory as 'noise'. An example would be using scientific jargon to communicate to a senior manager who does not have a scientific background.

Confidence

Information must be trusted by the managers who are expected to use it. However not all information is certain. An important problem is therefore how much uncertainty analysis should be incorporated into reporting systems, in order to make the information realistic. Some information has to be certain, especially operating information, for example, related to a production process. Information relating to the external environment is uncertain. However, if the assumptions underlying it are clearly stated, this might enhance the confidence with which the information is perceived.

Another way in which confidence may be undermined is if the information comes from a source that has been wrong in the past.

Communication

Within any organisation, individuals are given the authority to do certain tasks, and they must be given the information they need to do them. An office manager might be made responsible for controlling expenditures in his office, and given a budget expenditure limit for the year. As the year progresses, he might try to keep expenditure in check but unless he is told throughout the year what his current total expenditure to date is, he will find it difficult to judge whether he is keeping within budget or not.

Information that is needed might be communicated to the wrong person. In other words, it might be communicated to a person who does not have the authority to act on it, or who is not responsible for the matter and so does not see any need to act on it.

Volume

There are physical and mental limitations to what a person can read, absorb and understand properly before taking action. An enormous mountain of information, even if it is all relevant, cannot be handled. Reports to management must therefore be clear and concise. Often, managers only take action on the 'exception' principle.

Definition

The *exception principle* focuses attention on those items where performance differs significantly from what is expected, in other words on the things that are unusual, not on the things that are routine.

Timing

Information which is not available until after a decision is made will be useful only for comparisons and longer term control, and may serve no purpose even then.

Information prepared too frequently can be a serious disadvantage. If, for example, a decision is taken at a monthly meeting about a certain aspect of a company's operations, information to make the decision is only required once a month, and weekly reports would be a time-consuming waste of effort.

Channel of communication

There are occasions when using one particular method of communication will be better than others. For example, job vacancies should be announced in a medium where they will be brought to the attention of the people most likely to be interested. The channel of communication might be the company's in-house journal, a national or local newspaper, a professional magazine, a job centre or school careers office. Some internal memoranda may be better sent by 'electronic mail'. Some information is best communicated informally by telephone or word-of-mouth, whereas other information ought to be communicated formally in writing or figures.

Activity 2 [15 minutes]

One way of helping to ensure that information has these properties is to have well designed data collection tools such as paper forms and computer data entry screens.

Think about the sort of information that you should try to get if you are taking a telephone message on behalf of a colleague.

Design a form to encourage telephone messages to contain good information.

Cost

Information should have some value, otherwise it would not be worth the cost of collecting and filing it. The benefits obtainable from the information must also exceed the costs of acquiring it, and whenever management is trying to decide whether or not to provide information for a particular purpose, this should always be borne in mind.

We shall look at the value of information and its costs and benefits in more detail later in this chapter. Now we are going to think about where businesses get information from.

2 DATA CAPTURE

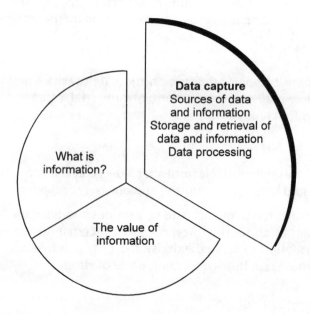

2.1 Sources of data and information

Collecting and keeping hold of information is sometimes called 'data capture'.

For discussion

Criminals and wild animals are also 'captured'. Based on what you have read so far, do you think there is any reason to see information as something elusive?

Data and information come from sources both inside and outside an organisation, and an information system should be designed so as to obtain all the relevant data and information from whatever source.

Internal information

Capturing data/information *inside* the organisation involves the following.

(a) Establishing a system for collecting or measuring transactions data - for example measuring output, sales, costs, cash receipts and payments, asset purchases, stock turnover etc. In other words, there must be established procedures for what data is collected (how frequently, by whom, by what methods) and how it is processed, and filed or communicated.

(b) Relying to some extent on informal communication of information between managers and staff (for example, by word-of-mouth or at meetings).

(c) Communication between managers.

External information

Tracking down information from *outside* the organisation might be entrusted to particular individuals, or might be 'informal'.

Formal collection of data from outside sources includes the following.

(a) A company's tax specialists will be expected to gather information about changes in tax law and how this will affect the company.

(b) Obtaining information about any new legislation on health and safety at work and about employment regulations should be the responsibility of a particular person such as the organisation's legal expert or the personnel department. They should pass information on to any managers to whom it may be relevant.

(c) Some legislation applies specifically to computerised information systems. The UK Data Protection Act 1984 requires that organisations who wish to hold and process personal information on computerised systems must register with the Data Protection Registrar and comply with certain principles in the way the data is stored and used. Organisations are recommended to appoint a data registration officer to ensure compliance with the Act. The Computer Misuse Act 1990 was introduced to try to combat unauthorised access to computerised information systems. The Copyright (Computer Software) Amendment Act was introduced to try to prevent the unauthorised copying of programs.

(d) Research and development (R & D) work often relies on information about other R & D work being done by another company or by government institutions. An R & D official might be made responsible for finding out about R & D work outside the company.

(e) Marketing managers need to know about the opinions and buying attitudes of potential customers. To obtain this information, they might carry out market research exercises.

Informal gathering of information from the environment goes on all the time, consciously or unconsciously, because the employees of an organisation learn what is going on in the world around them from newspapers, television reports, chats in the pub and so on.

Activity 3 [15 minutes]

Make a list of all the sources of internal and external information that you use in your job.

Much of the information that you use from day to day you store in your head. Someone working in a buying department, for example, would soon learn the names of different suppliers and probably the prices of regularly purchased things. The amount of information used by an organisation is so large, however, that a more reliable system than human memory is needed.

2.2 Storage and retrieval of data and information

Often, when data is processed, the information is communicated immediately to the person who wishes to use it. However, there is no reason why processed information should be used straightaway. It might be kept for later use. If it is, it must be stored, or filed away, and then retrieved when it is eventually needed.

Storage and retrieval of data are 2 interrelated aspects of holding data for a later use because data must be stored in such a way that it can be found again when it is eventually wanted. To assist with storage, data (or information) is often stored in a pre-sorted order (for example alphabetical order). Alternatively, it is given a reference number and filed in reference number order. Sometimes, an index helps the storage and retrieval process. In business, vast quantities of data are stored and then retrieved when required. In accounting systems, there are many such examples, including the data recorded in the sales ledger, purchase ledger and payroll systems.

We have jumped the gun a little here, since 'capturing' data nearly always involves doing something to the data.

2.3 Data processing

A data processing system might be described as follows.

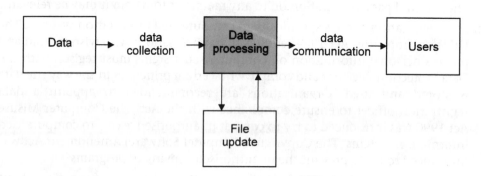

Figure 9.1 A data processing system

Processing data can be said to have the following features (for both manual and computerised systems).

(a) Data is *collected*. There must be data to process and this may arise in the course of operations. There has to be a system or procedure for ensuring that all the data needed for processing is collected and made available for processing. The quality, accuracy and completeness of the data will affect the quality of information produced.

(b) Data is *processed* into information, perhaps by summarising it or classifying it and/or producing total figures. For example, a sales system might be required to process data about goods despatched to satisfy customer orders so as to:

(i) produce and send out invoices;

(ii) record the invoices sent out in the customers' individual accounts with the company;

(iii) produce a report of the total value of invoices sent out in the day/week etc.

(c) Data is *communicated*. Continuing the example of the sales system, the output consists of invoices and figures for sales totals (ie management information). Updating the customers' accounts is a file updating activity to keep the debtors' records up to date. Communication might involve the *routine* dissemination of information to users. This includes routine monitoring information for example comparing actual and budgeted results for the month. Communication also involves the provision of *non-routine* information to users on request.

(d) Files are *updated* to incorporate the processed data, or information. The example of sales department work has already been mentioned. Updating files means bringing them up to date to record current transactions.

3 THE VALUE OF INFORMATION

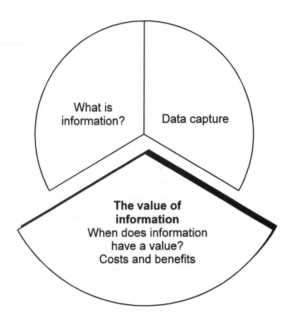

3.1 When does information have a value?

For information to have value, it must lead to a decision to take action which results in reducing costs, eliminating losses, increasing sales, better utilisation of resources, or providing management with information about the consequences of alternative courses of action.

Information which is provided but not used has no actual value. A decision taken on the basis of information received also has no actual value. It is only the *action* taken as a result of a decision which realises actual value for a company. The cost of collecting information bears no relation to its value. An item of information which leads to an actual increase in profit of £90 is not worth having if it costs £100 to collect.

Activity 4   **[20 minutes]**

The value of information lies in the action taken as a result of receiving it. What questions might you ask in order to make an assessment of the value of information?

If information costs more to produce than the economic benefits derived from it, then there is no point in producing it. This issue is particularly pertinent when considering the substantial amounts of money and management time invested by large organisations in information systems. However, there are two complicating factors.

3.2   Costs and benefits

In simple terms the cost of information consists of the wages paid to people to collect and process it, the costs of the equipment and stationery they need and storage and retrieval costs.

However, the *cost* of an individual item of information is not always easy to quantify. For example, if a manager uses an information system to enquire into the company's store of data, what is the cost of this enquiry?

(a) The information is already existent anyway, as it is used for a number of different purposes. It might be impossible to predict how *often* it will by used, and hence the economic benefits derived from it.

(b) The information system which is used to process these requests has also been purchased. Its cost is largely fixed.

It is not too hard to assess the *benefits* if comparisons are being made between one type of information system and another. For example the amount of *time* saved by computerising a processing task rather than doing it by hand could be worked out.

However, why is the information produced *needed* in the first place? If it is needed, for example, because it has to be disclosed in company accounts by law, then the *benefit* of having the information is that it allows the company to be a company. This probably is a benefit, but it is very hard to say what its value is and how a proportion of that value could be allocated to individual items of information.

We shall continue to refer to the various costs and benefits of information and information systems where appropriate throughout the next few chapters.

Chapter roundup

- An important distinction can be made between data and information. Data is the complete range of raw facts and measurements which exist within and outside an organisation. Information is data which has been processed in some way so as to make it meaningful to the person who receives it.

- Good information has a number of specific qualities, including relevance, completeness, accuracy, clarity and timeliness. It should inspire confidence, it should be communicated to the right person through the right channel, it should be of a manageable volume and it should not be too expensive to provide.

- Data is captured from both inside and outside the organisation. It may be used immediately or stored for later use. Processing entails collecting data, summarising or classifying it in some way, communicating it and keeping it up to date.

- For information to have value it must lead to a decision to take action that brings about some improvement. Costs and benefits are simple to identify in broad terms but more difficult in specific cases.

Quick quiz

1   Define data and information. What is business information?

2   What processing operations might be carried out on data?

3   Why is accuracy important?

4   When may it be acceptable to omit some information?

5   How is data captured inside an organisation?

6   How might data be stored?

7   What are the costs of information, in simple terms?

8   What is the exception principle?

9   Give an example of legislation which relates to computerised information systems.

10 Give an example of information which has to be stored for a substantial period of time even though it may never be referenced?

Answers to quick quiz

1   Data and information are discussed in Section 1.2; business information in Section 1.1.

2   Data is captured or collected, processed and stored, communicated and updated.

3   The importance of accuracy is discussed in Section 1.3.

4   There are many reasons why it may be acceptable to omit some information; for example if it is irrelevant, excessive, too detailed, or confidential.

5   The ways that data could be captured inside an organisation are discussed in Section 2.1.

6   Storage of data is discussed in Section 2.3.

7   Costs of information include wages, stationery, and equipment for its capture, processing, storage and retrieval.

8   The exception principle focuses attention on information which indicates that performance differs significantly from what is expected.

9   Examples of legislation which relates to computerised information systems are discussed in Section 2.1.

10 Organisations are required by law to keep many of their accounting records for several years.

Answers to activities

1   It *might* be good enough information depending on the situation. If Dave and Liz are people you only contact once or twice a year - to send them a Christmas card, say - then there are problems with it. If you see them or chat to them on the phone regularly this is probably all you need: it is *clear* enough for your purposes.

Potential problems include the following.

(a) There is no indication of when the information was last known to be up to date.

(b) Dave and Liz's surnames are not given.

(c) Dave and Liz may have split up.

(d) One or both of them may have moved.

(e) Their phone number may have changed (at the very least the dialling code is probably 01462).

(f) The postcode is not shown.

In other words the information may not be *accurate,* it certainly is not *complete,* it is difficult to have *confidence* in it (because it is not complete). If you never see or hear from them these days it is not really *relevant* to you. It is, however, of a manageable volume, it is *timely* in the sense that it is there when you need it. The channel is appropriate unless you contact them frequently in which case it might be better to store the phone number in your telephone's memory.

2   A form for recording telephone messages should encourage the person taking the call to record details of:

(a) the time of the call;

(b) the caller's name and organisation;

(c) the intended recipient's name;

(d) the nature of the call;

(e) a return telephone number or address;

(f) any action that the caller has been promised.

In addition, the message should be legible and promptly delivered to the appropriate person

3   Your answer will be specific to your *own* job.

Internal information sources are likely to include verbal or written instructions from your boss, verbal exchanges with colleagues, memos, notices, files, procedures manuals, brochures and price lists.

External sources may have included letters, invoices from suppliers, suppliers' brochures etc, trade magazines, newspapers, conversations with non-work friends, reference books, external libraries and information services.

You probably have many other examples.

4   (a) What information is provided?

(b) What is it used for?

(c) Who uses it?

(d) How often is it used?

(e) Does the frequency with which it is used coincide with the frequency with which it is provided?

(f) What is achieved by using it?

(g) What other relevant information is available which could be used instead?

An assessment of the value of information can be derived in this way, and the cost of obtaining it should then be compared against this value. On the basis of this comparison, it can be decided whether certain items of information are worth having.

Assignment 9 [1½ hours]

Scenario

The following is an extract from a conversation with the Sales Manager of a medium sized manufacturing company. Read through it.

I get so much information that I seem to spend most of my time studying documents and I rarely get the chance to act upon any of them. Every week all the managers get performance figures from all the departments including lots of data about the production processes which I find very difficult to interpret, and the reports from the Research and Development manager contain lots of technical terms relating to things that are not really my area of expertise. Some information is considered sensitive and only one copy of the document is made and is passed around the managers. It can take a long time to get to me and even longer for me to find time to read it properly.

Recently I was caught unawares when one of our main competitors introduced a special bulk order discount and I lost two of our major clients to them; it made my monthly predictions look a bit silly. Our Managing Director was not very pleased and he said he assumed I had known about it because it had been mentioned in the trade press a month previously. He also criticised me for overspending on the advertising budget when really it was the accounts people that had made an error in the figures they gave to me.

With all this information to absorb I seem to have no time to plan anything so I end up just trying to cope with one crisis after another. The latest problem came when a computer software supplier queried how many copies of some software package we are using - I have never really tried to keep records of who is using the package.

Task

This extract illustrates how information can fail to be useful if it does not have all the necessary qualities of good information. Read the extract again and identify each place where the qualities of good information seem to be lacking. In each case explain what qualities are missing and suggest how the manager and the business can try to improve on the situation.

Chapter 10

REVIEWING INFORMATION PROVISION

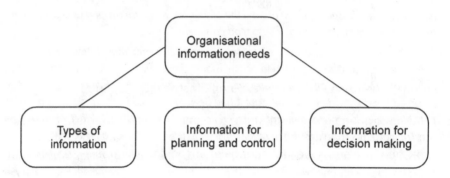

Introduction

What sort of information needs to be provided in an organisation? The answer to this question will affect the design of systems for collecting information and systems for processing it and disseminating it.

In this chapter we look at information needs from three angles: who needs it, why they need it and what sort of information they need.

In the next chapter we will start to look at the design of systems to provide the information that is needed.

Your objectives

After completing this chapter you should:

(a) be able to list the users of an organisation's information;

(b) know the various reasons why information is needed;

(c) be able to describe the decision-making process;

(d) understand the need for organisations to plan and control their activities in the face of change;

(e) be able to classify information according to what it is used for and according to the nature of the information itself.

1 ORGANISATIONAL INFORMATION NEEDS

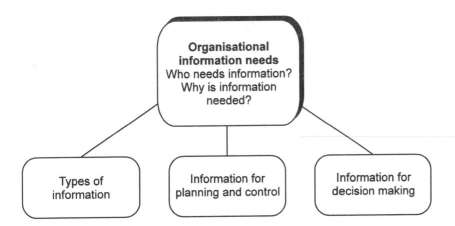

1.1 Who needs information?

The information generated by an organisation can be valuable to many different people. Users of an organisation's information can be *external* or *internal*.

Activity 1 [15 minutes]

It is important to bear in mind that information may be relevant to people outside the organisation as well as to its internal management and employees. In fact, decisions relating to an organisation can be taken by outsiders. Give four examples of outsiders who need information about a business.

Internal users of information include the following.

(a) The board of the company, or the equivalent of a board in other organisations.

(b) Directors with functional responsibilities.

(c) Divisional general managers, reporting to these directors.

(d) Divisional heads.

(e) Departmental heads.

(f) Section leaders or foremen.

(g) Discretionary employees, those who are expected to act on their own initiative to some extent.

(h) Non-discretionary employees, who work under instruction all the time with little scope for initiative.

Internal users of information can also be classified by function.

(a) Marketing

(b) Finance

(c) Administration

(d) Production

(e) Technical

(f) Personnel

(g) Research

(h) Design

With so many people interested in it, there clearly is a need for information. Let's think about what all these users do with their information.

1.2   Why is information needed?

The information requirements of the organisation can be categorised as follows.

(a) Information for decision making.

(b) Information for planning.

(c) Information for monitoring and controlling.

(d) Information for recording transactions.

Decision making

Information is required for decision making. The entire decision-making process can be viewed as the acquisition and processing of information.

Planning

Once any decision has been made, it is necessary to plan how to implement the steps needed to make it effective. (This involves further decisions.) Planning requires a knowledge of, among other things, available resources, possible timescales for implementation and the likely outcome under alternative scenarios.

Monitoring and controlling

Actual performance must be monitored to enable comparisons against budget or plan. This may involve the collection of information on, for example, the following.

(a) Costs

(b) Revenues

(c) Volumes

(d) Timescale

(e) Profitability

Information is required to assess whether things are proceeding as planned or whether there is some unexpected deviation from plan. It may consequently be necessary to take some form of corrective action (more decisions!).

Recording transactions

Information about each transaction or event is required for a number of reasons.

(a) Documentation of transactions can be used as evidence in a case of dispute.

(b) There may be a legal requirement to record transactions, for example for accounting and audit purposes.

(c) Detailed information on production costs can be built up, allowing a better assessment of profitability. Similarly, labour utilised in providing a particular service can be measured.

(d) It may be needed later for reference or further processing.

The first three uses of information - decision making, planning and controlling - are described in more detail in the next two sections of this chapter.

Activity 2   [15 minutes]

This simple activity may help you to understand the terminology that we are using.

Mr and Mrs Average need to go to Sainsbury's to buy food and other household items. They make a list beforehand which sets out all the things they need. As they go round the supermarket they tick off the items on the list. If any particular item is not available they choose an alternative from the range on the shelves. They also buy a bottle of wine and two bars of chocolate. These were not on their original list.

(a) What part or parts of this activity would you describe as planning?

(b) There are several examples of decision making in this story. Identify three of them.

(c) What part or parts of this activity would you describe as control?

2   INFORMATION FOR DECISION MAKING

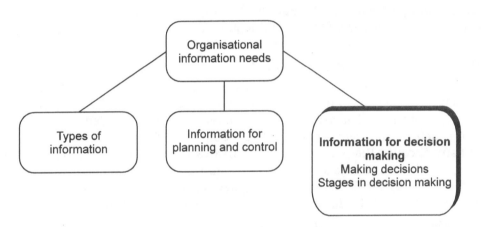

2.1   Making decisions

Decisions are made in different ways in different situations.

(a) In some organisations decisions are arrived at *collectively* through negotiation or voting. A referendum is a means of taking such a decision. In many cases, the right to make decisions is delegated to certain *individuals*. In most limited companies, the owners will appoint directors to act on their behalf, and to manage the organisation's activities.

(b) Within an organisation, different types of decision are taken at different *levels*. Decision making is one of the main functions of management, and many decisions will be delegated from the top to middle and junior management.

(c) Certain kinds of decision are *routine*, in that the same remedy will be applied to a situation which recurs regularly, or which is relatively simple. For example, an organisation might have a policy of sending out reminder notes if its customers have not paid their bills after 30 days. If customer Y is late in payment, the conditions specifying the organisation's response have been determined in advance. Such a decision can be called a *programmed* decision. (This does not necessarily refer to computer programs. A set of clerical procedures laid down in a manual would be just the same.) Programmed decisions:

   (i) respond to simple problems (where only a few factors are relevant);

   (ii) have few possible solutions (for example to send or not to send reminder notes);

(iii) are easy to make, as the relationship between the problem and the decision is easy to determine.

So how are decisions made? We can analyse the process into a series of steps.

2.2 Stages in decision making

The stages in making a decision are as follows.

(a) Problem recognition.

(b) Problem definition and structuring.

(c) Identifying alternative courses of action.

(d) Making and communicating the decision.

(e) Implementation of the decision.

(f) Monitoring the effects of the decision.

Problem recognition

Decisions are not made without information. The decision maker needs to be informed of a problem in the first place. This is sometimes referred to as the *decision trigger*. Normally further information is required.

Problem definition and structuring

This further information can be analysed so that the problem can be defined precisely. Consider, for example, a company with falling sales. The fall in revenue would be the trigger. Further information would be needed to identify where the revenue deficiencies were occurring. The problem can therefore be defined. If our company discovers that sales of product X in area Y are falling, the problem can be defined as 'decline of sales of product X in area Y due to new competitor: how can the decline be reversed?' Some 'problems' may be more vague, however. There are a number of ways of defining and structuring a problem, for example:

(a) as a mathematical model, for example the EOQ (economic order quantity) model for stock control; or

(b) as a scenario in 'what-if?' analysis.

One of the purposes of *defining* the problem is to identify the relationships between the various factors in it, especially if the problem is complex.

Definition

What-if? analysis looks at a problem by considering what would happen in different circumstances (or 'scenarios'). For example, *what if* sales demand is 10,000 units, or 20,000 units? What are the different implications for staffing the production department?

A *model* is something that represents the real thing as closely as possible. For example, the government uses a computerised mathematical 'model' of the economy so that it can assess, say, the impact of a rise in interest rates on people's buying habits.

Identifying alternative courses of action

Where alternative courses of action are identified, information is needed about them so they can be assessed. So, in a situation where there are a number of alternatives, the decision maker will glean information as to their likely effect. As a simple example, if our company wishes to review the price of product X in area Y, information will be needed as to the effect of particular price levels on the public's demand for the product. Such information can include external information such as market research (demand at a particular price) and the cost of the product, which can be provided internally.

Making and communicating the decision

The decision is made after review of the information relating to alternatives. However, the decision is useless if it is not communicated. So, in our example, if the sales director decides to lower the price of product X and run an intensive advertising campaign, nothing will happen unless the advertising department is informed, and even the manufacturing department, who will prepare new packaging showing the lower price.

Implementation of the decision

The decision is then implemented. For large-scale decisions (for example to relocate a factory 100 miles away from the current site), implementation may need substantial planning and review. Information is needed to ensure that implementation is going according to plan.

Monitoring the effects of the decision

Once a decision has been made, information is needed so that its effects can be reviewed. For example, if a manufacturing organisation has installed new equipment in anticipation of savings in costs, then information will need to be obtained as to whether these savings are being made in practice.

Decisions would rarely be necessary if every day was the same as yesterday, and everybody was content with this. In reality the world is constantly changing and organisations want to grow and do new things. We must consider how this affects information needs.

3 INFORMATION FOR PLANNING AND CONTROL

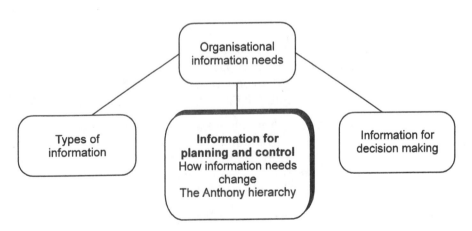

3.1 How information needs change

Organisations face a changing environment which they cannot always control, but to which they must relate. At the same time an organisation itself is a complex system which converts resources into products, or services, or money. Most complex organisations have some sort of management structure, to plan and control the activities of the organisation, both as a whole in relation to its environment, and in its separate units.

The environment is variable, so the organisation has often in some way to adapt to it. For example, if anti-pollution legislation affects an organisation's production activities, then the organisation will have to adapt to these new legal requirements. It may adapt in a number of different ways. Similarly, as the organisation is a complex social system, on a day to day basis, the conflicting demands of the various departments must be harmonised in some way and priorities must be established. There may be a number of options or choices available.

Activity 3 [15 minutes]

What changes have there been in the last year or so internally in your own organisation and your section and externally in the environment in which your organisation operates? If you are not at work, consider your college or an organisation with which you are familiar.

How have these changes affected your own information needs, if at all?

Decisions must therefore be taken in response to choices and options regarding how the organisation responds to the environment, and how its internal activities are to be run. There is a wide variety of decisions that can be taken: we shall now look at a way of classifying these decisions, which helps us to understand what information will be needed.

3.2 The Anthony hierarchy

A well known writer on management, Richard Anthony identified three areas of decision making as a hierarchy (Figure 10.1).

(a) Strategic planning.

(b) Management control.

(c) Operational control.

Figure 10.1 A hierarchy of decision making

Strategic planning, management control and operational control may be seen as a hierarchy of planning and control decisions. Management control is always in the middle of the range.

(a) Top level management make strategic plans, and low level managers make operational control decisions.

(b) Strategic planning tends to cover a longer time period than management control, whereas operational control is exercised day-to-day.

(c) The most important decisions are usually strategic, and the least important are operational.

Strategic planning decisions

Strategic planning is a process of deciding on objectives of the organisation, on changes in these objectives, on the resources used to attain these objectives and on the policies that are to govern the acquisition and use of these resources.

Definition

Objectives are the things that an organisation is trying to achieve, for example, increase sales by 10% or increase market share by 20%.

Strategic planning involves choosing objectives and planning how to achieve those objectives. Although much strategic planning is done with a view to the long term future, its consequences and results might also be short term.

Strategic planning is largely a process of formulating plans, but it also includes an important element of control. A board of directors might set as a policy objective diversification of the business, so that a decision might be taken to purchase a company which manufactures umbrellas (say) with a view to acquiring a 50% share of the market for umbrella sales and obtaining a financial return on investment of 20%. Strategic decision making therefore:

(a) is long term;

(b) involves high levels of uncertainty and risk (the future is unpredictable);

(c) involves situations that do not necessarily recur;

(d) deals with complex issues.

Management control decisions

Anthony defined management control as ensuring that resources are obtained and used effectively and efficiently in the accomplishment of the organisation's objectives. Management control decisions are taken within the framework of strategic plans and objectives which have previously been made, or set.

Definitions

Efficiency means that resources input to a process produce the optimum (maximum) amount of outputs.

Effectiveness means that the resources are used to achieve the desired ends.

This type of decision can encompass planning activities. A decision about how to price a new product, given that a lower price offers a lower unit profit but prospects of higher sales volumes, would be 'management control' planning.

Operational control

Operational control decisions ensure that specific tasks are carried out effectively and efficiently. It focuses on individual tasks, and is carried out within the strictly defined guidelines issued by strategic planning and management control decisions.

Many operational control decisions can be automated or programmed. 'Programmed control' exists where the relationship between what resources go in and what result comes out is clearly defined, so that an optimal relationship can be specified for every activity. Mathematical models can be designed to provide optimal solutions to problems, and many physical procedures can be controlled by automatic devices. Programmed control will always be a form of operational control.

Activity 4 [10 minutes]

Consider management decisions as they affect work in a purchasing department. Classify each of the following three decisions according to the three types of decision identified by Anthony.

(a) The payment cycle (the time between receiving an invoice and paying for it) will be extended by five days to improve cash flow.

(b) On receipt of an invoice, the purchase order form and goods received note relating to the order must be checked to the invoice. Specified details must be checked, and the invoice stamped to show that the checks have been carried out fully and satisfactorily.

(c) Major suppliers will be asked to join the company's EDI (electronic data interchange) network.

In the next section we think about information needs in terms of the types of information available. To begin with we look at the information needed for the different levels of decision that we have just described.

4   TYPES OF INFORMATION

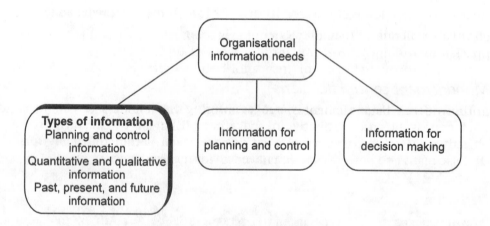

4.1   Planning and control information

One way of classifying information is in terms of the level of decision that it is used for.

Strategic information

Strategic information is used by senior managers to plan the objectives of their organisation, and to assess whether the objectives are being met in practice. Such information includes overall profitability, the profitability of different segments of the business, future market prospects, the availability and cost of raising new funds, total cash needs, total manning levels and capital equipment needs.

Strategic information therefore:

(a) is derived from both internal and external sources;

(b) is summarised at a high level;

(c) is relevant to the long term;

(d) deals with the whole organisation (although it might go into some detail);

(e) is often prepared on an 'ad hoc' basis (ie as and when needed, but only then);

(f) is both quantitative and qualitative (see below);

(g) is incapable of providing complete certainty, given that the future cannot be predicted.

Tactical information

Tactical information is used by middle management to decide how the resources of the business should be employed, and to monitor how they are being and have been employed. Such information includes productivity measurements (output per man hour or per machine hour) budgetary control or variance analysis reports, and cash flow forecasts, manning levels and profit results within a particular department of the organisation, labour turnover statistics within a department and short term purchasing requirements.

Tactical information therefore:

(a) is derived from a more restricted range of external sources, so is thus primarily generated internally;

(b) is summarised at a lower level - a report might be included with summaries and raw data as backup;

(c) is relevant to the short and medium term;

(d) describes or analyses activities or departments;

(e) is prepared routinely and regularly;

(f) is based on quantitative measures.

Operational information

Operational information is used by 'front-line' managers such as foremen or head clerks to ensure that specific tasks are planned and carried out properly within a factory or office. In the payroll office, for example, operational information relating to labour will include the hours worked each week by each employee, his rate of pay per hour, details of his deductions, and for the purpose of wages analysis, details of the time each man spent on individual jobs during the week. In this example, the information is required weekly, but more urgent operational information, such as the amount of raw materials being input to a production process, may be required daily, hourly, or in the case of automated production, second by second. Operational information relates to the level of decision making previously referred to as operational control.

Operational information:

(a) is derived almost entirely from internal sources;

(b) is highly detailed, being the processing of raw data;

(c) relates to the immediate term;

(d) is task-specific;

(e) is prepared constantly, or very frequently;

(f) is largely quantitative.

We have used the terms 'quantitative' and 'qualitative' a number of times. This distinction provides another way of classifying types of information.

4.2   Quantitative and qualitative information

Information may be quantitative or qualitative. Quantitative information is provided in numerical form such as amounts of money, lengths of time or amounts of raw materials. On the other hand, qualitative information relates to things like people's attitudes, ideas and opinions and often these are not normally or easily expressed in numerical form. In an organisation, examples of qualitative information which may be of interest are motivation, employee morale, and public perception of the organisation.

Quantitative information (numbers) can be built into mathematical models and formulae. Mathematical computer models (such as financial planning models) which are used extensively by management, require some method of quantifying 'variables' in the situation under review.

Qualitative information depends on the experience and judgement of a manager, whereas quantitative information simply depends on the accuracy of the measured data and the assumptions used in a mathematical formula or a computer model.

When qualitative factors will influence a decision, the manager has two options.

(a) To use his or her judgement in reaching the final decision, trying to balance quantitative and qualitative factors. This is what normally happens.

(b) To use a technique, if one is available in the organisation, for converting qualitative values into quantitative values, and making the decision on the strength of estimated quantified costs and benefits. This is the principle underlying so-called 'cost-benefit analysis' or CBA, which is sometimes used by a government to make decisions (for example about road-building) by putting money values to social costs and benefits. As we saw in Part A of this book, however, it is extremely difficult to do this, and the values can *always* be disputed.

In certain areas progress has been made in creating quantitative information by measuring qualitative information. For example attitudes can be measured according to their strength: a scale of 0-6 might be used to quantify the motivation of employees, with 0 representing poor morale and 6 high morale.

For discussion

The Conservative government in the 1980s and 1990s tried hard to find ways of measuring things that had not previously been measured. Examples are the performance of schools and hospitals.

Do you think things like this can be measured meaningfully? Do you think they should be?

4.3   Past, present and future information

Another useful categorisation of information, finally, is between past, present and future information.

Past information

This is record keeping, the storing of information about what has been done or what has happened in the past. This historical information will subsequently be used again at some time in the future. Much past information is information of a transaction processing nature. Recording transactions is a function of the operational level of management.

(a) In the case of a company, there is a statutory requirement of the Companies Act for a company to maintain proper accounting records of past transactions.

(b) Records that are kept of past transactions might be used to generate further routine operations at a later date. For example, a record of a sale to a customer, and details of the invoice sent out, will be kept, and if the customer does not pay on time, a statement or reminder will be sent out, chasing payment.

Present information

This is information about what is happening now, so that decisions can be taken about what, if anything, to do next. Present information is therefore most readily associated with control information. Much control information relates to the comparison of historical with current data.

Future information

This is forecasting information about what is expected to happen in the future. It is most readily associated with planning decisions, possibly for a budget, but also for longer term strategic information. Future information is also likely to include a significant proportion of environmental information, because the future of any organisation will not be secure unless it continues to adapt to changes in its environment.

Past information should be the most accurate of the three categories, and future information the least accurate of the three. The degree of accuracy expected from information should therefore vary according to whether it is past, present or future.

Chapter roundup

- Users of information include both internal and external users.

- One of the key uses of information is in the decision-making process. Decision making has a number of identifiable stages.

- The decision making process has three distinct stages: recognising a problem, thinking of ways of dealing with it, and choosing the best way.

- All staff in an organisation may make planning and control decisions. Anthony identifies a hierarchy of decision making, which comprises the three areas of strategic planning, management control and operation control. Strategic planning involves deciding on the organisation's objectives and planning how to achieve them. Management control seeks to ensure that resources are obtained and used efficiently and effectively in achieving those objectives. Operational control ensures that specific tasks are carried out efficiently and effectively.

- Different types of information are used at each level of the decision making hierarchy. In general, strategic information is highly summarised internal and external information, is often of a long term nature, and may be both quantitative and qualitative. Tactical information is more detailed short and medium term information, and operational information is highly detailed and immediate and tends to be quantitative.

- Other ways of classifying information are according to whether it is qualitative or quantitative and according to whether it is past, present or future.

Quick quiz

1　List five internal users of information.

2　What are the six stages in making a decision?

3　What are the three levels of decision making identified by Anthony?

4　What is management control?

5　Distinguish between efficiency and effectiveness.

6　What are the characteristics of strategic information?

7　What are the characteristics of operational information?

8　What is qualitative information?

9　How can an organisation attempt to quantify attitudes such as motivation of its staff?

10　In general, which of past, present and future information is the least accurate?

Answers to quick quiz

1　Examples of internal users of information are listed in Section 1.1.

2　The stages of decision making are discussed in Section 2.2.

3　The three levels of decision making identified by Anthony are strategic planning, management control, and operational control.

4　Management control is discussed in Section 3.2.

5　Efficiency and effectiveness are defined in Section 3.2.

6　Strategic information is discussed in Section 4.1.

7　Operational information is discussed in Section 4.1.

8　Qualitative information is information about things which are difficult to measure precisely and often relates to things such as attitudes and opinions.

9　An organisation can attempt to quantify attitudes such as staff motivation by asking people to put their motivation level on a numerical scale such as from 0 to 6.

10　In general, future information is less accurate than past or present information.

Answers to activities

1　There are many possible suggestions, including those given below.

(a) The organisation's *bankers* take decisions affecting the amount of money they are prepared to lend.

(b) The *public* might have an interest in information relating to an organisation's performance because they have invested in its shares or are thinking of doing so.

(c) The *media* (press, television etc) use information generated by organisations in news stories, and such information can adversely or favourably affect an organisation's relationship with its environment.

(d) The *government* (for example the Department of Trade and Industry) regularly requires organisational information.

(e) The *Inland Revenue* and *HM Customs and Excise* authorities require information for taxation and VAT assessments.

(f) An organisation's *suppliers* and *customers* take decisions whether or not to trade with the organisation.

2　(a) Making the list is an example of planning.

(b) Examples of decision making are choosing the items to put on the original list, selecting which alternatives to purchase and deciding to purchase additional items.

(c) Deciding to buy alternative and additional items are examples of control.

3   Your answer depends on your own experiences. Internal changes might include a change in your own role due to promotion or re-organisation, new colleagues, new products or services and so on. External changes could be new laws affecting what you do, new markets that your organisation has entered, or many others.

4   The first is a management control decision, the second is an operational control decision and the third is a strategic planning decision.

Assignment 10   [1½ hours]

Scenario

SuperBooks Limited run a chain of 23 large book shops in Scotland. Jean Jones is the Chief Executive of SuperBooks, Sam Green is the manager of the Glasgow shop, and Pat Smith is a supervisor in the Glasgow shop.

Tasks

1   Describe the Anthony hierarchy of decision making, using SuperBooks as an example organisation to illustrate the sorts of decisions and information dealt with at each level in the hierarchy.

2   SuperBooks are under increasing pressure from other retail outlets and the Board of Directors are meeting to discuss marketing strategies and set sales targets for the next financial year. It has been suggested that SuperBooks should take on new products such as publications on computer CD-ROM.

   (a) Describe the stages of decision making that the Board will have to go through, at the meeting and subsequently, including the sorts of information they will need and how they can get it.

   (b) Describe the sorts of transaction data that SuperBooks will need to record and explain how this transaction data may be processed into information that can be useful to all levels within the Anthony hierarchy.

Chapter 11

INFORMATION SYSTEMS

Introduction

In this chapter we introduce the concept of an information *system,* and in particular what is known as a management information system (MIS).

We shall look at what a system is, what data flows are involved, how systems are designed and how they are used for various management purposes.

These days information systems tend to be computerised, but they need not be and, in any case, a large amount of work is still done and stored on paper. We shall look specifically at computerised systems and their implications in the next chapter.

Your objectives

After completing this chapter you should:

(a) be able to explain what an information system is;

(b) understand the data flows that occur in an organisation;

(c) know what a management information system is;

(d) recognise the significance of transactions processing for management information systems;

(e) be able to describe issues surrounding the design of an MIS;

(f) understand the implications for an MIS of different levels of control and decision making.

1   INFORMATION SYSTEMS

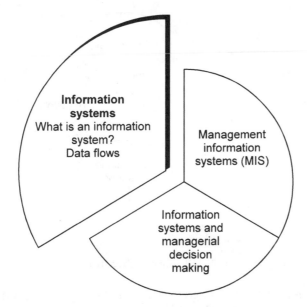

1.1   What is an information system?

An information system is an example of both a 'technical' system and a 'social' system. It is a technical system in that it may contain a large amount of machinery (plant, computers, telephones etc), but it is also a social system given that it may reflect, in the way it is used, the social structure of the organisation. For example, an information system not only exists to record transactions for operational managers but is also used to provide summary information to senior management to assess whether the organisation is following its long-term strategic objectives.

Definitions

A *system* is a set of connected things. Systems are a way of organising activities. For example, a sales system may consist of documents and procedures used for: taking customer orders; despatching goods; invoicing; recording debts; and accepting payments.

A *sub-system* is a smaller part of a larger system. For example, there may be a despatch sub-system with its own set of documents and procedures.

Figure 11.1 shows the organisation as a system with departments - manufacturing, personnel - as sub-systems.

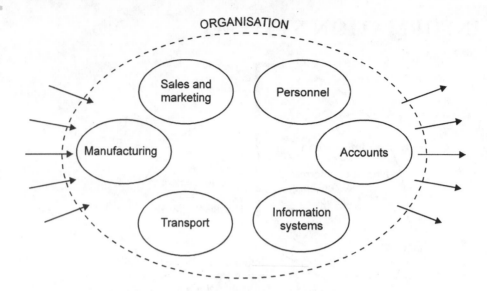

Figure 11.1 The organisation (system) with departments (sub-systems)

Information systems of varying degrees of formality may be encountered. Whereas computer output is a well-defined and formal way of passing information, informal communications channels (such as the telephone, or the 'grapevine') may be just as important.

Even at a technical level, an information system may feature a number of sub-systems (for example a data processing system, a management information system and a decision support system). The information system links the various parts of the organisation together.

Activity 1   [15 minutes]

A school or college can be viewed as a group of related functional sub-systems ie each of the sub-systems carries out a particular function. Enrolment could be one of the sub-systems. Try to think of several other functional sub-systems.

Note that an information system does not *have* to be a computer system.

Information systems do not need to be *permanent,* either. Many are developed in order to collect and process data and produce information to users on a regular basis, for example as part of monthly or daily reporting procedures. However, an organisation may need to obtain information about a situation for a specific period only; for example while there is industrial action by distributors or while one salesman is covering two sales areas pending a new appointment. In these cases, a temporary information system will be established and then discontinued once the specific situation for which it was set up no longer exists.

It can be seen that information systems may vary a great deal, for example in terms of their formality, their period of usefulness, the use they make of computers and the range of sub-systems they include. So what are the common features of all information systems?

An information system is really a series of activities or processes.

(a) Identification of data requirements

(b) Collection and transcription of data (data capture)

(c) Data processing

(d) Communication of processed data to users

(e) Use of processed data (as information) by users

A system, therefore, connects things up and this means that they can move more easily from where they are to where they are needed. Let's look at how data and information flows through an organisation.

1.2   Data flows

Data flows represent the movement of data or information from one person, group, department or organisation to another. There can be:

(a) *formal* and *routine* data flows;

(b) *formal* but *irregular* and *non-routine* data flows;

(c) *informal* data flows.

Data flows may be internal or external.

(a) Internal flows occur between sub-systems of the same organisation, usually between one department and another, one section and another, or one person and another. Most data flows in a business organisation are internal flows between its sub-systems.

(b) External flows occur between the organisation and its environment (for example customers, suppliers, government authorities or agencies).

Figure 11.2 shows the basic data flows between some of the sub-systems in an organisation, taking the receipt of a customer's order as the starting point. The organisation's boundary is shown by the dotted line. Each sub-system may itself be considered a system in its own right.

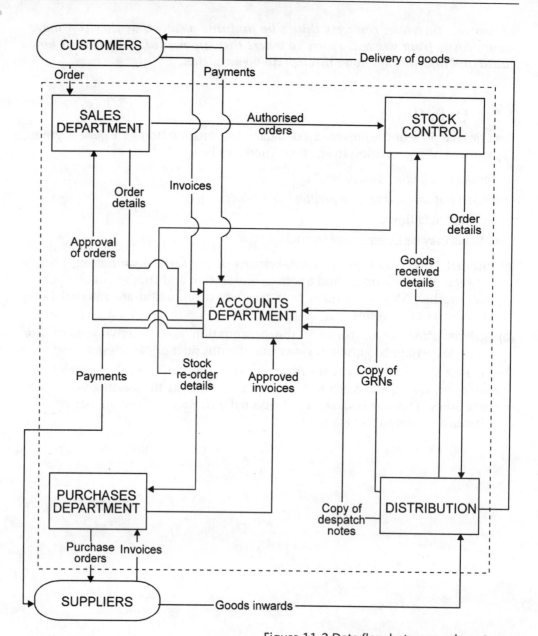

Figure 11.2 Data flow between sub-systems

Examples of transactions which transfer data from *one sub-system to another* are as follows.

(a) Order details received from customers in the sales department will be passed to the accounts department in order that the credit rating of the customer may be checked before the order is processed further.

(b) A copy of despatch notes will pass from distribution to the accounts department in order to start the process of raising an invoice to be sent to the customer.

(c) Details of goods received will be notified to stock control in order that they may update the stock records and their outstanding orders file.

Transactions which transfer data *to or from the external environment* might include the following.

(a) Re-order details will be sent by the purchases department to suppliers so that the company's stocks can be replenished.

(b) Money sent by customers will be received by the accounts department who will then be able to update the sales records with the fact that the customer no longer has a liability to the company for that amount.

The information system itself is likely to function as a number of sub-systems, for example as:

(a) functional information systems or *transaction processing systems* (sales order processing, creditors records etc);

(b) *management information systems* (for strategic, tactical and operational levels of management), whereby data and information go up and down the management hierarchy.

These are almost certain to overlap, and each functional information system can be used to provide information for any level of management. This is hardly surprising as management information is often extracted from operational data (usually in summary form). A sales system is a useful example. Note that the purchases functional system and sales functional system might be linked together (Figure 11.3)

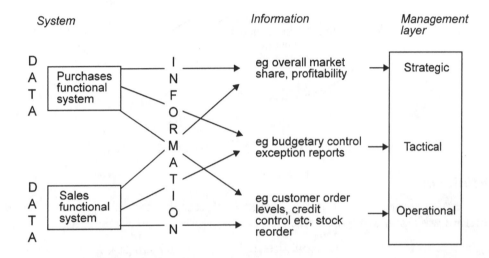

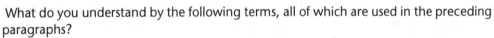

Figure 11.3 Sales and purchases systems

Activity 2 [20 minutes]

What do you understand by the following terms, all of which are used in the preceding paragraphs?

(a) Data
(b) Information
(c) Liability
(d) Functional
(e) Strategic levels of management
(f) Tactical levels of management
(g) Operational levels of management

Use the index to find the place where the term is first defined or explained if necessary.

We use most of these terms frequently in this chapter, so it is worth taking the trouble to do this activity now.

2 MANAGEMENT INFORMATION SYSTEMS (MIS)

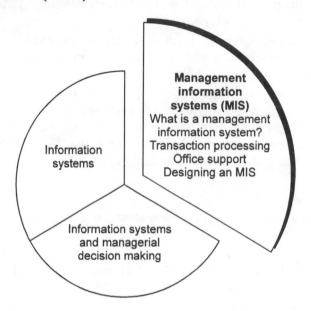

2.1 What is a management information system?

Definitions

The term *management information system* (MIS) can be defined in a number of different ways, some of which are listed below.

(a) 'A system to convert data from internal and external sources into information and to communicate that information, in an appropriate form, to managers at all levels in all functions to enable them to make timely and effective decisions for planning, directing and controlling the activities for which they are responsible.'

(Lucey, *Management Information Systems*)

(b) 'A computer system or related group of systems which collects and presents management information to a business in order to facilitate its control.'

(CIMA, *Computing Terminology*)

(c) 'A system which may perform routine commercial processing functions, but which is designed so that such processing will also produce information that will be presented to management, including top management, to assist in decision making. The implication is that the results will be produced speedily ... to enable management to ascertain the progress of the organisation in terms of satisfying its major objectives.'

(Penguin, *Dictionary of Computers*)

What is common to these definitions is that information is presented to management. However, this is not the only function of an organisation's information systems. A number of tasks might be performed simultaneously.

(a) Initiating transactions (for example automatically making a purchase order if stock levels are below a specified amount).

(b) Recording transactions as they occur (for example a sale is input to the sales system).

(c) Processing data.

(d) Producing reports.

(e) Responding to enquiries.

The scope of an MIS, potentially, is to satisfy all the informational needs of management. A good MIS will provide good information to those who need it. Whether this is possible will depend to some degree on the nature and type of information provided. An MIS is good at providing regular formal information gleaned from normal commercial data. For example, an MIS relating to sales could provide managers with information on the following.

(a) Gross profit margins of particular products.

(b) Success in particular markets.

(c) Credit control information (aged debtors and payments against old balances).

It may be less efficient at presenting information which is relatively unpredictable, or informal, or unstructured. So, for example, an MIS could not (without adjustment) provide information relating to the sudden emergence of a new competitor into the market.

While an MIS may not be able to provide all the information used by management, it should be sufficiently flexible to enable management to incorporate unpredictable, informal or unstructured information into the decision-making processes. For example, many decisions are made with the help of financial models (such as spreadsheets) so that the effect of new situations can be estimated easily.

We ought to give a little more consideration to the regular formal information collected by an organisation that can be used for management purposes.

2.2 Transaction processing

Transaction processing systems, or data processing systems, could be said to represent the lowest level in an organisation's use of information systems. They are used for routine tasks in which data items or transactions must be processed so that operations can continue. Handling sales orders, purchase orders, payroll items and stock records are typical examples.

Transaction processing systems generally contain at least two categories of file.

(a) A file (or files) of master records

(b) A file of transactions to be used in updating the master records

Consider a bank. The master records would consist of some identification data, historical transactions and the current balance for all the accounts.

The transactions file would consist of a day's transactions and would include deposits, withdrawals, cheques, direct debits, bank charges and so on. The transactions file would then be used to update the master file records of customer accounts, so that the master file continues to reflect the latest position.

Most organisations generate a large volume of transactions which need to be processed efficiently and effectively. Computerised transactions processing systems have clear cost and performance advantages over manual systems for all but the most trivial applications. Small businesses are using desk top personal computers to provide these functions just as larger companies earlier acquired huge mainframe computers for these purposes.

Activity 3 [15 minutes]

Why do computerised systems have cost and performance advantages over manual systems?

Transaction processing systems provide the raw material which is often used more extensively by management information systems. In other words, transaction processing systems might be used to produce management information, such as reports on cumulative sales figures to date, total amounts owed to suppliers or owed by debtors, total stock turnover to date, value of current stock-in-hand, and so on, but the main purpose of transaction processing systems is operational, as an integral part of day-to-day operations.

An information system is made up not only of transactions: it is also a series of processes, or ways of doing things. Records of transactions have always been collected, but the way in which this is done has changed radically in recent years.

2.3 Office support

Many of an organisation's MIS activities are enhanced through the use of information technology (IT). Information technology is a term used to describe the coming together of computer technology with data transmission technology, to revolutionise information systems. Cheap computer hardware, based on microchip technology with ever-increasing power and capacity, has been harnessed to an extensive telecommunications network.

Computers are able to 'talk' to each other over telecommunications links, or can transmit data to and from terminals located elsewhere. Terminals can send data to a computer and receive output messages. Small computers have spread rapidly in the home and the office. Information technology also involves other equipment and information transmission systems, not just computers; for example, there are electronic mail, fax, cable television, teletext, electronic telephone exchanges, satellite communications and data transmission using laser technology.

IT therefore involves the electronic acquisition, storage and dissemination of vocal, pictorial, textual and numerical information.

The emergence of the electronic office means that management information can be provided more quickly and cheaply than before, and that managers can be involved in information production and report design. Some typical applications are:

(a) text processing (word processing systems, graphics);

(b) computing (cheap microcomputers);

(c) telecommunications and networks;

(d) data storage and reference (databases).

Computerised systems are the topic of the next chapter. For now we shall concentrate on some of the issues that affect the type of MIS an organisation chooses to have.

2.4 Designing an MIS

Most management information systems are not formally 'designed', but grow up informally, with each manager making sure that he gets all the information he thinks he needs to do his job. It is virtually taken for granted that the necessary information flows to the job, and to a certain extent this is so. Much accounting information, for example, is easily obtained, and managers can often get along with frequent face-to-face contact and co-operation with each other. Such an informal system works best in small companies, but is inadequate in a large company, especially one which spreads over several industries, areas or countries.

The consequences of a poor MIS might be: dissatisfaction amongst employees who believe they should be told more; a lack of understanding about what the targets for achievement are; and a lack of information about how well the work is being done.

Some information systems *are* formally designed or planned, often because the introduction of computers has forced management to consider its information needs in detail. This is especially the case in large companies.

For discussion

It is likely that some of your colleagues on your course work for large companies and some for smaller ones. This presents an ideal opportunity for you to share knowledge about the applications of MIS in different forms and sizes of organisations.

Think about the equipment used (a manual system or a single PC in the smallest of businesses, a network of PCs in small to medium-sized one, a huge 'mainframe' computer in a large business like a bank). What sort of information can you and others obtain from the system? Is it your job to turn low-level detailed information into higher-level summary reports? Does the system cover all the activities of the organisation or just a specific part or parts of it? You will find lots of other differences to discuss.

Management should try to design the management information system for their business with care. If they allow the MIS to develop without any formal planning, the MIS will almost certainly be inefficient because data will be obtained and processed in a random and disorganised way. The communication of information will also be random and hit-and-miss. For example, without formal planning and design of the MIS, the following situations are likely.

(a) Some managers will prefer to keep data in their heads and will not commit information to paper. When the manager is absent from work, or is moved to another job, his stand-in or successor will not know as much as he could and should about the work because there will be no information to help him.

(b) Not all data is collected and processed that ought to be, and so valuable information that ought to be available to management will be missing.

(c) Information is available but not communicated to the managers who are in a position of authority and so ought to be given it. The information will go to waste because it would not be used. In other words, the wrong people will have the information.

(d) Information is communicated late because the need to communicate it earlier is not understood and appreciated by the data processors.

(e) Information may be unnecessarily duplicated in several places which wastes resources in collecting, storing and processing the information. In addition, there is the danger that the information held at different places may be inconsistent.

Whether a management information system is formally or informally constructed, it should have certain essential characteristics.

(a) The functions of individuals and their areas of responsibility in achieving company objectives should be defined.

(b) Areas of control within the company (eg cost centres, budget centres) should also be clearly defined.

(c) Information required for an area of control should flow to the manager responsible for it.

Finally in this chapter we shall return to the idea of different levels of management activity in an organisation and see how this affects the use of the MIS.

3 INFORMATION SYSTEMS AND MANAGERIAL DECISION MAKING

3.1 Operational level MIS

We saw in the previous chapter that operational decisions are essentially small-scale and programmed, and that operational information is often highly formal and quantitative. Many operational decisions can, in fact, be incorporated into computer processing itself.

Most MIS at operational level, however, are essentially used for processing transactions, updating files and so forth. The inputs will be basic transaction data, and outputs will be simple reports, which have sorted or listed the input data, or documents as records of transactions, or further instructions.

3.2 Tactical level MIS

A variety of systems can be used at this level, and there may be a greater reliance than at operational level on:

(a) exception reporting;

(b) informal systems;

(c) investigation and analysis of data acquired at operational level;

(d) externally generated data.

At tactical level the MIS will interact with the same systems as at operational level, and in fact tactical information may be generated in the same processing operation as operational level information. For example, tactical level information comparing actual costs incurred to budget can be produced by a system in which those costs are recorded. Functional MIS at tactical level are typically related to other functional MIS. Information from the sales department's MIS will affect the accounting department's system, for example.

3.3 Strategic level MIS

At strategic level the information system is likely to be informal, in the sense that it is not always possible to quantify or program strategic information, and much of the information might come from environmental sources. The MIS will provide summary level data from transactions processing. Human judgement is used more often at this level, as many strategic decisions cannot be programmed.

Definition

The *environment* means the organisation's surroundings, not just the 'green' environment. For example an organisation's technological environment is all the developments that are taking place in the world in technology. Similarly there is a legal environment, an economic environment and so on.

In short, formal systems are likely to be less important at this level. However, they can be used in the gathering of information. In a finance sub-system the operational level would deal with cash receipts and payments, bank reconciliations and so forth. The tactical level would deal with cash flow forecasts and working capital management. Strategic level financial issues are likely to be integrated with the organisation's commercial strategy, but may relate to the most appropriate source of finance (for example debt or equity).

Table 11.1 shows typical inputs, processes and outputs at each level of a management information system.

	Inputs	Processes	Outputs
Strategic	Plans Competitor information Market information	Summarise Investigate Compare Forecast	Key ratios Ad hoc market analysis Strategic plans
Tactical	Historical data Budget data	Compare Classify Summarise	Variance analyses Exception reports
Operational	Customer orders Programmed stock control levels	Update files Output reports	Updated files Listings Invoices

Table 11.1 Inputs, processes and outputs

We introduced information technology earlier in this chapter and suggested that it has had a huge impact on MIS. We explore this topic in much more detail in the next chapter.

Chapter roundup

- An information system connects up the diverse sources at which information is collected or produced in an organisation. It will consist of a number of sub-systems.

- Data must flow between sub-systems until it reaches the person who needs it. There are both internal flows and external flows and data flows in both directions.

- There are various definitions of an MIS, but basically an MIS presents information to management. The raw material of an MIS is provided by the transactions processing system.

- Systems often grow informally, but the larger they get the more inefficient this will be unless some formal attention is given to the design of the system.

- The way in which the MIS is used will vary depending upon the level of control and decision making that the information is required for.

Quick quiz

1 What is a sub-system?

2 What sort of data flows may occur in an organisation?

3 Define an MIS.

4 What information may *not* be provided by an MIS?

5 Give an example of management information that might be derived from a transaction processing system.

6 What are some applications of information technology?

7 What might be the consequences of a poor MIS?

8 What are the essential characteristics of an MIS?

9 What sort of systems might be used at a tactical level?

10 Draw up a table showing inputs, processes and outputs at each management level.

Answers to quick quiz

1 A system is a set of connected things. A sub-system is a system which is a smaller part of a larger system.

2 Data flows within an organisation are discussed in Section 1.2.

3 An MIS is a management information system; several definitions of a management information system are given in Section 2.1.

4 An MIS may not be able to provide information which is relatively unpredictable, or informal, or unstructured and will not generally provide information relating to the organisation's external environment.

5 A transaction processing system can often summarise detailed operational information to provide management information such as cumulative sales figures to date.

6 Applications of information technology are discussed in Section 2.3.

7 The possible consequences of a poor MIS include employee dissatisfaction and lack of information about planned and actual performance.

8 The main characteristics of a typical MIS are that it provides regular formal information derived from normal commercial data.

9 The systems used at the tactical level are discussed in Section 3.2.

10 A table showing inputs, processes and outputs is shown in Section 3.3.

Answers to activities

1 A school or college may have functional sub-systems dealing with things such as:

(a) teaching

(b) external examinations

(c) student social functions

(d) student grants

(e) student accommodation

(f) induction

(g) catering

(h) cleaning and maintenance

2 (a) Data are facts and figures.

(b) Information is data when it has been processed in some way to make it meaningful to the intended user.

(c) A liability is an amount that you owe to someone else.

(d) Functional (in this context) refers to different functions of the business such as production, personnel, sales, research, distribution and so on.

(e) Strategic levels are the top levels who decide the overall direction of the business.

(f) Tactical levels are the middle levels who decide how resources should be used in order to go in the required direction.

(g) Operational levels are the junior levels who implement and control the tactical plans from day to day.

3 Computerised systems are *faster* and so able to deal with greater volumes of information in less time, and they are more *accurate*. These are the essential points. You may have thought of others, and we shall pose this question again at the beginning of the next chapter.

Assignment 11 [1½ hours]

Scenario

Chris Williams is a qualified accountant who has built up an accountancy business, JW Financial Services (JWF), specialising in providing accountancy services to small businesses. The range of services includes financial advice, preparation of annual accounts, and general book-keeping work. The business now has three qualified accountants, two part qualified accountants and four book-keepers; all of these people work on clients' accounts. In addition there are three administrators and an office manager.

In the early days of the business, Chris went into partnership with John Dawson, an accountant who had been given early retirement from the accounts office of a large department store. John has always resisted Chris's attempts to introduce computerised information systems into the business and Chris suspects that the reason is really John's anxiety about coping with modern technology. John is soon to retire fully. Chris feels that the time is right to try to modernise JWF's information systems.

Currently all work is done manually with a paper-based information system, except that Chris and the other remaining accountants use PCs for some of their work. They each have their own systems and cannot easily exchange information from one system to the other. Chris has tried to run the business using informal face-to-face communications but has found that, as the business has grown and employed more people, this is becoming increasingly unsatisfactory.

Tasks

1 Chris has asked you to provide an informal report entitled 'The Electronic Office', which should explain what the electronic office consists of, and what are its potential benefits and disadvantages to JWF.

2 Chris also wants you to explain what functional sub-systems are, in relation to JWF, and compare the use of formal and informal data flows internally within JWF and externally with JWF's environment.

Chapter 12

IT AND MANAGEMENT INFORMATION SYSTEMS

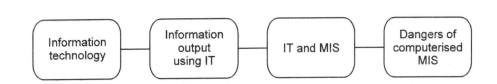

Introduction

In this chapter we are going to discuss a variety of issues arising from the uses of computers and telecommunications (information technology) in an information system.

We begin by looking at the advantages of IT and consider some specific ways in which computers (especially personal computers or PCs) can improve an MIS.

Next we discuss some of the ways in which computers affect the sort of output obtainable from an MIS and look at the most common applications of MIS - decision support systems, executive information systems and expert systems.

Finally we consider the problems that can arise in a computerised information environment.

Your objectives

After completing this chapter you should:

(a) be aware of the advantages and disadvantages of IT;

(b) understand the differences between manual and electronic processing;

(c) be able to describe some common applications of computers;

(d) know about the impact of IT on the output produced by an information system;

(e) be able to describe decision support systems, executive information systems and expert systems;

(f) recognise the dangers of using computers in an MIS.

1 INFORMATION TECHNOLOGY

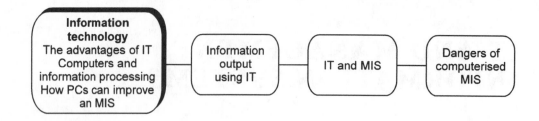

1.1 The advantages of IT

Definition

IT (Information technology) can be broadly defined as the convergence of computer technology and communications technology.

Information systems may be manual, computerised or a combination of the two. What are the potential advantages of the use of information technology?

(a) The *accuracy* of information is improved.

(b) The *volume* of information which can be processed is increased.

(c) The *speed* at which information becomes available is higher.

(d) The *workforce* is freed up for more skillful and judgmental work.

(e) There is *greater access* to information available to more people.

(f) *Consistency.*

Activity 1   [15 minutes]

What are the potential disadvantages of the use of information technology in an organisation?

1.2 Computers and information processing

The principles of data processing are essentially the same, no matter whether it is done manually or electronically. There are differences, as noted above, and these can be explained as follows.

(a) *Accuracy.* Computers are generally accurate, whereas humans are prone to error. The errors in computer data processing are normally human errors (errors in the input of data) although there can be software errors (errors in the programs) and hardware errors (faults or breakdowns in the equipment itself).

(b) *Volume.* As businesses grow and become more complex, their data processing requirements increase in volume and complexity too. More managers need greater amounts of information. More transactions have to be processed. The volume of data processing (DP) work is often beyond the capability of even the largest clerical workforce to do manually within a useful timescale. Clearing banks, for example, would be unable to function nowadays without electronic data processing to ease the demands on their workforce.

(c) *Speed.* Computers can process data much more quickly than a human. This means that a computer has a much higher productivity level and so it ought to be cheaper for large volumes of data processing than doing the work manually. As computer costs have fallen, this cost advantage of the computer has become more accentuated. The ability to process data more quickly means that a computer can produce more timely information, when information is needed as soon as possible.

(d) *Judgement*. Although a computer can handle data in greater volumes, and do more complex processing, the 'manual' or 'human' method of data processing is more suitable when human judgement is involved in the work.

(e) *Access to information*. The use of databases and the ability to link a number of users via a multi-user system or some form of network improves the distribution and dissemination of information within, and beyond, an organisation.

(f) *Consistency*. Properly developed and tested computer systems will always produce the same answer from the same input and will produce the output in a consistent manner. Thus an operation can be performed consistently many times and by several users.

Definitions

Hardware refers to the physical computer and communications equipment. A *personal computer* (PC) system usually contains hardware such as:

> a visual display unit (VDU) or screen
> a keyboard and a mouse
> a system unit housing the central processing unit (CPU), memory, storage such as disk drives, and network communications equipment

In addition, further hardware such as scanners, printers and plotters may be connected to the system unit and these devices are sometime known as *peripherals*.

Larger computer systems can be accessed by many users at the same time and are called *multi-user systems*. This requires more powerful hardware than a PC. Large central computers which can support hundreds of users are called *mainframe* computers, and smaller systems which can still support tens of users are called *mini-computers*. Equipment consisting of a VDU and keyboard is known as a *terminal* and it is used for accessing multi-user systems.

Software is the coded instructions which the computer carries out. *Systems software* carries out the basic operation of the computer such as managing keyboard input and loading and storing disk files. The main part of the systems software is the operating system such as Microsoft Windows or UNIX. *Applications software* is the programs that users run such as spreadsheets like Lotus 1-2-3 and Microsoft Excel.

A *database* is a group of related items of data. Computerised *database management* systems (DBMS) include facilities for setting up and maintaining the database and also incorporate security and access facilities so that several users can have simultaneous access to the information in the data, provided they have the appropriate access permission.

Computer networks can be classified in two main sorts. *Local Area Networks* (LAN) which connect a limited number, perhaps 30 computers together over a relatively short distance such as within one building. *Wide Area Networks* (WAN) which can connect thousands of computers together and can be world wide using the telephone system as its communication links.

1.3   How PCs can improve an MIS

Some examples of how personal computers (PCs) can improve a management information system might help to illustrate these advantages. Personal computers, also referred to as microcomputers, are particularly beneficial because:

(a) they allow an individual to use a desk-top computer himself/herself and so have direct access for input of data and receipt of output information;

(b) modern software is very flexible. For example, applications such as spreadsheets enable individual users to easily develop models of aspects of their organisation such as its cashflow or stock control.

Most organisations, whatever their size, make extensive use of PCs nowadays.

Managing cash flows

If a manager has direct access to information about the organisation's current cash position via a computer terminal, he can make quick decisions about transferring cash (eg transferring surplus cash from a current account to an interest-bearing deposit account).

Spreadsheet models

Computers have improved the ability of managers to develop models to help with planning and decision making.

Spreadsheet software packages can be used by managers to develop a range of planning and forecasting models. Planning models are particularly valuable MIS tools: managers can develop computer budgets, sales forecasts, and cash flow forecasts, etc. They can then carry out intensive sensitivity analysis using the model, by asking 'what if?' questions.

Definition

A *spreadsheet* is like a very large sheet of paper with a grid drawn on it. Numbers can be entered into the boxes on the grid and very sophisticated calculations and analyses can be performed.

Access to information

Terminals linked to a network, or central computer file, or to information of an external organisation (eg Reuters) give managers access to more information than they would otherwise have. Comprehensive information which is readily available (in good time) contributes, as we have seen already, to an effective MIS.

Word processing

Word processing systems include the facility for producing standard letters and mailshots, which can be of great assistance to:

(a) sales managers - sending out personalised mailshots or amended price lists to potential customers;

(b) account managers - sending out reminder letters to late payers.

Modern word processors are capable of producing very attractive looking documents and have features like spell-checking and indexing (and many others) which considerably enhance the quality of the finished product.

For discussion

Over the last couple of years a great deal of attention has been given to the Internet (or World Wide Web, or 'Information Superhighway') which links up millions of computers world wide. Most large companies now have 'sites' on the Internet so that you can, for example, buy airline tickets, go to the bank or do the weekly shopping while sitting at your computer.

Share your personal experience of the Internet with your colleagues or fellow students and discuss the implications for the businesses of the future.

If you look back through the files of your organisation from no more than 10 years ago you will be amazed at how much work was done with pen and paper and at how amateurish the typed and printed documents look. IT has had a huge impact on the output of an information system as well as on the processing methods.

2 INFORMATION OUTPUT USING IT

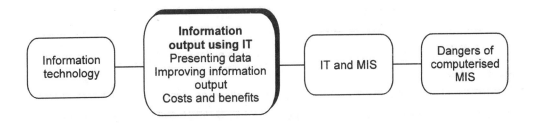

2.1 Presenting data

One of the qualities of good information is *clarity*. Modern technology has greatly expanded the techniques for displaying management information. Management information can be presented in a number of ways.

Computer printouts

Management information can be presented in printed computer reports, or summaries. For relatively simple information this is cheap and easy to prepare. Once the information becomes complicated, rows of figures become harder to use.

Desktop publishing

More advanced printing technology has greatly expanded the scope and flexibility for the visual presentation of management information. Graphs, charts, maps and so forth can be used to enhance the subject. This book is a product of desktop publishing.

VDU

Much management information is computer-generated. Managers can access information with a VDU and keyboard. The advent of powerful graphics software means that the information can be manipulated, converted into graphical format, and made easier to understand.

Video

If senior management wish to communicate, say, a change in strategy to middle management, this can be achieved by group presentations. Videos, for example, can be used to present this type of information. Moreover, some computer graphics packages are able to manipulate video-based information so that a combination of graphics and pictures can be prepared relatively cheaply.

E-mail

Electronic mail (E-mail) is another way of distributing management information from computer to computer. Instead of sending you a memo on paper your boss can simply type it into his computer and send it via your organisation's network to your computer or even a particular group of computers. You can call the message up on screen whenever you like.

Bulletin boards

Another source of information is the 'bulletin board' which becomes possible with e-mail systems, so that managers can communicate information to all their colleagues. This is a good way of sharing ideas. Computers are arranged in a network, and everybody has access to the bulletin board.

Activity 2 [15 minutes]

What form of output is most appropriate in the following cases and why?

(a) A customer rings up and asks a member of the sales team what is the current balance on his account.

(b) The Board of Directors has decided to introduce a just-in-time (JIT) production and stock control system which will involve radical changes to working procedures. The Board wants employees to understand the principles and benefits of JIT.

(c) Two of your main competitors have just merged. Everybody in the company will be interested to know this.

(d) A detailed record of the whole month's transactions needs to be kept for examination by the company's auditors later in the year.

(e) A mailshot to certain customers will contain a leaflet giving details of a new product

---

We shall consider the presentation of data in much more detail in the final chapter of this book. For now we are interested in how information systems can be designed to produce particular kinds of output.

2.2 Improving information output

A review of the possibilities of making improvements to output should cover three separately identifiable types of results.

(a) *External results* - results that will be sent out to people outside the organisation. These include customer invoices and statements and remittance advices to suppliers.

(b) *Internal results* - results that will be distributed within the organisation. These include management reports, error reports and audit listings etc.

(c) *Internal system results* - information relating to the operations of the system itself, such as system operating statistics and reports.

A review of existing output should cover the following aspects.

(a) *Identification of output.* All output report documents and VDU screen displays must be clearly specified and uniquely identified.

(b) *Content and format.* Obviously, this is a fundamental part of output design work, and you should refer back to our discussion of the qualities of good information to find the key issues that need to be addressed.

(c) *Frequency of production.* The frequency with which the output will be produced must be specified, including whether there might be a requirement for urgency in its production. Reports might be routinely produced (every week, month, year etc) or produced only on demand.

(d) Where appropriate, the *conditions* giving rise to the production of output should be specified ie what needs to happen for a particular report or item to be produced as output?

(e) The *volume* of expected output must also be specified. When output volumes are very large, and a large computer is being used, the systems designer will probably have opted for high-speed printer output. When output volumes are low and a paper copy of the output is required, the systems designer might have chosen to use a low-speed printer.

(f) The *sequence* in which output is produced must be specified. (This is another aspect of form design, even when output is not produced in hard copy but is displayed instead on a screen.)

(g) The *output medium* must be specified (eg screen, printer, graph plotter etc). Also the number of copies might have to be considered. Output which will be used as input to another program or module will need a computer readable medium, such as magnetic floppy disk. The choice of output medium will have regard to whether a paper copy is required and what quality the output should be, whether paper copy or VDU display.

Before leaving this topic we should remember that there is no point in producing information if it does not have a value.

2.3   Costs and benefits

The *costs and benefits* of output information should also be considered. The user might ask for information that would be too costly to produce in view of the benefits obtainable from it. The designer needs to consider questions such as the following.

(a) Is the user asking for too much information?

(b) Can two or more required outputs be combined into a single multi-use output?

(c) Is the output required as frequently as specified, or can the frequency be reduced?

(d) Should output be produced automatically, or only on demand (thus reducing output regularity and so output volume)?

(e) Should the user be allowed some control over the format and sequence of output, or should format and sequence be rigidly designed?

We can now move on to look at some ways in which concepts of a management information system are applied in practice. Three particular types of MIS deserve special mention and these are covered in the next section.

3 IT AND MIS

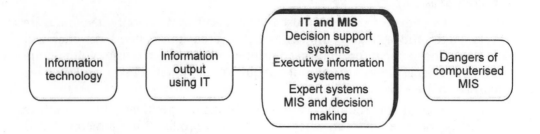

3.1 Decision support systems

Definition

Decision support systems (DSS) are a form of management information system. Decision support systems are used by management to assist in making decisions on complex problems, which are often very poorly defined with high levels of uncertainty about the true nature of the problem.

DSS specify the various responses which management could undertake or the likely impact of those actions. These highly ambiguous situations do not allow the easy application of many of the techniques or systems developed for better defined problems or activities. Decision support systems are intended to provide a wide range of alternative information gathering and analytical tools with a major emphasis upon flexibility and user-friendliness.

The term 'decision support system' is usually taken to mean computer systems which are designed to produce information in such a way as to help managers to make better decisions. They are now often associated with information 'at the touch of a button' at a manager's personal computer or workstation. DSS can describe a range of systems, from fairly simple information models based on spreadsheets to expert systems.

Decision support systems do not make decisions. The objective is to allow the manager to consider a number of alternatives and evaluate them under a variety of potential conditions. Managers using these systems often develop scenarios using earlier results to refine their understanding of the problem and their actions.

Some decision support computer systems are composed of three elements. These sub-systems then combine to provide the capabilities required for an effective decision support system.

(a) A *language* sub-system used by the manager to communicate interactively with the decision support system.

(b) A *problem processing* sub-system which provides analytical techniques and presentation capabilities.

(c) A *knowledge* sub-system which holds internal data and may access external data.

A decision support system *integrates* many of the functions supplied by information systems so that managers may use them more easily and on a wider range of problems.

A development of the decision support system is the executive information system (EIS), sometimes referred to as an enterprise information system.

3.2 Executive information systems

Definition

An *executive information system* (EIS) provides top level managers within an organisation with the underlying performance facts and figures about the organisation. Since the information is often very comprehensive and covers all aspects of the organisation or enterprise, an EIS may be known as an enterprise information system.

EIS is a type of DSS which is accessed via a personal computer on the manager's desk and provides easy access to key internal and external data. EISs have been made possible by the increasing cheapness, power and sophistication of microcomputer and network technology. An EIS is likely to have the following features.

(a) Provision of summary-level data, captured from the organisation's main systems.

(b) A facility which allows the executive to 'drill-down' from higher (summarised) levels of information to lower (more detailed) levels.

(c) Data manipulation facilities (for example comparison with budget or prior year data, trend analysis).

(d) Graphics, for user-friendly presentation of data.

(e) A template system. This will mean that the same type of data (eg sales figures) is presented in the same format, irrespective of changes in the volume of information required.

The basic design philosophy of executive information systems is as follows.

(a) They should be easy to use ('idiot-proof', not just user-friendly) as an EIS may be consulted during a meeting, for example.

(b) They should make data easy to access, so that it describes the organisation from the executive's point of view, not just in terms of its data flows.

(c) They should provide tools for analysis (including ratio analysis, forecasts, what-if analysis, trends).

(d) They should provide presentational aids so that information can be conveyed without bothering the executive with too many trivial choices of scale, colour and layout.

Executive information systems have also been more generically described as *executive support systems (ESS)*. Typical applications include the following.

(a) Provision of data on the performance of the organisation. This would include actual, budget and forecast figures for key areas such as sales, production and profitability.

(b) Provision of internal communications facilities. This would include storage and retrieval of personal correspondence, minutes of meetings and financial and other reports.

(c) 'Environmental scanning'. An organisation needs data on the political and economic environment. It will also collect information about competitors and markets.

An ESS, by supporting all the major responsibilities and activities of senior executives, can be used for strategic planning.

Some types of problem faced by managers are not difficult in themselves, except that they require considerable knowledge and experience of specialist subjects. This is where expert systems come in.

3.3   Expert systems

Definition

Expert systems are computer programs which allow users to benefit from expert knowledge and information, and also advice. An expert system therefore includes a reference file that holds a large amount of specialised data, for example on legal, engineering or medical information, or tax matters.

The user keys in certain facts and the program uses its information on file to produce a decision about something on which an expert's decision would normally be required.

(a) A user without a legal background can obtain guidance on the law without having to consult a solicitor for example, on property purchase matters, or for company law guidance.

(b) A user without much tax knowledge could consult an expert system for taxation for guidance on particular matters of tax.

(c) As a non-business example, doctors can use an expert medical system to key in symptoms and arrive at a diagnosis.

Applications of expert systems include the following.

(a) In some database systems they can speed up the process of retrieving data from a database file.

(b) Diagnostic systems can identify causes of problems, for example in production control systems, or in medical applications.

(c) They can provide advice to a decision maker. Expert systems can give facts, but they can also indicate to the user what a decision ought to be in a particular situation, and in this respect, expert systems can be a form of decision support system for managers in business.

(d) Tax advice.

(e) Credit scoring (deciding whether to lend money to people or let them buy on credit good lending risks have certain characteristics such as good security and good earning ability).

Figure 12.1 is a diagram of an expert system.

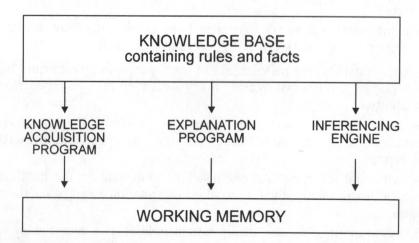

Figure 12.1 An expert system

The *knowledge base* contains facts (assertions like 'a rottweiler is a dog') and rules ('if you see a rottweiler, then run away'). Some facts contradict rules, of course, or even each other ('all birds can fly' is contradicted by the existence of ostriches and kiwis). The *knowledge acquisition program* is a program which enables the expert system to acquire new knowledge and rules. The *working memory* is where the expert system stores the various facts and rules used during the current enquiry and the current information given to it by the user. The *inferencing engine* is the software that carries out the reasoning. It needs to work out which rules apply, and allocate priorities. The *explanation program* presents the results of the enquiry to the user along with explanations of how results were arrived at.

Activity 3 **[15 minutes]**

Read the following extracts.

(a) 'Direct Line's speed of response and cost advantage derive from its policy of only accepting low risk business and the use of sophisticated computer systems which allow telesales staff to key in essential details and respond to applications for insurance instantly rather than having to spend days waiting for a decision from an underwriter.' (*Financial Times*, November 1992)

(b) 'Know-How has set out to formulate and make accessible a wealth of internal information. The map references to such information previously existed only in the heads of experienced solicitors. Now, documents are analysed before data entry by experts who predict how they are likely to be of use in the future and encapsulate carefully-coded keywords in the text.

Typically, the information on the system is used to shed light on new situations and interpret them in the light of previous experience.' (*Financial Times*, February 1993: article on Linklater & Paines, solicitors)

(c) 'Instant access to summary information, the potential for highlighting exceptions or variances with budget and the ease with which executives can find the reasons for a variance, in terms of an individual salesman's performance, have thrown up major implications for entire organisations'. (*Financial Times*, October 1992)

Which of these extracts describes a decision support system, which an executive information system and which an expert system?

3.4   MIS and decision making

A management information system cannot realistically provide all of the information needs of management, but computer technology means that tools for decision support can be provided in the form of a computer system.

(a) Executive information systems are used at strategic level for unstructured problems, or perhaps even to identify problems rather than solve them.

(b) Decision support systems are not often used by top executives, being less 'user friendly' and requiring more expertise. They are used by middle managers for routine modelling, but also to analyse unstructured problem situations for senior executives.

(c) Normal MIS provide structured information from transactions data for all three levels of management.

(d) An expert system could be used at all levels within an organisation depending on the area of expertise that it covers. For example, a credit control expert system could be used at the operational level while an investment appraisal expert system could help strategic management to make long term policy decisions.

Activity 4 [15 minutes]

A decision support system has been described as having the following characteristics.

Objective:	Assist management
Who makes the decision:	Manager
Orientation:	Decision-making
Applications:	Functional areas
Database:	Factual

(Beaumont & Sutherland: *Information Resources Management*)

Using the same five criteria, describe the features of an EIS and an expert system.

With so many benefits there have to be some drawbacks. We cannot leave the topic of computerised information systems without giving some thought to the problems that computers can cause. If you use one yourself you have probably experienced the frustration of a computer crash, or a power cut or a damaged floppy disk.

4 DANGERS OF COMPUTERISED MIS

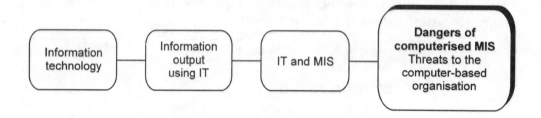

4.1 Threats to the computer-based organisation

Threats might arise from events which are accidental or deliberate. Data processing by computer creates extra problems because of its special characteristics, which are as follows.

(a) Large volumes of data are concentrated into files that are physically very small, much smaller than a corresponding manual filing system would be to hold the same data.

(b) The processing capabilities of a computer are extensive, and enormous quantities of data are processed without human intervention, and so without humans knowing what is going on. This places great reliance on the accuracy of programs and of data on file.

(c) It is easy to lose data on file. Equipment can go wrong and malfunction, data files can become corrupt and store meaningless data, bits of information can get lost when files are copied, and data files are always susceptible to loss through theft, flood or fire.

(d) Unauthorised people can gain access to data on files, and read classified data or tamper with the data on file (for example insert bogus data). It is even possible for 'hackers' to use their home computers to gain access to the files and programs of other systems. A well-publicised problem in the past has been the ease with which some schoolboys in the USA have gained access to the Pentagon's top secret military data processing systems using their home computers.

(e) Information on a computer file can be changed without leaving any physical trace of the change. In comparison, a change to a manual file would often involve leaving a trace eg crossing out data on a card file to insert new data.

It does not help matters that computers lack judgement, and errors in data processing by computer can go undetected when this would not be the case with manual data processing. For example, a payroll system might produce a salary cheque for an employee of £0.00 or for £1 million, and would not know that it had done something wrong. (This sort of problem can be overcome by building reasonableness checks into a program, however.)

A further problem is that programmers are experts, and with careful planning, a dishonest programmer can tamper with a program to his own benefit. A case has been recorded, for example, of a programmer who arranged for salary payments to be rounded down and for all halfpennies in salaries to be paid into a bogus bank account which the programmer opened and from which he took the money. Thousands of halfpenny payments mounted up over time into substantial sums of money.

Accidental error can cause problems too, for example, accidentally overwriting an important file. This is such an important source of potential error that controls to prevent this from happening should be built into any computer system.

Activity 5 [15 minutes]

The risks to data set out in the box below are relevant to manual as well as computerised systems. With computers however, the risks are greater, because data is held on magnetic files, and cannot be seen or read by the human eye. What risks do you think are particularly relevant to data storage on a magnetic medium such as a floppy disk or tape?

EXAMPLE: RISKS TO DATA

The risks to data are set out in the Institute of Chartered Accountant's *Information Technology Statement No 1*, as follows.

Human error

'This is the risk with the highest incidence. Examples of human errors are entering incorrect transactions, failing to correct errors, using wrong data files during processing, and failing to carry out instructions in respect of security procedures.'

Technical error

'This is probably the second most common risk after human error. Technical error can involve malfunctioning of hardware, system software, application software or communications software. System software includes the operating system, file management software and database software. Hardware includes not only computers and disk drives but communication equipment, normal and emergency power supplies and air conditioning units.'

Natural disasters

'Fire, flooding, explosion, impact and lightning are examples of natural disasters, the possible consequences of which should be foreseen.'

Deliberate actions

'The scope for fraud needs particularly careful consideration if data is held on magnetic media, because such data is not immediately legible and it may therefore be difficult to obtain evidence of improper data amendment. Also, there is a wide variety of different methods by which such fraud can be committed.'

Commercial espionage

'When considering the value of data to competitors the organisation should consider how a particular item of data might complement other data which a competitor has obtained from publicly available sources.'

Malicious damage

'There are many cases of disaffected employees destroying data or software. Sabotage also falls under this heading.'

Industrial action

'The more concentrated the processing and storage of data the more vulnerable an organisation can be to industrial action.'

In the last two chapters of this book we are going to discuss some of the techniques used in managing information. The next chapter looks at some statistical techniques for compiling and interpreting data. The final chapter describes ways of presenting data.

Chapter roundup

- Information technology is often defined as being the convergence of computer technology and communications technology.

- Computers have the advantages, compared with manual data processing, of speed, accuracy, the ability to process large volumes of data and the ability to perform complex operations. In the past the main commercial use of computers was to process large volumes of transactions data. Over time, computers have been used increasingly to provide management information.

- Modern technology has greatly expanded the techniques for displaying information, as well as for processing it.

- There are a number of identifiable types of information systems, including transaction processing systems, decision support systems, executive information systems and expert systems.

- The risks to data may be classified as human error, technical error, natural disaster, deliberate action, commercial espionage, malicious damage and industrial action.

Quick quiz

1 What are the advantages of the use of information technology in the development of information systems?

2 What are the particular benefits of PCs when used in an information system?

3 What should be covered in a review of the existing output of an information system?

4 Describe an EIS.

5 How are the various types of MIS used in decision making?

6 How might a computerised information system be threatened?

7 What does technical error involve?

8 What is a VDU?

9 What does an expert system do?

10 What sorts of checks need to be incorporated into a transaction processing system allow for a computer's lack of judgement?

Answers to quick quiz

1 The advantages of using information technology in the development of information systems are discussed in Section 1.2.

2 The benefits of using PCs (personal computers) in information systems are discussed in Section 1.3.

3 The review of the existing output of an information systems is discussed in Section 2.2.

4 EIS (executive information systems) are discussed in Section 3.2.

5 The ways that various types of MIS are used in decision making are discussed in Section 3.4.

6 The threats to computerised information systems are discussed in Section 4.1.

7 Technical error may involve the malfunction of hardware, systems software, applications software, or communications software.

8 A VDU is a visual display unit sometimes referred to as the computer screen or monitor.

9 An expert system is a computer program which allows users to benefit from expert knowledge, information and advice.

10 Since computers lack judgement, reasonableness checks should be incorporated into transaction processing systems.

Answers to activities

1 You may well have examples of your own, based on experience. Some suggestions are given below.

   (a) There may be a tendency to produce information for its own sake, rather than because it is required.

   (b) Users may not be able to cope with complex technology, resulting in reduced efficiency.

   (c) Development staff and users may not communicate well with each other, so that user requirements are not properly met.

   (d) Wider access to data increases the risk of threats to security, particularly where data is transmitted between sites.

2 (a) This is best looked up on the *VDU screen* because this will probably be the quickest way of finding the information and the information will be most up-to-date.

   (b) A *video* would be a good way of conveying the information a way that has maximum impact. Companies such as Melrose produce excellent training videos of this kind.

   (c) An *e-mail* message on the bulletin board would be one way. Actually, however, this is probably such hot news that word of mouth will be just as quick. A formal message from senior management would help to dispel any worries people may have and prevent rumours.

   (d) A *print-out* on paper is the best choice: it will be easy for the auditors to consult and they will not be taking up your company's computer time. (Disk format might be better if the auditors have a compatible system and their own lap top computers.)

   (e) *Desktop publishing* will allow you to produce an attractive leaflet incorporating text and pictures.

3 Decision Support System: (b)

   Executive Information System: (c)

   Expert system: (a).

4 The objective of an EIS (executive information system) is to provide easy access to comprehensive internal and external information. It is used by top-level management and orientated towards presenting information in as much detail as appropriate. Its application is towards the planning and monitoring of the organisations' progress within its environment. The database in an EIS is factual.

   The objective of an expert system is to provide the benefit of specialist knowledge and experience. The actual area of knowledge will determine what level it is used within an organisation. It is orientated towards decision making and each expert system will have a fairly narrow specific area of application such as investment appraisal or credit control. The database in an expert system is procedural as well as factual.

5 The dangers associated with information storage on a magnetic medium include the following.

   (a) *Physical security.* Tapes or disks can be stolen or mislaid or damaged or destroyed by fire, flood or vandalism.

(b) *Environmental security.* Tapes and disks are susceptible to magnetic fields, dust and extremes of temperature and humidity. Although in modern mini- and microcomputer systems the problems of environment have been reduced, they are still quite important.

(c) *Loss of confidentiality.* Information stored in magnetic files may be accessed by unauthorised persons. This is a particular problem in larger systems with remote terminals, or in time sharing/computer bureau applications.

(d) *Processing the wrong file.* Since data is in magnetic form, and not visible, the wrong file could be read, or a file overwritten when its data is still needed.

(e) *Hardware or program corruption.* Hardware or software faults may damage or destroy the information on the files, as can updating a file with incomplete or inaccurate data.

Assignment 12 [1½ hours]

Tasks

1 Describe the purposes and applications of the following types of information system.

(a) Transaction processing systems.

(b) Decision support systems.

(c) Expert systems.

(d) Executive information systems.

2 A company executive for a large multi-national organisation travels widely between offices in various countries. The executive relies heavily upon the information that is processed and stored on a portable computer system. Describe the risks to such a system and outline appropriate procedures for minimising those risks.

Chapter 13

TECHNIQUES FOR COMPILING DATA

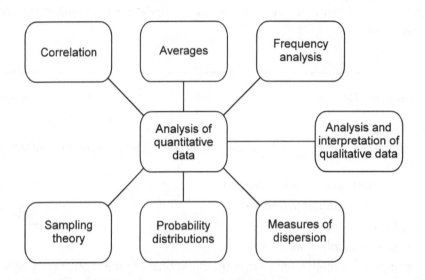

Introduction

We won't beat about the bush: this is a chapter about statistics, a subject that many people hate! Please don't worry. There is not room within a single chapter for things to get very complicated. If you need to become proficient at statistical analysis you will have to work through a whole book on the subject.

The aim of this chapter is simply to introduce the ideas of statistical analysis and interpretation of data. This puts you in a position of strength the next time an accountant in your organisation tries to persuade you that his or her figures are correct.

Some topics, such as averages and percentages and the idea of probabilities, will be pretty familiar from every day usage in any case. Others, such as sampling distributions, will not. You will need to work slowly and concentrate hard at certain points, so make sure you are fresh and have plenty of time for this chapter.

Your objectives

After completing this chapter you should:

(a) understand that there are several different types of average;

(b) know how the most typical values in a large number of measurements can be expressed;

(c) be aware of ways in which the variation of values in a number of measurements can be analysed;

(d) understand that the mean, the standard deviation and the normal distribution can be used to draw valid conclusions from samples of data;

(e) know about ways of assessing how closely variables are related to each other.

1   ANALYSIS OF QUANTITIVE DATA

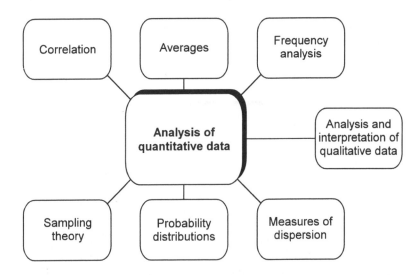

Analysing raw data - the words and sentences, or the metric or non-metric measurements taken in the collection phase - requires three processes:

(a) *data reduction:* summarising data in order to identify the key features;

(b) *data presentation:* illustrating the data's key features in a way that will be understood by the target audience; and

(c) *drawing conclusions.*

In this chapter we will concentrate on (a) and (c). We shall look at data presentation in the next chapter.

Definitions

Quantitative data are data that can be measured. For example, the temperature on each day of August (which can be measured in degrees (fahrenheit or celsius) or the time it takes you to travel to work each day (which can be measured in hours and minutes) are quantitative data.

Contrast this with *qualitative data*, which cannot easily be measured but reflects some quality of what is being observed. Whether somebody is male or female is qualitative data: there is no measure of *how* male or *how* female somebody is.

Data analysis involves analysing masses of data so as to summarise its essential features and relationships in order that, by generalising, patterns of behaviour, particular outcomes or future results can be determined.

A useful way of think about data analysis is to separate it into problems where:

(a) we have more than one value for only one set of variables or unit of analysis (*univariate analysis*);

(b) we have more than one value for two sets of variables/units of analysis (*bivariate analysis*); and

(c) we have more than one value for more than two sets of variables/units of analysis (*multivariate analysis*).

This is not nearly as scary as it sounds.

In *univariate* analysis we concentrate on reducing techniques the raw data to meaningful figures and looking at what is typical. In *bivariate* analysis we concentrate on how the values of two variables are related, and in *multivariate* analysis we attempt to see how three or more variables interact together: seeing how things typically respond to one another.

If a group of people are aged 24, 19, 27 and 19 what age is representative of the group or, in other words, what is their average age? In fact we will examine 3 different ways of selecting a representative or average.

2 AVERAGES

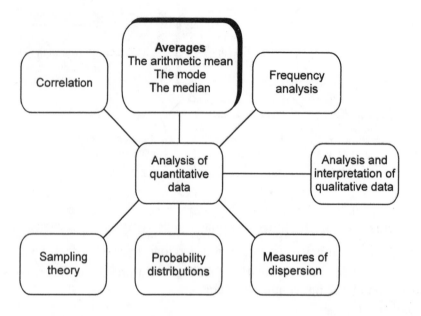

2.1 The arithmetic mean

This is the best known type of average. It is calculated by the formula

$$\text{Arithmetic mean} = \frac{\text{Sum of values of items}}{\text{Number of items}}$$

For example, if three bakers sell bread, the *mean* price of a loaf of bread is the 3 individual prices added together and divided by three.

Example: the arithmetic mean

The demand for a product on each of 20 days was as follows (in units).

3 12 7 17 3 14 9 6 11 10 1 4 19 7 15 6 9 12 12 8

The arithmetic mean of daily demand is

$$\frac{\text{Sum of demand}}{\text{Number of days}} = \frac{185}{20} = 9.25 \text{ units}$$

The advantages and disadvantages of the arithmetic mean

The advantages of the arithmetic mean are as follows.

(a) It is widely understood.

(b) The value of every item is included in the computation of the mean.

(c) It is supported by mathematical theory and is suited to further statistical analysis.

The disadvantages of the arithmetic mean are as follows.

(a) Its value may not correspond to any actual value. For example, the 'average' family might have 2.3 children, but no family has exactly 2.3 children.

(b) An arithmetic mean might be distorted by extremely high or low values. For example, the mean of 3, 4, 4 and 6 is 4.25, but the mean of 3, 4, 4, 6 and 15 is 6.4. The high value, 15, distorts the average and in some circumstances the mean would be a misleading and inappropriate figure.

Activity 1 [15 minutes]

What is the arithmetic mean of the following figures?

12   46   1   77   25

2.2 The mode

The mode is an average which means 'the most frequently occurring value'.

Example: the mode

The daily demand for a product in a 10 day period is as follows.

Demand Units	Number of days
6	3
7	6
8	1
	10

The mode is 7 units, because it is the value which occurs most frequently.

The advantages and disadvantages of the mode

The mode will be a more appropriate average to use than the mean in situations where it is useful to know the most common value. For example, when we want to know what sort of product is most in demand with customers the mode is easy to find, it is uninfluenced by a few extreme values and it can be used for data which are not even numerical (unlike the mean and median). The main disadvantage of the mode is that it ignores dispersion around the modal value, and unlike the mean, does not take every value into account. There can also be two or more modes within a set of data and it is unsuitable for further statistical analysis.

2.3 The median

The third type of average is the median. The median is the middle value of a set of values when the values have been placed in numerical order.

Example 1: the median

What is the median of the following nine values?

8   6   9   12   15   6   3   20   11

We must firstly put the values in order:

3   6   6   8   9   11   12   15   20

Now we select the middle value, which in this case is the fifth value, so the median is 9.

Example 2: the median

What is the median of the following 10 values?

8   6   7   2   1   11   3   2   6   2

We must firstly put the values in order:

1   2   2   2   3   6   6   7   8   11

Now we select the middle value but in this case we have an even number of values so there is no value in the set which is on its own in the middle. We need to select halfway between the fifth and sixth values, so half way between 3 and 6. In this case the answer is 4½ which we could have calculated as (3 +6)/2 = 9/2 = 4½.

The advantages and disadvantages of the median

The median is only of interest where there is a range of values and the middle item is of some significance. Perhaps the most suitable application of the median is in comparing changes in a 'middle of the road' value over time where most values inevitably fall close to the middle value. An example might be the age at which women marry: the median would show a gradual rise during the twentieth century. The median (like the mode) is unaffected by extremely high or low values. On the other hand, it fails to reflect the full range of values, and is unsuitable for further statistical analysis.

Activity 2   [15 minutes]

A group of hourly paid workers are paid at the following hourly rates:

£2.50   £2.75   £2.75   £2.75   £3.00   £3.40   £3.75   £3.90   £5.75   £9.50

The workers claim their average wage is £2.75 but the management claim it is actually just over £4. Which type of averages are they talking about and which type of average do you think is the best or fairest representative of the workers' hourly rates?

For discussion

In the previous activity you may have realised that there are often different ways to process or interpret data to produce statistics. Another example is when an advertiser states 'In tests to compare product X with product Y, 8 out of 10 people who expressed a preference said that they preferred product X'. This seems at first glance to mean 80% preferred product X but how many people were asked? If 100 people were asked then only 8% preferred product X, 2% preferred product Y and 90% did not care which product they had and expressed no preference.

You are probably starting to understand why many people mistrust statistics and market research results. In the vast majority of cases, the statistics that are presented are accurate and true but sometimes the way they are presented emphasises certain aspects and omits to show other aspects. Try to think of ways that unscrupulous people could use this to their own advantage.

Averages are not the only way of analysing data to find out what is most typical. You will often hear an analysis such as 70% said Yes, 25% said No and 5% were Don't Knows. Data is expressed in this way when a large number of people have been asked.

3 FREQUENCY ANALYSIS

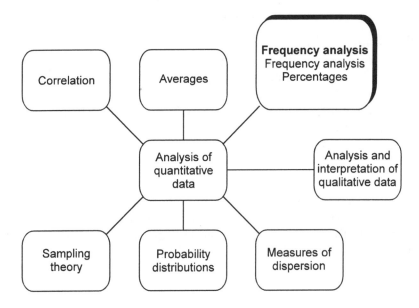

3.1 Frequency analysis

If a large number of measurements of a particular variable is taken (for example the number of items purchased per customer per week) some values may occur more than once. A frequency distribution (or frequency table) is obtained by recording the number of times each value occurs.

Definition

A *variable* is something that can have different values. For example the number of customers that come into your shop per hour is a variable: the number of customers changes, while the things it is measured against (your shop, per hour) do not.

Example: a frequency distribution

The quantity of items purchased by 20 customers during one week was as follows.

65	69	70	71	70	68	69	67	70	68
72	71	69	74	70	73	71	67	69	70

If the number of occurrences is placed against each purchase quantity, a frequency 'distribution' is produced.

Items purchased	Number of customers (frequency)
65	1
66	0
67	2
68	2
69	4
70	5
71	3
72	1
73	0
74	1
	20

The number of customers corresponding to a particular volume of purchases is called a frequency. When the data are arranged in this way it is immediately obvious that 69 and 70 units are the most common volumes of purchases per customer per week.

Activity 3   [10 minutes]

There is a deliberate error in the frequency distribution shown above. What is it?

Make sure you have noted the term distribution as illustrated above. It is important over the next few pages.

3.2   Percentages

Percentages are used to indicate the *relative* size or proportion of items, rather than their absolute size. For example, if one car salesman sells ten Fords, six Vauxhalls and four Renaults, the *absolute* values of car sales and the *percentage* of the total sales of each type would be as follows.

	Fords	Vauxhalls	Renaults	Total
Absolute numbers	10	6	4	20
Percentages	50%	30%	20%	100%

The idea of percentages is that the whole of something can be thought of as 100%. The whole of a cake, for example, is 100%. If you share it out equally with a friend, you will get half each, or 100%/2 = 50% each.

To turn a percentage into a fraction or decimal you divide by 100. To turn a fraction or decimal back into a percentage you multiply by 100%. Consider the following.

(a) $0.16 = 0.16 \times 100\% = 16\%$

(b) $4/5 = (4/5) \times 100\% = (400/5)\% = 80\%$

(c) $40\% = 40/100 = 2/5 = 0.4$

There are three main types of situations involving percentages.

(a) You may want to calculate a percentage of a figure, having been given the percentage.

Question: What is 40% of £64?

Answer: 40% of £64 = 0.4 × £64 = £25.60.

(b) You may want to state what percentage one figure is of another, so that you have to work out the percentage yourself.

Question: What is £16 as a percentage of £64?

Answer: £16 as a percentage of £64 = (16/64) × 100% = 25%

In other words, put the £16 as a fraction of the £64, and then multiply by 100%.

(c) You may have to fill in the missing number.

Question: If the price with a 20% discount is £5, what is the full price?

Answer: £5 must be 80%, so the full price is (£5 ÷ 80) × 100 = £6.25.

Proportions

A proportion means writing a percentage as a proportion of 1 (that is, as a decimal).

100% can be thought of as the whole, or 1. 50% is half of that, or 0.5. Consider the following.

Question: There are 14 women in an audience of 70. What proportion of the audience are men?

Answer: Number of men   =   70 − 14 = 56

              Proportion of men   =   56/70 = 0.8

(a) 56/70 is the *fraction* of the audience made up by men.

(b) 0.8 is the *proportion* of the audience made up by men.

(c) 80% is the *percentage* of the audience made up by men.

Note that 56/70 is not very meaningful to most people. It can be simplified to four-fifths. A scientific calculator or a spreadsheet will do this for you.

One of the problems with averages that we identified above was that they do not give a very clear idea of the variation or spread of values they represent. This is called 'dispersion' and there are several ways of taking account of it.

4   MEASURES OF DISPERSION

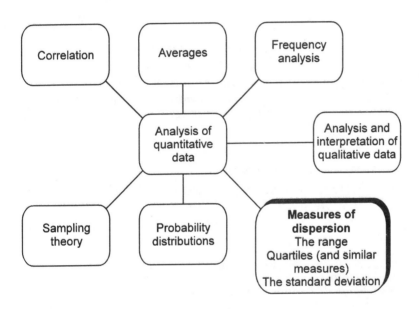

4.1   The range

The range of a set of values is the difference between the highest and the lowest values in the set. If a group of people are aged 28, 25, 32, 21 and 29 then the range of their ages is (32 − 21) = 11. The main properties of the range as a measure of the spread of a set of values are as follows.

(a) It is easy to find and to understand.

(b) It is easily affected by one or two extreme values.

(c) It gives no indication of spread between the extremes.

(d) It is not suitable for further statistical analysis.

4.2   Quartiles (and similar measures)

Quartiles are one means of identifying the range within which proportions of the values being analysed occur. The lower quartile is the value below which 25% of the values fall and the upper quartile is the value above which 25% of the values fall. It follows that 50% of the total number of values fall between the lower and the upper quartiles. The quartiles and the median also divide the values into four groups of equal size, hence the term quartiles.

In a similar way, the values could be divided into ten equal groups, and the value of each dividing point is referred to, not as a quartile, but as a *decile*. When a series of values is divided into 100 parts, the value of each dividing point is referred to as a *percentile*. For example, in a series of 200 values, the percentiles would be the second, fourth, sixth, eighth and so on, up to the 198th item, in rising order of values.

Quartiles, deciles and percentiles, and any other similar dividing points for analysis are referred to collectively as *quantiles*. The purpose of quantiles is to analyse the dispersion of data values: how widely the values are dispersed about the mean.

For example, a marketing researcher might find that the mean number of bottles of cola consumed per household per month was three. This *could* mean that every household consumes between two and four bottles, but equally it could mean that a sizeable number consume no bottles and a sizeable number consume ten or more bottles. Not every household, therefore, is an equally good target for marketing activities.

The most important measure of spread in statistics is the standard deviation. It is denoted by s or σ. The symbol s is used for the standard deviation of a sample of values (cola-consuming households in Swindon, say), and σ is used for the standard deviation of a population of values (all cola-consuming households).

4.3 The standard deviation

The standard deviation is used in conjunction with the arithmetic mean (the simple average that we described right at the beginning of this chapter). The standard deviation provides a measure of how widely spread the values used to calculate the mean are around that central point.

The standard deviation's main properties are as follows.

(a) It is based on *all* the values measured and so is more comprehensive than dispersion measures based on quantiles, such as the quartile deviation.

(b) It is suitable for further statistical analysis.

(c) It is more difficult to understand and calculate than some other measures of dispersion.

The importance of the standard deviation lies in its suitability for further statistical analysis, as we shall see in the following sections.

We use words like 'probably' or 'unlikely' all the time without being precise about what we mean. If you think about it though, probability can be measured. If you have always done x in the past except on one or two occasions you will 'probably' do x again next time. You could, of course, count up the number of occasions and work out how probable it is you will do it in numerical terms.

5 PROBABILITY DISTRIBUTIONS

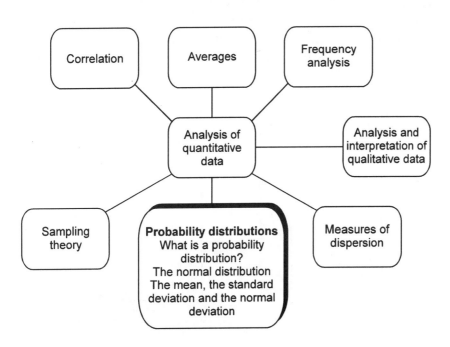

5.1 What is a probability distribution?

We have seen that a frequency distribution gives an analysis of the number of times each particular value occurs in a set of items. A probability or sampling distribution simply replaces actual numbers (frequencies) with proportions of the total. For example, in a survey, the ratings out of 10 given to a product by customers might be as follows.

Ratings out of 10	Number of customers (frequency distribution)	Proportion or probability (probability distribution)
0	0	0.00
1	0	0.00
2	1	0.02
3	2	0.04
4	4	0.08
5	10	0.20
6	15	0.30
7	10	0.20
8	6	0.12
9	2	0.04
10	0	0.00
	50	1.00

A graph of the probability distribution would be the same as the graph of the frequency distribution, but with the vertical axis marked in proportions rather than in numbers. In our example, this would be as follows (Figure 13.1).

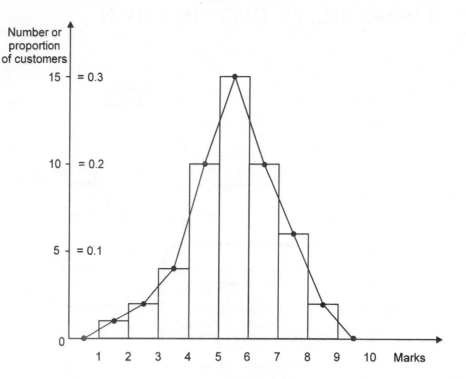

Figure 13.1 Frequency and probability distribution

The area in the bars in the frequency distribution represents the total number of customers whose views have been recorded, 50 people. The area under the curve in a probability distribution is 100%, or 1 (the total of all the probabilities).

There are a number of different types of probability distribution but we shall confine our attention to just one: the so-called 'normal' distribution.

5.2 The normal distribution

Definitions

A *continuous variable* is one that may be restricted by upper and lower limits but can take any value in between, although we may not be able to measure accurately enough to distinguish between values that are very close. For example, peoples' ages could be stated very accurately down to fractions of a second. A child may walk through the gates of senior school for the first time when they are 315,361,465.4 seconds old. In this example we are much more likely to consider treating it as a *discrete variable* by simply saying that the child started senior school at 11 years old.

The normal distribution is an important probability distribution which is often applied to 'continuous variables': variables that do not have to be a whole number.

Examples of continuous variables include the following.

(a) The heights of people. The height of a person need not be an exact number of centimetres, but can be anything within a range of possible figures.

(b) The temperature of a room. It need not be an exact number of degrees, but can fall anywhere within a range of possible values.

The normal distribution can also apply to 'discrete variables' which can take many possible values. For example, the volume of sales, in units, of a product might be any whole number in the range 100 to 5,000 units. There are so many possibilities within this range that the variable is, for all practical purposes, continuous.

The normal distribution can be drawn as a graph, and it would be a bell-shaped curve (Figure 13.2)

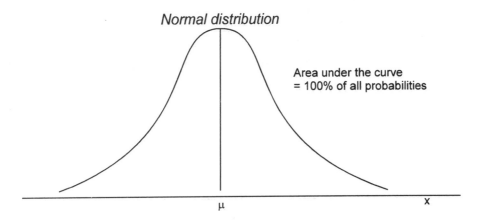

Figure 13.2 Normal distribution

The normal curve is symmetrical. μ is the mean, or average of the distribution. The left hand side of the area under the curve to the left of μ is the mirror image of the right hand side. Because it is a probability distribution, the area under the curve totals exactly 1, or 100%.

The normal distribution is important because in the practical application of statistics, it has been found that many probability distributions are close enough to a normal distribution to be treated as one without any significant loss of accuracy.

Now we shall begin to see how the statistical measures that we have identified as being particularly important come together.

5.3 The mean, the standard deviation and the normal distribution

For any normal distribution, the dispersion around the mean of the frequency of occurrences can be measured exactly in terms of the standard deviation.

The entire frequency curve represents all the possible outcomes and their frequencies of occurrence and the normal curve is symmetrical; therefore 50% of occurrences have a value greater than the mean value, and 50% of occurrences have a value less than the mean value.

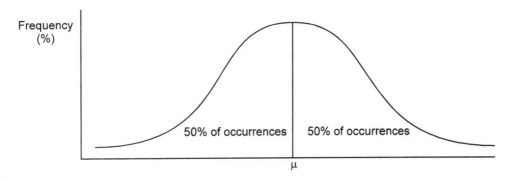

Figure 13.3 Frequency curve

Further conclusions can be drawn as follows.

(a) About 68% of frequencies have a value within *one* standard deviation either side of the mean.

Thus if a normal distribution has a mean of 80 and a standard deviation of 3, 68% of the total frequencies would occur within the range ± one standard deviation from the mean, that is, within the range 77 to 83.

Since the curve is symmetrical, 34% of the values must fall in the range 77 to 80 and 34% in the range 80 to 83.

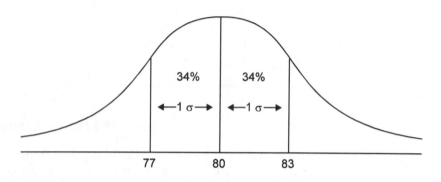

Figure 13.4 Frequency distribution where mean = 80 and standard deviation = 3

(b) 95% of the frequencies in a normal distribution occur in the range ± 1.96 standard deviations from the mean.

In our example, when the mean is 80, and the standard deviation is 3, 95% of the frequencies in the distribution would occur in the range:

$$80 \pm (1.96 \times 3)$$
$$= \quad 80 \pm 5.88 \quad \text{(the range 74.12 to 85.88)}$$

47½% would be in the range 74.12 to 80 and 47½% would be in the range 80 to 85.88.

(c) 99% of the frequencies occur in the range ± 2.58 standard deviations from the mean.

In our example, 99% of frequencies in a normal distribution with $\mu = 80$ and $\sigma = 3$ would lie in the range

$$80 \pm 2.58 \times 3$$
$$= \quad 80 \pm 7.74$$
$$= \quad 72.26 \text{ to } 87.74$$

These properties of the normal distribution are developed in the next section.

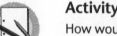

Activity 4   [15 minutes]

How would a researcher arrive at the following conclusion?

'Analysis of the data shows that 95% of people are willing to spend between £7 and £9 on a bottle of wine for a special occasion.'

6 SAMPLING THEORY

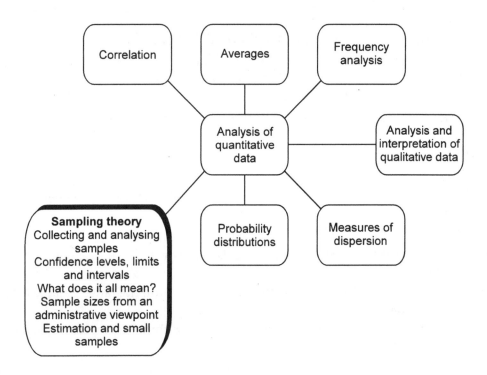

6.1 Collecting and analysing samples

Definitions

In statistical terms, the *population* is used to refer to the set of all the items we are interested in. Sometimes it is very difficult or impossible to gain data about every item in the population so we get data from just some of the items, in other words we use a *sample* of the population.

Descriptive statistics are used to summarise the actual data that we have collected. If we measure the height of everyone in a group and calculate the mean and standard deviation of these heights then we are using descriptive statistics. If we have statistics from a sample of the population we cannot say with certainty those statistics are true for the whole population. However, some sophisticated statistical techniques have been developed for making inferences or estimates about the population based on data from a sample of the population. These techniques are known as *inferential statistics* and usually include a *confidence level* which gives an indication of how certain we are about the accuracy of the results.

In the first part of this chapter we looked at distributions occurring as a result of considering a 'population' of items. We can also construct probability distributions, known as sampling distributions, for *samples* rather than whole populations and, when we start taking fairly large random samples (over 30) from a population and measuring the *mean* of those samples, we find an uncanny relationship with the normal distribution.

A distribution of the means of these samples has the following important properties.

(a) It is very close to being normally distributed. The larger the samples the more closely will the sampling distribution approximate to a normal distribution.

(b) The mean of the sampling distribution is the same as the population mean, μ.

(c) The sampling distribution has a standard deviation which is called the *standard error of the mean*.

6.2 Confidence levels, limits and intervals

From our knowledge of the properties of a normal distribution, together with the rule that sample means are normally distributed around the true population mean, with a standard deviation equal to the standard error, we can predict the following.

(a) 68% of all sample means will be within one standard error of the population mean.

(b) 95% of all sample means will be within 1.96 standard errors of the population mean.

(c) 99% of all sample means will be within 2.58 standard errors of the population mean.

Let us look at it another way.

(a) With 68% probability, the population mean lies within the range: sample mean ± one standard error.

(b) With 95% probability, the population mean lies within the range: sample mean ± 1.96 standard errors.

(c) With 99% probability, the population mean lies within the range: sample mean ± 2.58 standard errors.

These degrees of certainty (such as 95%) are known as *confidence levels*, and the ends of the ranges (such as sample mean + 2.58 standard errors) around the sample mean are called *confidence limits*. The ranges (such as sample mean ± one standard error) are called *confidence intervals*.

6.3 What does it all mean?

What it means is that, if you take a reasonably large sample of representative items and find out something about them, you can be confident up to a certain level that something is true of the whole population of items.

Suppose, for example, you measured the height of 100 mature labradors and found that the average was, say, 30cm with a standard deviation of 2cm. You could then be 99% certain that the average height of all mature labradors was in the range of $30 \pm (2.58 \times 2) = 24.84$cm to 35.16cm. (This gives you a basis for designing a range of labrador leisure-wear, or whatever!)

In practice you will probably be able to leave the figurework to marketing research specialists or company statisticians. The important thing is that you understand enough of the jargon to appreciate the scientific basis of such an analysis rather than be blinded by it.

For discussion

The media are very keen to publicise opinion poll statistics. Try to find some examples and discuss how the data may have been collected and how the statistics quoted could have been arrived at.

The practical implication in terms of managing information is that a vast amount of time, effort and money can be saved if you only have to consider a sample rather than every single item in a population.

6.4   Sample sizes from an administrative viewpoint

Although it is possible to calculate an ideal sample size from a statistical point of view, administrative and practical factors have to be taken into account. These factors are summarised below.

(a) The amount of money and time available.

(b) The aims of the survey.

(c) The degree of precision required.

(d) The number of sub-samples required.

(e) The larger the sample size, the more precise will be the information given about the population, but above a certain size, little extra information is given by increasing the size. A sample therefore only need be large enough to be reasonably representative of the population.

6.5   Estimation and small samples

Be aware that although we can calculate the standard error using the standard deviation of the sample, this is only true for very large samples. Smaller samples may not be as closely representative of the population as a whole.

Activity 5   **[20 minutes]**

Can you think of five problems that might be experienced when trying to collect sample data?

It will be well worth pausing at this point and going back over points you do not understand.

In the next section we move on from what is typical and start to discuss the measurement of how variables are related to each other.

7   CORRELATION

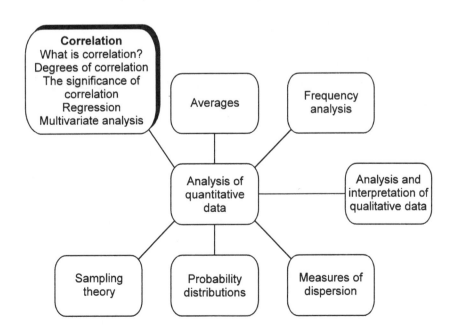

7.1 What is correlation?

When the value of one variable is related to the value of another, the variables are said to be correlated. Correlation therefore means an inter-relationship or correspondence.

If the variables are correlated then a change in the value of one of the variables corresponds to a change in the value of the other variable in a regular manner.

Examples of variables which might be correlated are as follows.

(a) A person's height and weight.

(b) The distance of a journey and the time it takes to make it.

One way of showing the correlation between two related variables is on a scattergraph or scatter diagram, plotting a number of pairs of data on the graph and using judgement to draw what seems to be a straight *line of best fit* through the data.

For example, a scattergraph showing monthly selling costs against the volume of sales for a 12 month period might be as follows (Figure 13.5).

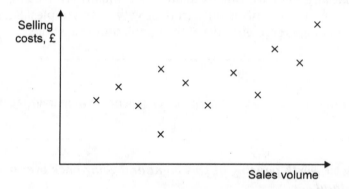

Figure 13.5 Scattergraph: selling costs and sales volume

This scattergraph suggests that there is some correlation between selling costs and sales volume, so that as sales volume rises, selling costs tend to rise as well.

7.2 Degrees of correlation

The relationship between two variables can be described as one of the following.

(a) Perfectly correlated (Figure 13.6)

(b) Partly correlated (Figure 13.7)

(c) Uncorrelated (Figure 13.8)

These differing degrees of correlation can be illustrated by scattergraphs.

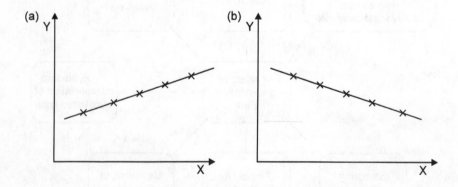

Figure 13.6 Perfect correlation

All the pairs of values lie on a straight line. An exact straight line or linear relationship exists between the two variables.

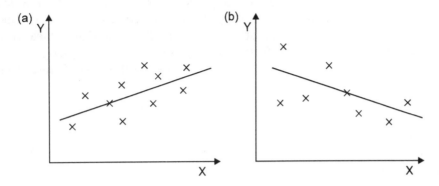

Figure 13.7 Partial correlation

In (a), although there is no perfect straight line relationship, low values of x tend to be associated with low values of y, and high values of x with high values of y.

In (b) again, there is no perfect straight line relationship, but low values of x tend to be associated with high values of y and vice versa.

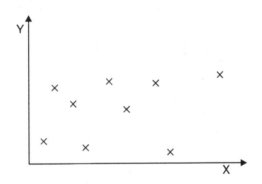

Figure 13.8 No correlation

The values of the two variables are not correlated with each other.

Positive and negative correlation

Correlation, whether perfect or partial, can be positive or negative.

Positive correlation means that low values of one variable are associated with low values of the other, and high values of one variable are associated with high values of the other - as illustrated in Figure 13.6(a) and Figure 13.7(a).

Negative correlation means that low values of one variable are associated with high values of the other, and high values of one variable with low values of the other - as illustrated in Figure 13.6(b) and Figure 13.7(b).

Activity 6   [15 minutes]

See if you can think of any potential examples of variables that are likely to be positively correlated and negatively correlated.

The correlation coefficient

The degree of correlation between two variables can be measured, and we can decide, using actual results in the form of pairs of data, whether two variables are perfectly or partially correlated and, if they are partially correlated, whether there is a high or low degree of partial correlation. The correlation coefficient measures the degree of correlation. It can range from -1 to $+1$, where -1 indicates perfect negative correlation, $+1$ indicates perfect positive correlation and values near 0 mean there is no correlation.

7.3   The significance of correlation

If two variables are well correlated, either positively or negatively, this may be due to pure chance or there may be a reason for it. The larger the number of pairs of data collected, the less likely it is that the correlation is due to chance, though that possibility should never be ignored entirely.

If there is a reason, it may not be causal. For example, monthly net income is well correlated with monthly credit to a person's bank account, for the logical (rather than causal) reason that for most people the one equals the other.

Even if there is a causal explanation for a correlation, it does not follow that variations in the value of one variable *cause* variations in the value of the other. For example, sales of ice cream and of sunglasses are well correlated, not because of a direct causal link but because the weather influences both variables.

Having said this, it is of course possible that where two variables are correlated, there is a direct causal link to be found.

The correlation coefficient measures the degree of correlation between two variables, but it does not tell us how to predict values for one variable (y) given values for the other variable (x).

7.4   Regression

To make use of correlation for forecasting purposes (for example in budgeting), we need to find a line which is a good fit for the points on a scattergraph, and then use that line to find the value of y corresponding to each given value of x.

There are a number of techniques for estimating a line of best fit. We will look at the scattergraph method only (other methods such as linear regression analysis are beyond the scope of this book).

The scattergraph method

The scattergraph method is to plot pairs of data for two related variables on a graph, producing a scattergraph, and then to use judgement to draw what seems to be a line of best fit through the data.

For example, suppose we have the following pairs of data about sales revenue and advertising expenditure.

Period	Advertising expenditure £	Sales revenue £
1	17,000	180,000
2	33,000	270,000
3	34,000	320,000
4	42,000	350,000
5	19,000	240,000
6	41,000	300,000
7	26,000	320,000
8	27,000	230,000

These pairs of data would be plotted on a scattergraph. It is conventional to use the x-axis (the horizontal axis across the graph) for the *independent* variable and the y-axis (the vertical axis up the graph) for the *dependent* variable. In this example, we would think that a change in sales revenue would *depend* on a change in advertising expenditure and therefore choose the sales value as the dependent variable. A line of best fit could be estimated and drawn in as shown in Figure 13.9.

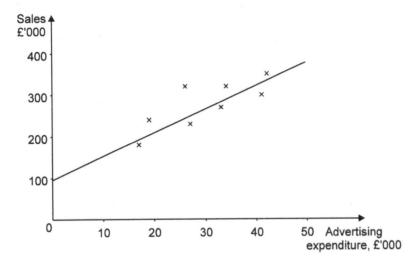

Figure 13.9 Straight line of best fit

You may well be thinking that it is not really valid to assert that sales revenue depends only on advertising expenditure: in practice things like the price, competitors' prices, word of mouth, the quality of the product and so on will all have an influence. How can these things be taken into account?

7.5 Multivariate analysis

In certain circumstances the simple linear model is not a good enough predictor. One possible course of action is to investigate the possibility that movements in the dependent variable are caused by *several* independent factors and not just one as in the basic model. For example, changes in demand for a product may depend on the following.

(a) Price of the product.

(b) Price of substitute products.

(c) Income levels.

(d) Consumer tastes.

If, after investigation, it is decided that there *is* a linear relationship between the dependent variable and a number of independent variables, then a linear multiple regression model can be used for prediction purposes.

Multiple regression analysis aims to improve predictions of the value of y by recognising that several different explaining factors might be involved when the correlation between the dependent variable and any single independent variable is not high.

The disadvantage of multiple regression analysis is its relative complexity. A computer program would be needed to derive estimates of the y function. But the use of a computer program is to be encouraged since, provided past estimates are a reliable guide to estimating the future, multiple regression analysis is likely to produce more accurate estimates than simple linear regression analysis, however it is performed.

Finally in this chapter we shall add a few words about the process of compiling and interpreting qualitative data. As we mentioned when we first considered qualitative information, there are some ways in which its analysis can be made more scientific.

8 ANALYSIS AND INTERPRETATION OF QUALITATIVE DATA

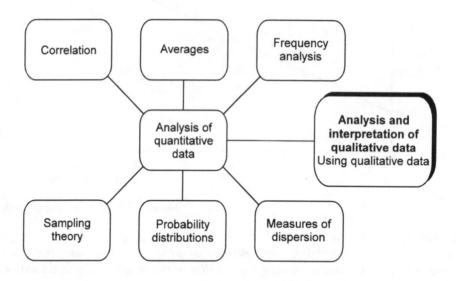

8.1 Using qualitative data

Collecting qualitative data means the recording of words, phrases, sentences and narrative which explains or describes people's thoughts, feelings and intentions. The key task in analysis is to summarise what people *said*. It is then possible to classify responses into categories, analyse them to some extent using statistics, and then analyse the content.

Summarising the wealth of data gathered may take some time. It involves scanning over the questionnaires or discussion transcripts and picking out:

(a) key ideas, on the grounds of novelty, excitement or conviction;

(b) key words and phrases, which seem to sum up the attitudes of the respondents.

It will then be possible to reduce the data to a logical sequence of key points.

Alternatively, it may be possible to identify categories into which responses fall, and classify all responses into these categories. While this is a more systematic method, it may not give due weight to those results which were perceived to be important at the time of the research.

If it is possible to categorise responses then the frequencies of each can be calculated and some degree of statistical method is possible. Thus, a response with which 'nearly all' the respondents agreed has a much higher frequency than one with which very few concurred. This method is particularly useful where differences in the 'demographics' of the groups are highlighted, such as language and humour variations between old and young.

Key words or phrases used in the research should be quoted in a report, but they must be regarded as illustrative rather than representative.

While qualitative data can generate hypotheses, researchers cannot test them easily. The conclusions which can be drawn are those to do with observing relationships, sequences and patterns, but how far these are causal would have to be tested by quantitative techniques.

Activity 7 [15 minutes]

Many of the statistical techniques that we have discussed in this chapter are mentioned in the extracts shown overleaf (from the *Daily Telegraph* in August 1995). Read through the articles and try to identify the techniques that have been used.

'THE MOST detailed survey ever published on the lives of British women appears today, presenting a broad-brush study of how they are managing their lives in a fast-changing society - from teenagers to pensioners.

Women are still under-represented at the top in business, it concedes, and they earn less than men.

But they are increasingly setting marriage aside in their younger years to play a more active role in commerce and the professions. Socially, they are going to pubs, night classes and sports clubs as never before. They exhibit greater self-reliance and are broader-minded (30,000 read *Penthouse*).

Fifty-five per cent of women work full-time; they are making inroads into the professions and are affected less by long-term unemployment than are men.

More women [are] on the Pill and delaying families until they are in their 30s and financially settled. Lone mothers may be a symbol of the times, it says, but more than three-quarters have husbands or partners.

Women are better off (three-quarters carry credit cards) and better housed (17 per cent are buying their own homes, twice the figure for a decade ago).

A wife who quotes the old epithet that a woman's work is never done, might find her attention drawn to page 54 which reveals that British females watch television for an average of 28 hours a week.

A husband's argument about politics might produce a reference to page 51 which shows that less than seven per cent of women show much interest in what is going on at Westminster. The document can also provide ready support for headaches. Stress is increasingly a female complaint, it says.'

'THOUGH THE roles and lifestyles of women may be changing, it is not always for the better.

The report says that more than half of women feel unsafe when walking home at night and one in five is worried about being at home alone at night - compared with only four per cent of men.

Burglary, mugging and car theft worried most women more than rape did, but those aged 16 to 29 said rape was what they feared most.

Nearly half of all women are said to be either overweight or obese even though 65 per cent drank skimmed or semi-skimmed milk and 73 per cent claimed to eat fruit at least three days a week.

The proportion of overweight women rose to 60 per cent of those aged 55 - 64, twice the proportion for 16 - 24 year olds.

They also reported high levels of stress, with nearly one in six saying they had experienced "quite a lot" or "a great deal" of stress in the previous four weeks.

Peak levels of stress - suffered by one in five women - affected women aged 35 - 54, the time in a woman's life, says the report, when she is most likely to be combining responsibilities for children, home and work.

The traditional female activities of dressmaking, knitting and needlework are declining: only 38 per cent of women have engaged in them in the previous four weeks compared with nearly half 10 years ago.

However, the proportion who do DIY has grown to 30 per cent (one in six mortgages is now held by women). Women tend not to read newspapers as much as men, but the most popular among them is *the Sun*.

Women read more books than men but their favourite weekly magazines are the quiz magazine *Take a Break* and *Woman's Own*.

The keenest cinema goers are young women: 87 per cent of 15 - 24 year olds go to the cinema at least once a year but just over half of those aged 45 and over never went to the cinema.

Walking is by far the most common physical activity for women, followed by keep fit, yoga classes and swimming.'

Chapter roundup

- To become meaningful, raw data must be analysed using three processes: data reduction, data display and the drawing of conclusions.
- We looked at different averages, or ways of selecting a representative value: the arithmetic mean, the mode and the median.
- A frequency distribution shows how many times a particular value occurred.
- Percentages show the size of items in relation to each other, while proportions are percentages expressed as decimals.
- Under measures of dispersion we encountered the range (including quartiles and centiles) and standard deviations.
- The normal distribution is a probability distribution which usually applies to variables with a continuous range of possible values (continuous variables), such as distance, time, length and weight. The distribution can be drawn as a bell-shaped curve, the area under the curve being exactly equal to one. The distance of a point above or below the mean is expressed in numbers of standard deviations and 68%/95%/99% of frequencies are ±1/±1.96/±2.58 standard deviations from the mean.
- We then looked at the process of relating results from samples to facts about the population from which they were taken. Armed with knowledge of the properties of the sampling distribution of the mean we can say, with a certain level of confidence and using sample data, whether or not the true population mean is in a particular range.
- Correlation measures how closely two variables are related to each other. If they are closely correlated this *may* be due to the same cause.
- Multiple regression analysis is a way of analysing the relationship between more than two variables. A computer is needed to do the calculations.

Quick quiz

1 How do you calculate (i) the arithmetic mean, (ii) the mode, (iii) the median?

2 'Six people like product A and 14 like product B'. Express this information as (i) a percentage (ii) a proportion

3 What is the purpose of quartiles?

4 What is the range of a set of values?

5 What are the advantages and disadvantages of using the range?

6 Describe the standard deviation of a set of numbers.

7 What are the properties of the normal distribution?

8 Explain what is meant by the confidence level of a statistic

9 What administrative factors need to be taken into account when deriving a sample size?

10 What is linear correlation used for?

11 Sketch a scattergraph showing perfect positive correlation

12 What does the correlation coefficient show us?

13 What is the purpose of regression analysis?

14 What problems does multiple regression analysis address?

15 Distinguish between quantitative and qualitative data.

16 How can qualitative data be analysed?

Answers to quick quiz

1 The different sorts of average are discussed in Section 2.

2 (i) 30% (ii) 0.3

3 Quartiles are one means of identifying the ranges within which 25%, 50% and 75% of the values lie.

4 The range is the difference between the highest and lowest of a set of values.

5 The advantages and disadvantages of the range are listed in Section 4.1

6 The standard deviation of a set of values is a measure of the amount of variation in the values.

7 The normal distribution is described and illustrated in Section 5.2

8 Confidence levels are discussed in Section 6.2

9 Administrative factors are summarised in Section 6.4

10 Linear correlation is used to establish whether or not two variables are related to each other in such a way that they lie on a straight line when be plotted on a graph.

11 A scattergraph showing perfect positive correlation is shown in Section 7.2.

12 The correlation coefficient shows how strong the linear relationship is between two variables.

13 Regression analysis is a mathematical technique used to find the line of best fit.

14 Multivariate analysis is discussed in Section 7.5

15 Quantitative data is expressed in numerical terms while qualitative data is expressed as feelings or opinions.

16 Analysing qualitative data is discussed in Section 8.

Answers to activities

1 12 + 46 + 1 + 77 + 25= 161

The mean is 161 ÷ 5 = 32.2

2 The workers are using the mode since £2.75 is the value that occurs most often. Six workers earn more than this and only one earns less.

The management have calculated the arithmetic mean which is (£40.05/10) = £4.00. Only two workers earn more than this but seven of them earn less.

Neither the mode nor the mean seem very fair or representative of the workers' rates. The median is half way between £3.00 and £3.40 which works out at £3.20. We may not consider this to be perfectly representative of the workers' rates but it would seem to be fairer than either the mode or arithmetic mean.

3 The frequency distribution is constructed by counting up the number of times (how frequently) a particular value occurs. If you look at the two *rows* of figures, for example, you can see that 68 occurs twice, both in the first line.

The mistake is the frequency of the value 73. This appears once, in the second line, but the distribution shows it appearing 0 times. The number of values does not total 20.

4 This information would be collected to help the wine producer with pricing its products. It shows that its best quality wines will sell well if they are priced in the range £7 to £9. (We include this activity because you are probably starting to wonder what the point of all these percentages and pluses and minuses is'!)

5   Problems with sampling include the following.

(a) The sample may be biased, for example if a questionnaire contains leading questions or an interviewer tries to get people to reply in a certain way.

(b) It might not be possible to collect enough data to have a representative survey.

(c) The data that is collected may not be representative of normal conditions.

(d) An important factor may be missed out when the questions are being designed. For example people may not like something because it is a horrible colour. The producer may not find this out unless a question about colour is included.

(e) People may not tell the truth when they are being questioned.

(f) Selecting who should be in the sample can be difficult without introducing bias.

You may have thought of further problems.

6   *Positively correlated*:   low cost, low quality; high temperature, high consumption of cold drinks.

Negatively correlated: low cost, high sales demand; high temperature, low use of hot water bottles.

There are, of course, countless other examples.

7   Each of the extracts presents a different finding from the survey. We should note that the data will have been collected from a sample of British women, and not from the whole population of British women. Inferential statistics will have been used to generalise from the sample data to make broad statements about the population. However, confidence levels have not been quoted.

Many of the statistics are described textually rather than in figures. For example, "women are still under-represented at the top in business": presumably the proportion of women in top jobs is less than the proportion of women in the whole British population of men and women.

There are a lot of items that are presented as fractions, proportions and percentages. Averages are mentioned; presumably the arithmetic mean was used. The results have often been broken down into age ranges, which suggests the use of frequency distributions. The paragraphs on stress are interesting in that a person's stress level is difficult to quantify, as it is more of a qualitative issue. But some attempt to gauge stress levels has been made by using categories like: 'stress', 'has been experienced "quite a lot" or "a great deal"'.

Assignment 13 [1½ hours]

Scenario

SureSafe Insurance Company has plans for upgrading the computer systems at its headquarters. The plans include the purchase of 200 PCs. Three suppliers (X, Y and Z) have been short-listed, and each have offered to loan four PCs for a three week trial period. The trial periods will all run simultaneously. SureSafe have selected 12 staff who will try out each suppliers' PC for one week. At the end of each trial week they must give the PC a score out of 10. The results from the trials were are follows:

Supplier	Staff Members											
	A	B	C	D	E	F	G	H	I	J	K	L
X	9	3	8	8	4	9	3	8	7	9	2	8
Y	7	6	6	8	5	7	8	6	7	6	5	-
Z	8	4	5	7	4	5	5	6	4	6	9	3

Staff member L was unexpectedly absent from work for the trial of supplier Y's PC.

The standard deviation has been calculated for X, Y and Z with results of 2.57, 0.99, and 1.71 respectively.

Tasks

1 Use suitable statistical methods to process the data and use the results to make, and justify, a recommendation about which supplier to use, bearing in mind that the management of SureSafe insist that only one supplier is used.

2 Comment on the way that the trials have been carried out and suggest alternative schemes for assessing the PCs, within the constraints of the suppliers' three week simultaneous trial period.

Chapter 14

PRESENTING DATA

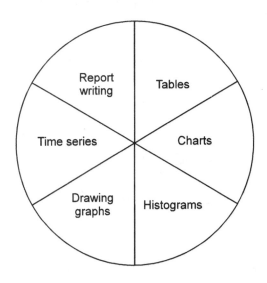

Introduction

Our final topic is the presentation of data. This is important because data and information will only be acted upon if it is presented in a way that helps users to understand it. If it is not acted upon it has no value.

We shall consider a wide variety of methods of presenting and interpreting data in this chapter. We look at ways of presenting numbers, graphical and pictorial presentation and presentation using the written word.

We will start with one of the most basic ways of presenting figures: a way that you have seen illustrated throughout this book - the table.

Your objectives

After completing this chapter you should:

(a) be able to tabulate data;

(b) recognise a variety of different types of chart including pie charts and bar charts;

(c) know what a histogram is;

(d) be able to draw graphs;

(e) understand the principles of report writing and good business writing in general.

1 TABLES

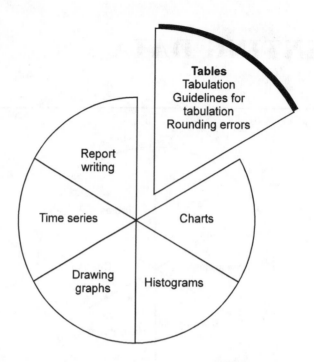

1.1 Tabulation

Tabulation means putting data into tables. A table is a matrix of data in rows and columns, with the rows and the columns having titles.

Since a table is two-dimensional, it can only show two variables. For example, the resources required to produce items in a factory could be tabulated, with one dimension (rows or columns) representing the items produced and the other dimension representing the resources.

Resources for production					£
	Product items				
	A	*B*	*C*	*D*	*Total*
Resources					
Direct material A	13	10	25	16	64
Direct material B	11	34	21	12	78
Direct labour grade 1	16	12	11	19	58
Direct labour grade 2	10	23	18	22	73
Supervision	8	6	7	11	32
Machine time	14	24	12	1	65
Total	72	109	94	95	370

To tabulate data, you need to recognise what the two dimensions should represent, prepare rows and columns accordingly with suitable titles, and then insert the data into the appropriate places in the table.

1.2 Guidelines for tabulation

The table shown above illustrates certain guidelines which you should apply when presenting data in tabular form. These are as follows.

(a) The table should be given a clear title.

(b) All columns should be clearly labelled.

(c) Where appropriate, there should be clear sub-totals.

(d) A total column may be presented; this would usually be the right-hand column.

(e) A total figure is often advisable at the bottom of each column of figures.

(f) Tables should not be packed with too much data so that reading the information is difficult.

1.3 Rounding errors

Rounding errors may become apparent when, for example, a percentages column does not add up to 100%. When figures in a table are rounded and then added up, the effect of rounding will depend on the method of rounding used.

(a) With *rounding to the nearest unit*, errors tend to cancel out giving *unbiased* approximation. We may therefore refer to *compensating errors* when figures are rounded to the nearest unit.

(b) With *rounding up*, errors will add together giving *biased* approximation. We may therefore refer to *cumulative errors* when figures are rounded up.

(c) With *rounding down*, as with rounding up, errors will add together giving *biased* approximation and are *cumulative errors*.

To avoid bias, any rounding should be to the nearest unit and the potential size of errors should be kept to a tolerable level by rounding to a small enough unit (for example to the nearest £10, rather than to the nearest £1,000).

Activity 1 [15 minutes]

Three different products can be made using materials X, Y and Z. The amounts required per unit are as follows.

Product A: 7 kg of Y; 4 kg of Z; 2 kg of X
Product B: 5 kg of X; 4 kg of Y; 3 kg of Z
Product C: 6 kg of Z; 3 kg of X, 2 kg of Y

Present this information in tabular form, following the guidelines given above.

Instead of presenting data in a table, it might be preferable to give a visual display in the form of a chart.

2   CHARTS

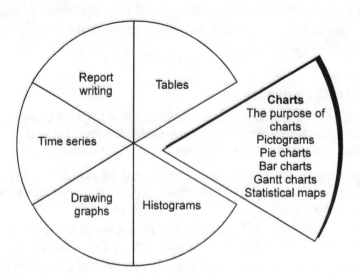

2.1   The purpose of charts

The purpose of a chart is to convey the data in a way that will demonstrate its meaning or significance more clearly than a table of data would. Charts are not always more appropriate than tables, and the most suitable way of presenting data will depend on the following.

(a) What the data are intended to show. Visual displays usually make one or two points quite forcefully, whereas tables usually give more detailed information.

(b) Who is going to use the data. Some individuals might understand visual displays more readily than tabulated data.

There are three main types of chart that might be used to present data.

(a) Pictograms.

(b) Pie charts.

(c) Bar charts.

We shall consider each of these in turn, and then take a brief look at some other types of chart you may encounter.

2.2   Pictograms

A pictogram is a statistical diagram in which quantities are represented by pictures or symbols.

Example: pictograms

A pictogram showing the number of employees at a factory would represent the quantities of employees using pictures of people.

Figure 14.1 Pictogram showing number of employees

In this example, each picture represents 10 employees, and to represent a smaller quantity, a part-picture can be drawn. Here, there were 45 men employed in 1996.

The guidelines for drawing a pictogram are as follows.

(a) The symbols should be clear and simple.

(b) The quantity that each symbol represents should be clearly shown in a key to the pictogram.

(c) Bigger quantities ought to be shown by more symbols, not by bigger symbols. For example, if sales of boxes of dishwasher powder double between 1995 and 1996, a pictogram should show:

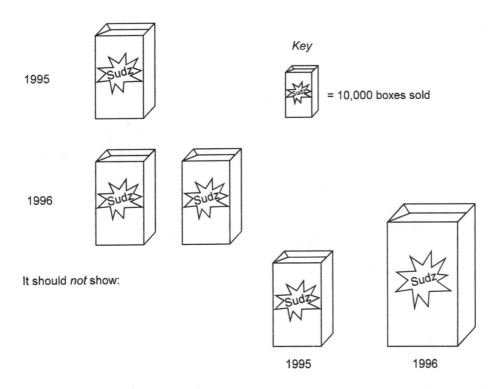

Figure 14.2 Pictogram showing sales of dishwasher powder

In this pictogram, the bigger symbol does not give a true impression of sales growth.

Activity 2   [20 minutes]

What are the advantages and disadvantages of pictograms?

2.3 Pie charts

A pie chart is used to show pictorially the relative sizes of component elements of a total. It is called a pie chart because it is circular, and so has the shape of a pie in a round pie dish, and because the 'pie' is then cut into slices. Each slice represents a part of the total.

Pie charts have sectors of varying sizes, and you need to be able to draw sectors fairly accurately. To do this, you need a protractor. Working out sector sizes involves converting parts of the total into equivalent degrees of a circle. Otherwise, speadsheet packages (such as Chart Wizard in Microsoft Excel) make the process very easy!

Example: pie charts

The costs of production at Factory A and Factory B during March 1996 were as follows.

	Factory A		Factory B	
	£'000	%	£'000	%
Direct materials	70	35	50	20
Direct labour	30	15	125	50
Production overhead	90	45	50	20
Office costs	10	5	25	10
	200	100	250	100

Show the costs for the factories in pie charts.

Solution

A pie chart could be drawn for each factory, as follows.

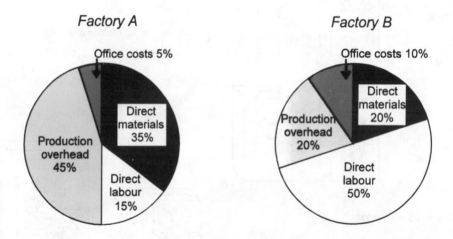

Figure 14.3 Pie chart showing costs of production

The advantages of pie charts are as follows.

(a) They give a simple pictorial display of the relative sizes of elements of a total.

(b) They show clearly when one element is much bigger than others.

(c) They can sometimes clearly show differences in the elements of two different totals. In the example above, the pie charts for Factories A and B show how Factory A's costs mostly consist of production overhead and direct materials, whereas at Factory B, direct labour is the largest cost element.

The disadvantages of pie charts are as follows.

(a) They show only the relative sizes of elements. In the example of the two factories, for instance, the pie charts do not show that costs at Factory B were £50,000 higher in total than at Factory A.

(b) They can involve calculating degrees of a circle and drawing sectors accurately, and this can be time consuming. Spreadsheets make this much less of a problem.

(c) It is sometimes difficult to compare sector sizes accurately by eye.

Activity 3 [unlimited time]

Modern spreadsheet packages offer numerous facilities for presenting information in the form of charts, including pie charts.

If possible, get access to a spreadsheet package and see if you can find out how to do this. (The latest packages take you step by step through the procedures.)

Bar charts are probably the commonest form of graphical presentation. Just look through a few newspapers and you will find plenty of examples. We shall therefore spend some time covering the various types of bar chart.

2.4 Bar charts

The bar chart is one of the most common methods of presenting data in a visual form. It is a chart in which quantities are shown in the form of bars.

There are three main types of bar chart.

(a) Simple bar charts.

(b) Component bar charts, including percentage component bar charts.

(c) Multiple (or compound) bar charts.

Simple bar charts

A simple bar chart is a chart consisting of one or more bars, in which the length of each bar indicates the magnitude of the corresponding data item.

Example: a simple bar chart

A company's total sales for the years from 1991 to 1996 are as follows.

Year	Sales
	£'000
1991	800
1992	1,200
1993	1,100
1994	1,400
1995	1,600
1996	1,700

The data could be shown on a simple bar chart as follows in Figure 14.4.

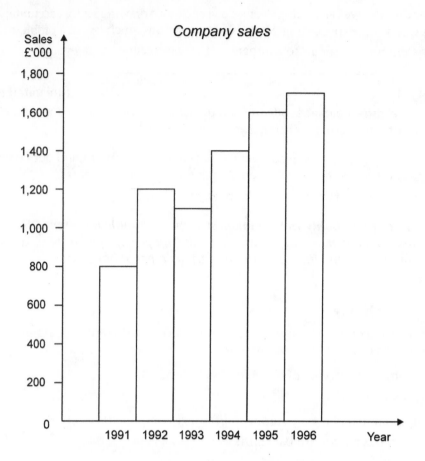

Figure 14.4 Simple bar chart: a company's sales

Each axis of the chart must be clearly labelled, and there must be a scale to indicate the magnitude of the data. In Figure 14.4, the y axis (the vertical axis) includes a scale for the amount of sales, and so readers of the bar chart can see not only that sales have been rising year by year (with 1993 being an exception) but also what the actual sales have been each year.

Simple bar charts serve two purposes.

(a) They show the actual magnitude of each item.

(b) They enable one to compare magnitudes, by comparing the lengths of bars on the chart.

Component bar charts

A component bar chart is a bar chart that gives a breakdown of each total into its components.

A component bar chart would show the following.

(a) How total sales have changed from year to year.

(b) The components of each year's total.

254

Charbart plc sales 1997-1999

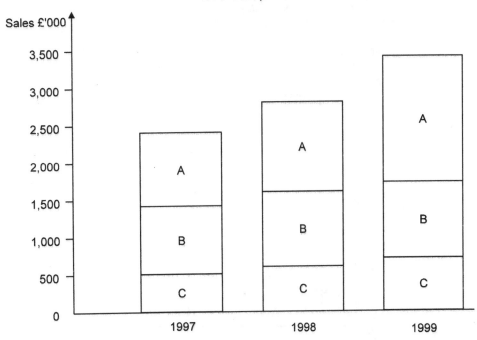

Figure 14.5 Component bar chart

The bars in a bar chart can either be drawn side by side, with no gap between them, or with gaps between them, as in the Figure 14.5. It does not matter which method is used.

In Figure 14.5 the growth in sales is illustrated and the significance of growth in product A sales as the reason for the total sales growth is also fairly clear. The growth in product A sales would have been even clearer if product A had been drawn as the bottom element in each bar instead of the top one.

Percentage component bar charts

The difference between a component bar chart and a percentage component bar chart is that, with a component bar chart, the total length of each bar (and the length of each component in it) indicates magnitude. A bigger amount is shown by a longer bar. With a percentage component bar chart, total magnitudes are not shown. If two or more bars are drawn on the chart, the total length of each bar is the same. The only varying lengths in a percentage component bar chart are the lengths of the sections of a bar, which vary according to the relative sizes of the components.

Example: a percentage component bar chart

The information in the previous example of sales of Charbart plc could have been shown in a percentage component bar chart in Figure 14.6.

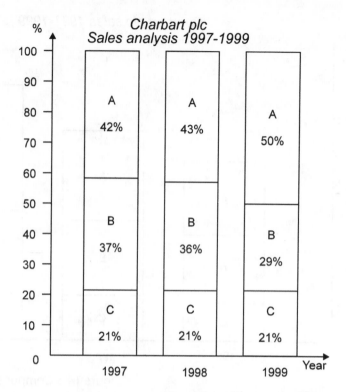

Figure 14.6 Percentage component bar chart

Figure 14.6 shows that sales of C have remained a steady proportion of total sales, but the proportion of A in total sales has gone up quite considerably, while the proportion of B has fallen correspondingly.

Bar charts are sometimes drawn with the bars horizontal instead of vertical.

Multiple bar charts (compound bar charts)

A multiple bar chart (or compound bar chart) is a bar chart in which two or more separate bars are used to present sub-divisions of data.

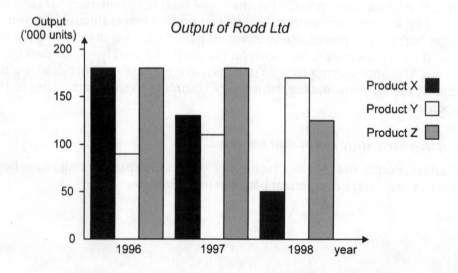

Figure 14.7 Multiple bar chart

A multiple bar chart uses several bars for each total. In Figure 14.7, the sales in each year are shown as three separate bars, one for each product, X, Y and Z.

Multiple bar charts present similar information to component bar charts, except for the following.

(a) Multiple bar charts do not show the grand total (in the above example, the total output each year) whereas component bar charts do.

(b) Multiple bar charts illustrate the comparative magnitudes of the components more clearly than component bar charts.

Two other types of chart that you may come across are Gantt charts, which are used in project management, and maps, which have a variety of applications.

2.5 Gantt charts

Gantt charts are named after their creator, Henry Gantt, a management scientist working in the early years of this century. They are a form of bar chart or line chart. A line chart is simply a bar chart which uses lines instead of bars.

The purposes of Gantt charts are to provide a diagrammatic tool to help project planning and to assist with monitoring the project once it has started. A simple example of part of a Gantt chart is shown in Figure 14.8.

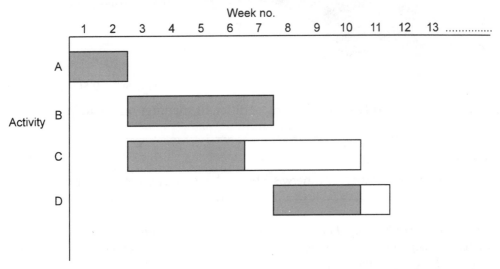

Figure 14.8 An example of a Gantt chart

On a Gantt chart the timescale (in days, weeks, or other appropriate units) is shown on the horizontal axis and the activities in the project (simply called A, B, C, etc. in our example) on the vertical axis. The weeks during which an activity is planned to take place are shown as a bar. As time progresses the bars can be shaded to show how much of each activity has been completed and thus progress can be monitored. In our example, activity C has been planned to take 8 weeks, running from week 3 to week 10, and the shading shows that it is currently half completed. Actual progress can be compared with planned progress, and so a Gantt chart gives a quick visual indication as to whether actual progress is ahead of or behind schedule.

2.6 Statistical maps or cartograms

Statistical maps, or cartograms, may be used to display geographical data. Figure 14.9 is an example, showing unemployment in England and Wales in a particular year (1993).

Unemployment in England and Wales, 1993

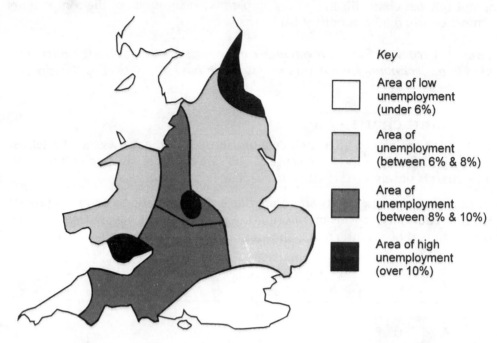

Figure 14.9 Statistical map

A key is needed to explain the meaning of different shadings on the map.

Activity 4   [15 minutes]

How could a map (statistical or otherwise) be used to convey business information?

A special type of bar chart called a histogram is used to present certain types of statistical information. Histograms can be hard to interpret so they deserve a short section to themselves.

3 HISTOGRAMS

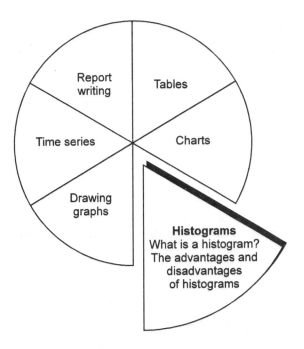

3.1 What is a histogram?

Histograms look rather like bar charts, but there are important differences. They are used when presenting data that is grouped into classes, for example people aged 12 or over but under 20, people aged 20 or over but under 30, and so on.

The number of observations in a class is represented by the *area* covered by the bar, rather than by its *height*.

3.2 The advantages and disadvantages of histograms

Histograms are frequently used to display grouped frequency distributions graphically.

(a) They display clearly the comparative frequency of occurrence of data items within classes.

(b) They indicate whether the range of values is wide or narrow, and whether most values occur in the middle of the range or whether the frequencies are more evenly spread.

Consider these two histograms (Figures 14.10 and 14.11).

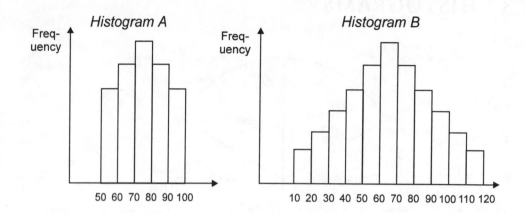

Figure 14.10 Example histograms I

In (A) there is a narrower range of values than in (B). Both have the most frequently occurring value somewhere in the middle of the range (70-80 with A and 60-70 with B).

Now compare these two histograms.

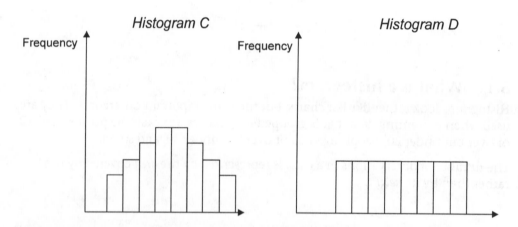

Figure 14.11 Example histograms II

The most frequently occurring values in C are towards the middle of the range, whereas, in histogram D, values occur with equal frequency across the entire range

The main disadvantages of histograms are as follows.

(a) If a histogram represents sample data, the measurements in the histogram might give a false sense of accuracy. The sample data will not be an exact representation of the population as a whole.

(b) If the histogram is showing data about a *continuous* variable, the sharp steps of the histogram blocks would be a little misleading.

(c) Histograms in which the class widths vary may not be readily understood by the lay person.

You will remember drawing graphs at school and you still see them constantly in newspapers and in television news and political analysis programmes. You may have forgotten the basic rules for drawing graphs, however, and may not appreciate when it is best to use them.

4   DRAWING GRAPHS

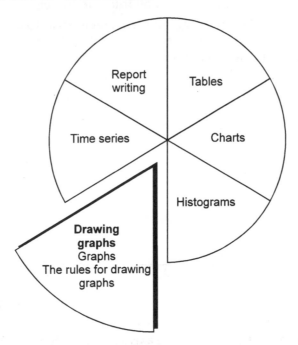

4.1   Graphs

A graph is a form of visual display. A graph shows, by means of either a straight line or a curve, the relationship between two variables. In particular, it shows how the value of one variable changes given changes in the value of the other variable.

For example, a graph might show how:

(a) sales turnover changes over time;

(b) a country's population changes over time;

(c) total costs of production vary with the number of units produced.

The relationship between variables can often be presented more clearly in graph form than in a table of figures, and this is why graphs are so commonly used.

Definitions

The variable whose value is influenced by the value of the other variable is referred to as the *dependent variable*. In the examples above, sales turnover, population and total costs would be the dependent variables in (a), (b) and (c) respectively.

The variable whose value affects the value of the dependent variable is known as the *independent variable*. In the examples above, these are time in (a) and (b) and number of units produced in (c).

4.2   The rules for drawing graphs

A graph has a horizontal axis, the x axis and a vertical axis, the y axis. The x axis is used to represent the independent variable and the y axis is used to represent the dependent variable.

If time is one variable, it is always treated as the independent variable. When time is represented by the x axis on a graph, we have a time series.

(a) If the data to be plotted are derived from calculations, rather than given in the question, make sure that there is a neat table in your working papers.

(b) The scales on each axis should be selected so as to use as much of the graph paper as possible. Do not cramp a graph into one corner.

(c) In some cases it is best not to start a scale at zero so as to avoid having a large area of wasted paper. This is perfectly acceptable as long as the scale adopted is clearly shown on the axis. One way of avoiding confusion is to break the axis concerned, as in Figure 14.12.

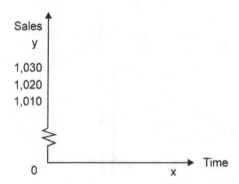

Figure 14.12 Graph with broken axis

(d) The scales on the x axis and the y axis should be marked. For example, if the y axis relates to amounts of money, the axis should be marked at every £1, or £100 or £1,000 interval or at whatever other interval is appropriate. The axes must be marked with values to give the reader an idea of how big the values on the graph are.

(e) A graph should not be overcrowded with too many lines. Graphs should always give a clear, neat impression.

(f) A graph must always be given a title and, where appropriate, a reference should be made to the source of data.

(g) Again, spreadsheet packages take a lot of the hard work out of preparing graphs!

Graphs are also a very good way of presenting information about trends over time.

5 TIME SERIES

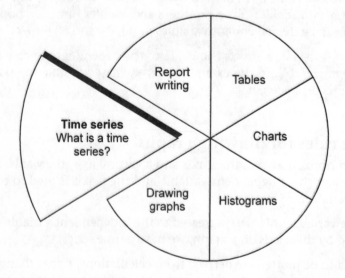

5.1 What is a time series?

A time series is a series of figures or values recorded over time such as monthly sales over the last two years. A graph of a time series is sometimes called a *historigram* (it deals with history!). The horizontal axis of a historigram is always chosen to represent time and the vertical axis represents the values of the data recorded. The graph will give some indication of the trend in the data over time.

Activity 5 [15 minutes]

The following data show the sales of a product in the period 1996-98.

Year	Quarter1 '000	Quarter 2 '000	Quarter 3 '000	Quarter 4 '000
1996	86	42	57	112
1997	81	39	55	107
1998	77	35	52	99

Required

Plot a time series of the above data.

Numbers and pictures can tell us a lot, but by far the most sophisticated medium of communication is the written word. Your numbers and graphics will almost always need to be accompanied by written commentary. In the final section of this book we look at report writing, because reports are perhaps the most elaborate form of data analysis and presentation. This section also ontains good advice for any sort of writing you have to do.

6 REPORT WRITING

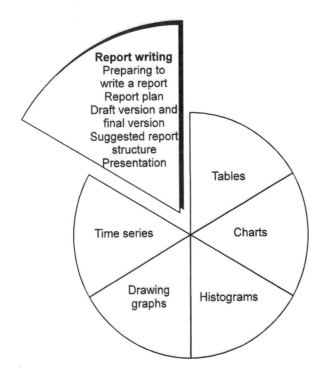

6.1 Preparing to write a report

For report writing to proceed efficiently, a logical structure for the report is needed. When you begin writing-up you might want to consider the following points.

(a) Is the *purpose* of the report clearly defined from the outset?

(b) Who or what is the *target* of your report? The intended target of the report can influence the way data is handled or the recommendations made.

(c) Is there a *wider audience* for the report? The likely audience could influence the style in which the report needs to be written (for example use of technical terms, diagrammatic presentation of information).

(d) Are any *recommendations* made likely to be considered for action by the targeted audience? The answer to this is almost certainly yes, given that your manager at work, who will be expected to testify to the validity and usefulness of your project, is part of the targeted audience.

You may not be able to judge a book by its cover but the nature and presentation of the final document will significantly influence the manner in which it is received.

The advantage of having a clear structure is that your ideas and material are forced into some sort of order. If there is a great deal you want to say then order is essential, and a good way of achieving it is to produce a report plan at an early stage.

6.2 Report plan

The best approach is to jot down all the things you want to say as a series of headings, with perhaps a little expansion of some points. Then look at them together and, by experiment if necessary, put them into a logical order by putting numbers against each. Only if you are very certain that your thoughts are logical and coherent as they stand should you omit putting them on paper as a plan - apart from any other reason, you are likely to forget vital material if you do not have a plan.

You might try writing 'network' notes to present your headings visually (see the diagram).

A network note

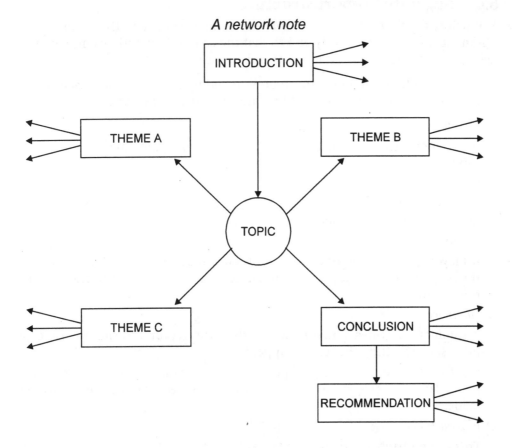

Figure 14.13 Network notes

Very few people can produce a perfect finished written document first time round: expect to produce at least two versions. (If you produce endless drafts, however, this is undoubtedly because you did not plan properly.)

6.3 Draft version and final version

Once you have assembled your material and established your plan, it is time to write the report itself along the lines of the plan. Many people suffer from 'writer's block' at this point and simply cannot get started, writing paragraph after paragraph of introduction and throwing each away. If you have this problem, try starting on the main body first, then go back to the introduction and end with the conclusion.

Once it is done, work on your draft so as to produce a finished report. The draft will have given you confidence and shown you, perhaps, any flaws in your argument. The break will have allowed your brain to sort things out into a better order and more fluent style. All new ideas should be noted on the draft copy before you start afresh to write the final version.

No strict version of report structure is, or could be, imposed. The topics of the report will, in part, determine the structure of the report. However, a generalised structure is suggested below, with appropriate guidelines as necessary.

6.4   Suggested report structure

Any report should be arranged so that the basic message and the main topics of argument emerge progressively and so that the conclusions and recommendations follow logically from those arguments and analysis.

All documents to be presented in a report, including any appendices, need to state clearly their contents, the source of the information and the date.

(a) *Title page*

A succinct but precise title is desirable. It should immediately identify the subject matter.

(b) *Contents page*

Besides detailing the chapters/sections involved, this should also include a list of tables, diagrams and so on.

(c) *Acknowledgments*

It may be just a matter of courtesy to acknowledge those who have assisted in the preparation of your project, but reference to them may also lend weight to the report.

(d) *Summary*

A summary provides a brief review of the main report and should also create interest by whetting the reader's appetite.

A brief review should note the purpose of the research, how it addressed the particular issue or topic and what conclusions and recommendations have been made.

(e) *Introduction*

This will probably briefly describe what the report is about and why it has been written.

(f) *Terms of reference*

This explains the purposes of the report and any restrictions on its scope: what is to be investigated, what kind of information is required and so on. If the report is self-initiated (rather than requested by someone else) however, it is more appropriate to call this section 'Objectives'.

(g) *Method of investigation*

This outlines the steps taken to make an investigation, collect data: telephone calls or visits made, documents or computer files consulted, expert advice obtained, computations or analyses made should all be briefly described. This is important because it gives credibility to the findings. Alternatively, if the report's audience do not like the conclusions, they will seek first to discredit the method of investigation, so it must be given.

(h) *Findings*

Presentation, analysis and discussion of data and other research information. There should be a logical flow, with ideas being presented in sequence. In some cases, a chronological sequence may be appropriate.

If there is any sort of problem situation in the question, your structure should be on the following lines:

(i)   analysing the facts of the situation;

(ii) stating the principles of the matter in hand and any exceptions to them;

(iii) applying those principles to the facts of the case;

(iv) identifying any ambiguities and problems thrown up by this process.

(i) *Conclusions*

The conclusions are directly drawn from the analysis and discussion.

(j) *Action taken*

This section may sometimes be necessary: it will outline the changes that the author has already implemented in response to the findings and conclusions.

(k) *Recommendations*

Strong, well-founded proposals for change will reflect a successful project and an impressive report. Avoid non-committal recommendations and try to present recommendations in a logical order, for example presenting recommendations for the short, medium and long term in sequence.

For each recommendation the following can be tabulated:

(i) *what* is recommended

(ii) *who* needs to act on the recommendation

(iii) *costs and benefits* of the recommendation, with figures if possible, indicating the time scale involved

(iv) *cross-references* to the points in the report leading to the recommendation

(l) *Appendices*

To be included here are a listing of any references, any other appropriate bibliography, glossaries of technical terms used, and copies of any important supporting documentation. It may be necessary to include in an appendix any body of material that is too large or detailed for the findings section (for example computer analyses).

Lastly, let's think about how a piece of writing should be presented. In essence, make it as easy as possible for your reader to read. The comments on writing style apply equally to other sorts of writing that you may do, such as letters or memos.

6.5   Presentation

The key is *organisation:* into sentences, into paragraphs, into chapters, into parts. A poorly organised report will be hard to read and it will be difficult for the reader to extract the value of the research you have done.

Whether your report is word-processed or typed, you may need to include graphs, charts or other diagrams where relevant. Be very neat when drawing them (they should be clearly labelled) and make sure you include all the visual material to which you refer. Spreadsheet software might be used for presenting tabular information, and most modern packages also have fairly sophisticated graphic capabilities.

Accuracy and unity

Accuracy is probably the most important requirement of any research project - not just in terms of the honest presentation of data, but also in giving the correct emphasis to the main themes - in order that an objective and useful report results.

Keeping within the terms of reference and only addressing the central issue at hand will enhance the *unity* of the report. Leave out material that is not really relevant and avoid discussions of marginal issues.

Writing style

It may worry you that you do not feel you can express yourself clearly in writing. This is a common problem but one which can be overcome if the following points are heeded.

(a) Write clearly and simply. Long sentences are no 'better' than short ones and often serve to confuse: many people lose track of what they wanted to say by the end of one! We need to communicate information in a way which other people will understand.

(b) Use vocabulary with which you are familiar. Do not be tempted to adopt a 'fancy style' of words which you would not use in normal life and which you may not fully understand.

(c) Try to vary your vocabulary and sentence structure as much as possible whilst keeping your meaning clear. You need to *develop* your style, and one of the best ways to do this is to read fairly widely. You will find that by reading books and newspapers you remember uses and meanings of words that you thought you had forgotten.

(d) Avoid the first person singular, for example 'I think that'. You will feel and sound more objective if you introduce an idea in another way 'it could be said that...'

(e) Write in short paragraphs - *nothing* is more off-putting to the reader than a dense area of intricately connected (or often totally unconnected) sentences. Each paragraph should relate to a central idea, introduced as early in it as possible (and possibly 'flagged' in a header).

(f) Paragraphs should connect smoothly with each other. Connecting words are often used for this purpose, such as 'therefore', 'however' and 'thus'.

(g) As an antidote to the above, do not be so conscious of your writing style that you are actually inhibited from writing what you think. If there is only one way to say a thing, say it how it is!

Chapter roundup

- Tables are a simple way of presenting information about two variables.
- Charts often convey the meaning or significance of data more clearly than would a table. Make sure that you are able to discuss the following:

    Pictograms
    Pie charts
    Bar charts
    Gantt charts
    Statistical maps

- There are three main types of bar chart: simple, component (including percentage component) and multiple (or compound).
- Histograms are used to present data when it is grouped into classes. The number of observations in a class is represented by the area covered by the block, rather than by its height.
- A time series is a series of figures or values recorded over time such as quarterly sales for the past three years. The graph of a time series is sometimes called a historigram.
- The rules for drawing graphs may seem obvious, but they are still important, and whenever you draw a graph you should check it carefully.
- Make sure that that you are aware of the information available from each method of presentation covered in this chapter. When selecting a method of data presentation remember to consider the type of information which must be shown and the presentation which the ultimate user of the information will find most helpful.
- When presenting research findings, it is important to follow the principles of report writing: *know* your purpose and audience, *organise* material, plan your report, *structure* your report and *present* it beautifully.

Quick quiz

1. What are the main guidelines for tabulation?
2. What are the advantages and disadvantages of pictograms?
3. What are the disadvantages of pie charts?
4. Name the three main types of bar chart.
5. What is the purpose of a Gantt chart?
6. Distinguish between a dependent variable and an independent variable.
7. What guidelines should be observed when drawing graphs?
8. What is a historigram?
9. What four points should be considered when preparing to write a report on your research findings?
10. Explain why the figures shown in a column of a table could add up to 98% but the total is shown as 100%.
11. What sort of method of rounding of figures is least likely to lead to cumulative errors?
12. Write down a list of the suggested headings for the sections of a formal report.
13. What type of chart would you choose to show how the current year's annual expenditure budget has been split between five departments?

14 What type of chart would you use to compare the annual sales of six products by five sales persons?

Answers to quick quiz

1 Guidelines for tabulation are discussed in Section 1.2.

2 The advantages and disadvantages of pictograms are explained in Section 2.2.

3 The disadvantages of pie charts are discussed in Section 2.3.

4 The three main types of bar chart are: simple bar charts, component bar charts and multiple bar charts.

5 A Gantt chart is used to show the when activities in a project are planned to take place and can be used to record and monitor the project's progress.

6 Dependent and independent variables are defined in Section 4.1.

7 The rules for drawing graphs described in Section 4.2.

8 A historigram is the graph of a time series.

9 The points to consider when preparing to write a report are discussed in Section 6.1

10 The figures may not add up to 100% due to rounding errors.

11 Rounding figures to the nearest unit is least likely to lead to cumulative errors, rather than always rounding up or always rounding down.

12 A suggested report structure is shown in Section 6.4.

13 A pie chart would be suitable as it enables the viewer to see what each department has been allocated as a proportion of the whole budget.

14 A multiple bar chart would enable to viewer to compare the figures for each product for each sales person.

Answers to activities

1

Materials required for products X, Y and Z				*kilograms*
	Material			
Product	X	Y	Z	Total
A	2	7	4	13
B	5	4	3	12
C	3	2	6	11
Total	10	13	13	36

Note. The total kg per product and the total kg of each material should be shown. The only point in totalling the total column, however, is as a cross check: the total itself tells us nothing useful.

2 The advantages of pictograms are that they present data in a simple and readily understood way. Pictograms are good for giving a general impression and they convey their message to the reader at a glance and are consequently often used on television and in the press.

The disadvantages of pictograms are that they can only convey a limited amount of information, and that they lack precision. Each symbol must represent quite a large number of items otherwise the pictogram would lose its simplicity and contain too many symbols. Using portions of a symbol to represent smaller quantities gives some extra precision, but not much.

3 Do try to do this Activity if you can: the graphics capabilities of modern software packages are fun to use and the experience will almost certainly be useful in your job and your course at some stage.

4   A map might show the location of a business's branches or factories, or it might divide the country into different sales regions, or areas with different market characteristics.

Street maps are widely used to guide customers precisely to the business premises.

You may have thought of other uses.

5   Graph of time series, called a historigram.

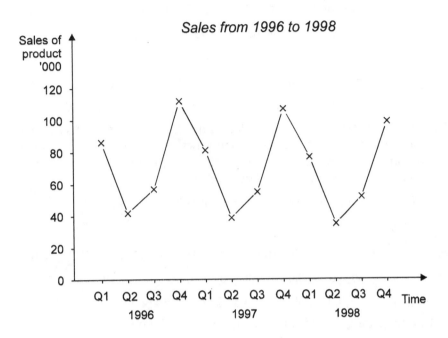

Sales from 1996 to 1998

Assignment 14 [1½ hours]

Scenario

This assignment covers techniques discussed in Chapters 13 and 14.

The marketing manager of a small retail company is preparing for the annual marketing meeting where the company's performance over the last year will be discussed.

The following table shows the monthly unit sales over the year.

Unit sales for period Jan 1995 - December 1995

1995

JAN	FEB	MAR	APR	MAY	JUN	JUL	AUG	SEP	OCT	NOV	DEC
1,050	1,375	1,630	485	1,205	1,538	530	1,570	1,105	1,460	635	1,615

The Marketing Manager has been placing monthly advertisements in the local press, and feels that the level of sales should increase according to the cost of the advertising campaign in the previous month. The advertising costs for the corresponding 12 month period were as follows.

Advertising costs for period Dec 1994 - Nov 1995 (£)

1994   1995

DEC	JAN	FEB	MAR	APR	MAY	JUN	JUL	AUG	SEP	OCT	NOV
400	1,050	1,750	0	750	1,480	0	1,265	745	1,590	260	2,015

(a) Present the unit sales figures in an appropriate graphical form.

(b) Draw a scattergraph of unit sales against advertising costs.

(c) Discuss whether or not the graph in (b) provides any evidence to suggest that the sales manager is correct in thinking that increasing advertising will lead to an increase in units sold in the following month.

ANSWERS TO ASSIGNMENTS

Answer to Assignment 4

Amongst the points to be covered:

The greater chances of over-trading if he operates his own outlets and grows rapidly

The far greater requirement for finance if buying all the properties, equipment, stock, etc. required for his own outlets

The inevitably longer time frame required if expanding with his own outlets

The far greater staffing and management problems of operating his own outlets

It may be more profitable to sell the franchises than attempt to operate nationwide.

On the other side of the coin:

Franchisees may be less controllable than employees

Quality may be more variable

He may later wish he owned outlets rather than having sold the franchises

Answer to Assignment 5

	Restaurant		Bar	
(a) *Variable costs*				
Food/drink	35%		50%	
Hourly wages	25%		15%	
	60%		65%	
Fixed costs are:	£		£	
Rent	40,000		30,000	
Management	25,000		20,000	
	65,000		50,000	
Therefore:	£		£	
Sales	350,000	100%	250,000	100%
Less variable costs	210,000	60%	162,500	65%
Contribution	140,000	40%	87,500	35%
Less fixed costs	65,000		50,000	
Net profit	75,000		37,500	

(b)
Total annual wages:

25% of £350,000	£87,500	15% of £250,000	£37,500
Average weekly wages (÷ 52)	£1,683		£721
Average weekly hours (÷ £4)	421 hours		180 hours

(b) Break even (work up from bottom, leading you to sales)

	£		£	
Sales	162,500		142,857	
Less variable costs	97,500		92,857	
Contribution	65,000	×100 / 40	50,000	× 100 / 35
Less: fixed costs	65,000		50,000	
Net profit	0		0	

Answer to Assignment 8

Amongst the points you could have made:

Sales dropped significantly.

Gross profit percentage dropped considerably.

Net profit percentage dropped considerably, resulting from both the gross profit % fall and an increase in expenses as a % of sales you could have looked at the expenses individually.

Current ratio drops, and quick ratio disappears (this is a retailer, with no debtors).

Stock turn falls.

Time taken to pay creditors increases.

Return on capital drops considerably; it should be appreciated that, in this scenario, Betty and Briando do not mind whether they are paid via directors' remuneration or via dividends - it all comes to them, as the only directors and shareholders. However, in 1994 their total rewards were less than the business profits, whilst in 1995 they removed more than the year's profits, which would drain the company of finance.

The business has had to start borrowing from the bank. The only expense to fall was advertising; was this responsible for the sales drop?

We don't know all the answers, but our examination of the accounts, helped by our ratio analysis, has raised our awareness of the apparent problems and given us a lot of information on the right questions to ask.

Answer to Assignment 9

There are several passages in the extract which highlight problems with the quality of the information. Some of them are commented upon here although you may have identified others.

> *'I get so much information that I seem to spend most of my time reading documents and I rarely get the chance to act upon any of them.'*

> *'With all this information to absorb I seem to have no time to plan anything so I end up just trying to cope with one crisis after another'*

The manager is suffering from information overload; too much information is being communicated. The Sales Manager must do something to reduce the volume of information and just ignoring some of it could lead to useful information being overlooked. The organisation should consider why all the managers need to receive specific details of each department's activities. It could be useful to adopt the exception principle and reduce all the contents of the reports to a short routine summary and only include details of particularly noteworthy items. Reducing the frequency of the reports may be helpful provided urgent information is still communicated quickly if necessary.

> *'...data about the production processes which I find very difficult to interpret,..'*

> *'...lots of technical terms relating to things that are not really my area of expertise..'*

For the Sales Manager, some of the documents contain data which should really be processed into useful information before it is communicated, and other information suffers from 'noise' because the meaning of the technical jargon is not clear. The organisation should either improve the general clarity of the documents or consider whether the Sales Manager needs to receive all of it.

> *'It can take a long time to get to me and even longer for me to find time to read it properly'*

The sensitive information is not being communicated in a timely manner. Either it should be passed on within a much more limited timescale or more copies will have to be circulated.

. '..one of our main competitors introduced a special bulk order..'

External information is not being routinely collected and communicated to the appropriate people. Perhaps a memo to staff is needed instructing them to pass on information rather than ignore it or assume that other people have received it.

'....it made my monthly predictions look a bit silly.'

'....had made an error in the figures they gave to me.'

Predictions about the future are always subject to uncertainty, unlike most present or past information. We should take into account the assumptions that underlie the information so that we can accept it with the appropriate degree of confidence. When information about the present or past is shown to be inaccurate then it may have the immediate effect of leading us to a wrong decision and, when shown to be inaccurate, it also reduces our confidence in any further information from that source.

'I have never really tried to keep records of who is using the package.'

The sales manager seems unaware of the need to have information about legal agreements, such as software licences, or legislation such as copyright on computer software. A tighter control is needed and the organisation could give a member of staff responsibility for maintaining records of software used and monitoring its usage.

It is often difficult to evaluate information in terms of its cost and value. However, in the example of the use of software, the organisation could try to cost the time needed for suitable record keeping and weigh it against the effects of possible court action and the potential damage to the organisation's reputation.

Answer to Assignment 10

Task 1

Richard Anthony suggested that decision making within an organisation could be categorised in the following hierarchy.

Strategic planning

Strategic decisions are made by top-level management and relate to the major, long-term issues concerning the main organisational objectives such as annual profit levels. Summary internal information about the organisation is needed to judge current performance and trends. External information about the organisation's sphere of operations and the general environment is also required.

In the case of SuperBooks, much of the Chief Executive Jean Jones's time will be spent on strategic issues such as considering whether to expand the business by individual purchase of more shops to add to the chain or to take over another smaller chain.

Management control

This is the middle management level which occupies the tactical role, taking decisions about medium term issues to try to realise the objectives that have been set at the strategic level. The information handled at this level will contain more detail, mainly concerning internal performance like monthly sales levels of different types of book.

Issues at this level would be the concern of Sam Green, the shop manager, who would be concerned with planning for several months ahead looking at things like whether to reorganise the layout of the shop to highlight a particular series of newly published books.

Operational control

This relates to the short term, everyday routine. It will require detailed internal, information about daily or weekly performance and the aim is to ensure that the plans made at the tactical level are smoothly carried through.

At SuperBooks, Pat Smith the supervisor will exercise operational control such as to make out the weekly shift rota and arrange for cover for absent staff.

Task 2

(a) Decision making can be considered to include the following stages.

Problem recognition: The SuperBooks board will need to recognise and react to the problem of competition from other retail outlets. This could become apparent initially as falling sales levels.

Problem definition and structuring: The board will need to try to gather information about things like their particular market, SuperBooks' market share and the predicted impact of increased competition.

Identifying alternative courses of action: The main objective may be to increase profitability but there may be several broad approaches to the problem. For example, SuperBooks may try to become more competitive on price, or diversify by expanding the product range to include computer CD-ROM titles, or become more specialised and market the shops accordingly.

Making and communicating the decisions: The alternatives which seem most feasible will be examined in more detail and a decision will be made. Suppose that the decision is to adopt some new product, like GD-ROM publication. This will probably have effects on most of the SuperBooks staff because a whole range of activities will be required: equipment will need to be purchased, marketing strategies will have to be organised, additional warehouse facilities may be required, shops will have to be rearranged to accommodate displays stands, and shop assistants will need training.

Implementing the decision: Detailed planning of activities like those mentioned above will need to be done and then the plans can be activated.

Monitoring the effects of the decision: SuperBooks will have to keep careful watch of how the public react to the new products and the way they are being marketed. Control action may be needed; for example it may be discovered that customers are asking lots of technical questions which takes up a lot of the general sales staff's time and it may be better to have one or two specialists to deal with the new products.

(b) At SuperBooks, the routine day-to-day transaction data will consist of mainly of details of individual books sold - title, author, publisher, price, customer's details, and so on. This will be collected for every sale and we have become accustomed to modern retail methods that use electronic point of sale (EPOS) terminals with bar code readers to input the information into their transaction processing system and use electronic funds transfer (EFT) to process the customers' payment. This information is vital to the low-level operation of the business.

The detailed transaction data needs to be processed into summarised lists and charts of sales on a weekly or monthly basis so that middle management can monitor actual performance, measure it against planned performance and maybe take control action at the tactical level. Sales will be analysed by product and if a review of sales levels for the new range of CD-ROM titles for the first three months exceeds expectations then the management could consider expanding the range.

At the strategic level, the transaction data will be further summarised to provide monthly, quarterly and annual sales figures which will be combined with other internal information such as direct costs and overheads to give an overall picture of the business. This can then be analysed, along with external data about the competition and market research predictions about future trends, to provide the basis for deciding upon long term strategies.

Answer to Assignment 11

Task 1

The electronic office

The use of office technology has grown rapidly in recent decades and most offices now include several forms of electronic equipment. Telex and telefacsimile machines are widely used, photocopiers have become more sophisticated, modern switchboards allow all kinds of internal configurations of the telephone system. These sorts of equipment have greatly improved communications, but the introduction of relatively low-cost, office-based personal computer systems (PC)has had an even greater effect on working practices.

The modern PC is a flexible tool that can be used for a variety of tasks in the office. Word processors allow the production of attractive looking documents that can be automatically checked for spelling and text can easily be revised and reused. They enable organisations to produce a consistent house style for documentation. Desk top publishing is now possible using PCs to produce booklets and marketing material. Graphics can be incorporated into documents and scanners can be used to input images such as photographs into documents. High quality output can be generated using ink-jet and laser printers attached to a PC. Other tools such as spreadsheets, accounts packages and database systems are also readily available to run on PCs.

A further development is the use of telecommunications equipment to form networks which allow staff to share information and to use electronic mail both internally between staff and externally with clients and other organisations.

All these features can be used by JWF and would allow all levels of staff to improve their productivity, as well as providing better quality information that is well-presented. However, in order to capitalise on the technology it is important that proper control is exercised to ensure that appropriate systems are implemented and then used properly. The systems should be compatible so that information is generated in formats which allow it to be easily transferred between systems. Compatibility will also mean that staff do not have too many systems to learn to use but it will be important to have a suitable training scheme so that staff regard the new systems in a positive manner and can make full use of them.

Once electronic office systems are implemented it is likely that the business will come to depend on them so it important that they are well maintained and proper backup procedures are adopted particularly for central database systems. Information should be secured from unauthorised access by using passwords and if personal information is stored then the systems will probably have to be registered under the Data Protection Act and the information used in accordance with that act's guidelines.

Task 2

Systems and data flows

A system such as an organisation may be regarded as a set of related sub-processes. Each of the sub-processes may be carried out by a smaller system which will form a sub-system of the organisation. Many organisations are structured into departments which actually form the functional sub-systems where each sub-system is responsible for a particular function. In the case of JWF the functional sub-systems could things like clients accounts, JWF's accounts, marketing, administration, and payroll.

Information must flow between the sub-systems in order for the organisation as a whole to function. The JWF accounts function needs to know how much work has been done for clients in order to charge them accordingly so the book-keepers and accountants working for clients must keep a log or time sheet of how they spend their time.

Information must also flow between JWF and its environment. JWF must advertise by sending information about itself into its environment, and must ensure that information is gathered from the environment such as changes to legislation which require that appropriate accounting procedures are adopted.

Some information flows are formal. Internally JWF may pass operational level information between departments on standard forms such as the time sheets previously mentioned. Strategic and tactical level information may flow formally in the form of end of year accounts and minutes of board meetings. Similarly, information may flow formally between JWF and the external environment in the way of things like tax returns, sales and purchase invoices.

Formal data flows play an important role in business communications and often they are recorded on paper. Since they are often governed by procedures and require authorisation, they may provide a slow means of communication.

Informal data flows can be quick and easy; a brief word on the telephone or chat after a formal meeting has concluded. They can be very cheap and effective means of communication. For example, word of mouth from satisfied clients is probably a very powerful vehicle for building JWF's reputation and securing more business without the need for costly and time-consuming marketing exercises. Another advantage of informal data flows is that they do not need to follow the formal hierarchy or chain of communication so they are speedier and may allow information to flow that would not otherwise have been transmitted.

However, most informal data flows do not have laid-down rules nor are they recorded, except possibly as a brief note or telephone number in someone's diary. This means that they are basically uncontrolled and can be difficult to trace or recall later which can be a disadvantage. Information may not get passed on to some or all of the appropriate staff.

JWF may have found that informal data flows were used extensively when only a few people worked together but as an organisation grows it becomes increasing difficult to rely on informal flows. So the communication flows become more formal and structured but if they become too cumbersome or slow then they will not be very effective and the uncontrolled informal flows take over again. Another point to consider is that the staff of JWF may have grown to like the culture of a small friendly firm with informal data flows between staff; changing to a more formal style of communication may change the culture and lead to dissatisfaction amongst staff.

Answer to Assignment 12

Task 1

(a) *Transaction processing systems*

Transaction processing systems are designed to handle the operational-level data of an organisation. The basic details of the transaction will be input into the system, via a keyboard or bar code for example, where they are processed and stored if necessary. Much of the routine manual work of a few years ago is now carried out partially or completely by computerised transaction processing systems. For example, banking is an area where lots of small details need to be input, recorded, checked and processed. Many of the processes associated with money, such as paying for goods in shops, transferring funds and withdrawing cash, are now carried out using computerised equipment. Transaction processing systems provide the raw data for many of the other types of information system to act upon.

(b) *Decision support systems*

Decision support systems are designed to provide managers with information about the options available so as to enable them to make better decisions. They are commonly used in semi-structured situations which involve some routine, easily predicted aspects and some more uncertain aspects. Computerised spreadsheets are commonly used as decision support tools. A model of some aspect of the organisation, such as predicted sales activity, is set up on the spreadsheet in such a way that a 'what-if?' analysis can be carried out by changing key variables and looking at the resulting situation. If a manager expects sales revenue to increase over the next year but is unsure what the percentage increase will be then several different percentages can be tried. This will give the manager a better idea about what the likely results are which will assist decisions about what staffing costs can be afforded at the different sales level.

(c) *Expert systems*

Expert systems are designed to provide the knowledge and experience in a narrow area of activity that would normally require the help of an expert. The user inputs basic data about the specific situation and the expert system integrates this with relevant facts that are contained in its built-in database and applies built-in rules to produce a result which will usually be in the form of a recommended course of action. Areas where expert systems have been developed are in medicine, taxation regulations, and investment appraisal.

(d) *Executive information systems*

An executive information system, or 'enterprise information system', provides comprehensive information about an organisation and its environment in a form that is easy to access at whatever level of detail the user requires. They have a large database of detailed internal information about the organisation and can process this information to provide an overview of the organisation's past, present and predicted performance. However, the user can also get at the detailed information if need be by 'drilling-down' into the database. For example, an executive information system for a multi-national sales organisation could display summaries of sales levels for various products world wide on a graph on the computer screen. If the user then wants to look at the sales levels of those products for a particular country then, with very little input from the user, this is made available in the same graphical format. The system may also include information about the organisation's environment such as the general financial climate and the state of the particular market area.

Task 2

Modern portable computers are becoming more commonplace but are still expensive items and an obvious threat is loss or theft motivated by the value of the hardware and software in the system, not the information it contains. So insurance to recover the cost and provide an immediate replacement should be considered. However, one of the main attractions of a portable computer is the large storage capacity. A person travelling on business can carry virtually all the information that would be available in a permanent office. This information will have a value to the organisation but may also have value to external people in a competitive market place. The executive should ensure that the system is not left unattended and is locked securely away in an unobtrusive place.

Although modern electronic equipment is reasonably reliable, it may still suffer hardware failure either through faulty components or accidental damage. The executive will suffer extreme embarrassment if the system fails just as it is about to be used for a key presentation to clients. The system should be handled carefully and kept away from hazards such as damp, heat from direct sunlight, magnetic fields and electrical power surges. Data may be stored on the system's internal disk but it should also be backed up onto floppy disk so that it can be restored onto the system, or onto another portable computer if necessary. The floppy disks should also be handled and stored properly to minimise the risk of damage to the disk or corruption to the data. The hardware and procedures needed to allow telecommunications from an ordinary telephone socket back to the executives head office will provide additional backup of data as well as the ability to make requests and gain additional information.

Unauthorised access to the data is a threat with the risk coming from the curious passer-by as well as the interested competitor. The computer should be kept in a locked case when not in use and a password should be required to log on to the system and further passwords used for particularly sensitive information. Passwords should not be easily guessed or simple to work out and should be changed regularly in case they have been inadvertently disclosed. Other procedures can be applied such as reducing the risk of leaving the system live but unattended by automatic logging out of the user if the system has been inactive for a few minutes.

Answer to Assignment 13

Task 1

We have been given the standard deviation of the scores for each type of PC but we should also calculate the averages.

Supplier	Total	Mean	Mode	Median	Standard deviation
X	78	6.50	8	8	2.57
Y	71	6.45	6	6	0.99
Z	66	5.50	4 & 5	5	1.71

We can now try to analyse the results.

The total score would be a useful indication of how well the users liked the systems, except that not all the PCs were tried by the same number of people.

The mean score for each PC shows X and Y quite close and clearly above Z.

The mode and median show X a clear favourite but with relatively few values in our data these can easily be distorted and we need to be careful about making judgements on the basis of them.

With relatively few values to examine we can scan the values by eye and try to form an overall impression. It looks like X has more extreme high and low values, whereas the values for Y are more concentrated in a middle area. We find that the statistics back up our intuitive view because the *standard deviation* indicates that the scores for Z are far more spread out then for Y, with X showing even more variation.

We should eliminate Z on the basis that it fares badly on all the statistics. We may be tempted to opt for X as it has the highest mean. However, the standard deviations show far more spread or variation in the scores for X than for Y. If we opt for X then some people will be very pleased with the PC but some will be very displeased, but if we opt for Y then we could expect most people to be at least fairly pleased with the PC.

Therefore we recommend PC Y as the best one to purchase if we are constrained to purchase from one supplier only.

Task 2

It would be rather surprising if the staff were only asked to give a single score for each PC after having tried it for a week. It would be better if several aspects of the PC were each evaluated and given a score. Perhaps the scores for each aspect have been combined in some way to give a single value but we do not know if or how this has been done. Having scores for different aspects could be useful because it gives us a richer picture of the staff's views. For example, it might show that the people who gave X very low scores were very dissatisfied with a single aspect of the PC such as a poorly laid out keyboard. It may be possible to rectify the single aspect and create a clear favourite with the staff.

It is difficult to generalise from the scores given by 11 or 12 staff as to what the overall views will be for all 200 staff who will have to use the system. We have not been told how the 12 staff were selected and would need to be reassured that at least they were from a cross-section of the whole company covering different grades of staff and different jobs. It would be difficult to justify using formal inferential statistical methods such as the standard error because from the data we have we cannot assume that the frequency of the scores would show the characteristics of the bell shaped normal distribution.

The 12 staff could have kept one PC for the whole three week trial in order to be able to give more in-depth reports of the PC. We would then have four scores for each of the types of PC. However, we would then have even more difficulty generalising to the whole staff of the company, and an additional problem in that we would need to try to ensure that the individuals in the trial were using a consistent scoring system.

Note: You were not asked to draw a chart or graph of the data but in this case a multiple bar chart of the frequency of the scores would be quite helpful. Graphs and charts are covered in Chapter 14 and you could usefully use the data in this assignment to practise drawing charts.

Answer to Assignment 14

Task 1

(a) The most suitable way to present this data would to use time as the independent variable ie the months on the x-axis and the unit sales as the dependent variable on the y-axis. We could do this on a bar chart but since we have time as the independent variable we should treat this as a time series and draw a historigram, as follows.

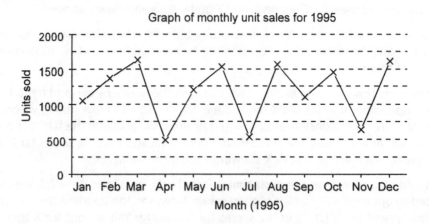

Graph of monthly unit sales for 1995

(b) The scattergraph of the data is shown below. The points represent each month's unit sales with the corresponding advertising costs (which occur in the previous month). Advertising costs are chosen as the independent variable on the x axis and the units sold as the dependent variable on the y axis.

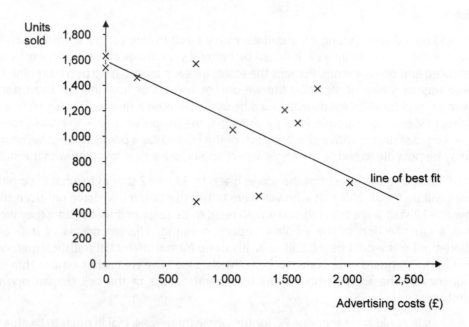

(c) If we examine the graph we can see that there seems to be a fairly strong positive correlation between the advertising costs and the units sold - as more is spent on advertising then more sales are made. There seems to be a base level of sales at about 500 units even when no advertising is done in the previous month.

An estimated line of best fit has been drawn on the graph. We are looking for linear correlation - is there a straight line that fits 'evenly' through the points? It may be tempting to say that the drawn line shows a good fit. However, it may lead us to believe that increasing advertising to £2,500 would lead to a further increase in units sold. Although we may feel intuitively that there is a causal relationship we do not know for certain. Perhaps more importantly in this example, the points seem to level off at about 1,500 units per month provided advertising costs are at least £1,300. This may indicate that the market becomes saturated at that level or that our sales or production operations cannot cope with higher demand. In either case, simply increasing advertising costs will probably be a waste of money.

GLOSSARY

Applications software The programs that users run such as spreadsheets like Lotus 1-2-3 and Microsoft Excel.

Asset Something *owned* by a business, for example a factory or a van.

Associated company A company in which a holding company has a very large interest, although it does not control it.

Bad debt A debt that is never repaid.

Bivariate analysis Analysis which concentrates on how the values of two variables are related.

Bonds Very large fixed interest loans. The term is often used interchangeably with debentures. *Commercial paper* is just another term for this sort of loan.

Budget committee Responsible for the co-ordination and administration of budgets (with the managing director as chairman). Every part of the organisation should be represented on the committee, so there should be a representative from sales, production, marketing and so on.

Budget period The time period to which the budget relates. Except for capital expenditure budgets, the budget period is commonly the accounting year (sub-divided into 12 or 13 control periods).

Budgetary control The practice of establishing budgets which identify areas of responsibility for individual managers (for example production managers, purchasing managers and so on) and of regularly comparing actual results against expected results.

Capital Capital is used with a number of slightly different meanings.

(a) *Capital* is the *money* with which a business starts up - your life savings, for example, or a large redundancy payment might be used to set up a business.

(b) *Capital* is the also the name given to the assets that are used in a business. If you use your reduncancy money to buy a pub and all its contents then the building, the furniture, the beer stocks and so on are all your capital.

(c) Sometimes *capital* is the name given to money invested, for example £10,000 savings in a building society or £10,000 worth of ICI shares.

Computer networks A set of computers connected together. Networks can be divided into two main sorts: Local Area Networks (LANs) and Wide Area Networks (WANs).

Contribution (or contribution to fixed costs) The difference between an item's selling price and its variable costs. In decision making contribution is more important than 'profit', which is sales minus *all* costs, because some costs have to be paid no matter what decisions are taken.

Cost centre A location, a function, an activity or an item of equipment. Each cost centre acts as a collecting place for certain costs before they are analysed further.

Cost unit 'A unit of product or service in relation to which costs are ascertained' (CIMA, *Official Terminology*).

Current assets Cash, stocks and debtors.

Current liabilities Amounts that must be paid out within one year.

Data The raw material for data processing. Data relates to facts, events, and transactions and so forth.

Database A group of related items of data.

Database Management Systems (DBMS) Databases which include facilities for setting up and maintaining the database and incorporate security and access facilities so that several users can have simultaneous access to information in the data, provided they have the appropriate access permissions.

Debentures Amounts loaned to a company. Debentures are usually secured: ie lenders have the right to seize assets if the loan is not repaid.

Dependent variable The variable whose value is influenced by the value of the other variable.

Depreciation A measure of how much a fixed asset wears out until it is completely useless.

Director (of a company) A person who takes part in making decisions and managing a company's affairs. Private companies *must* have at least one director and public companies must have at least two. Directors have to be re-elected by the shareholders at regular intervals.

Effectiveness When resources are used to achieve the desired ends.

Efficiency When resources input to a process produce the optimum (maximum) amount of outputs.

Environment The organisation's surroundings, not just the 'green' environment. For example an organisation's technological environment is all the developments that are taking place in the world in technology. Similarly there is a legal environment, an economic environment and so on.

Equity The ordinary shares of a company.

Eurobonds Bonds that are bought and sold on an international basis.

Exception principle A way of focusing attention on those items where performance differs significantly from what is expected, in other words on the things that are unusual, not on the things that are routine.

Fixed assets Things, like buildings and machines, that a business intends to keep and use for a long period.

Fixed cost That part of cost which does not vary with the level of activity or volume of production.

Fixed overheads Overheads which do not change no matter how much is produced.

Goodwill The amount paid to buy a business in excess of the value of its assets.

Hardware The physical computer and communications equipment.

Holding company A company which controls another, its subsidiary, by holding the majority of its shares. The term *parent company* is sometimes used instead.

Independent variable The variable whose value affects the value of the dependent variable.

Information Data that has been processed in such a way as to be meaningful to the person who receives it.

Information technology The convergence of computer technology and communications technology.

Intangible fixed asset A fixed asset that does not have a physical existence. It cannot be 'touched'. A good example is a trade mark. 'Coca-Cola' is a trade mark. It is an asset because it helps the Coca-Cola company to make profits - people buy things with the trade mark Cola-Cola in preference to other types of cola.

Lead time The time between starting something and finishing it. Thus supply lead time is the time between placing an order for an item and actually receiving it. Production lead time is the time between starting to make something and completing it.

Liability A debt *owed* by a business, for example an overdraft at the bank.

Liquid assets Assets that are easily converted into cash. For example Sainsbury's can easily convert packets of washing powder (stock) into cash by selling them. Cash itself is included when measuring the liquidity of a business.

Local Area Networks (LANs) Networks which connect a limited number, perhaps 30, computers together over a relatively short distance such as within one building.

Mainframe computers Large central computers which can support hundreds of users.

Management information system A computer system or related group of systems which collects and presents management information to a business in order to facilitate its control. (CIMA, *Computing Terminology*)

Mini-computers Small central computers which can support tens of users.

Minority interest The shares held in a subsidiary by people other than the holding company. For example a holding company may own 95% of the shares and another person or company may own the other 5%.

Model Something that represents the real thing as closely as possible. For example, the government uses a computerised mathematical 'model' of the economy so that it can assess, say, the impact of a rise in interest rates on people's buying habits.

Multi-user systems Larger computer systems that can be accessed by many users at the same time.

Mutivariate analysis Analysis which attempts to see how three or more variables interact together: seeing how things typically respond to one another.

Objectives Things that an organisation is trying to achieve, for example increase sales by 10% or increase market share by 20%.

Opportunity cost The value of the alternative action which you go without because you do the first action.

Overheads Expenses on things not used directly in the production of the finished item, for example factory rental or the cost of lighting a factory.

Peripherals Hardware which is connected to the system unit, such as scanners, printers and plotters.

Private company A company that is prohibited from offering its shares to the general public.

Profit centre A location, or a function accountable for costs and income. It may also be called a *business centre, business unit* or *strategic business unit.*

Public company (plc) A company that can invite the general public to subscribe for shares.

Published accounts Accounts are not published in the sense that you can go and buy a copy in a bookshop or a newsagents. 'Published' means that they are available for consultation by the general public. You have to pay a small fee to a government body called Companies House to see them. *All* companies have to publish their accounts in this way.

Raw materials Things that are processed to make the finished product. For example steel is a raw material used to make cars.

Resource A means of doing something. A business's resources are sometimes referred to as the four Ms - men, machinery, materials and money. (We should say 'people', not 'men'.)

Securities This term is commonly used to mean any sort of investment that can be bought and sold in the financial markets. (Some would object to this definition, but this is how you will find the word used in financial writing.)

Semi-variable costs Costs which are partly variable and partly fixed.

Share premium The amount paid for a new share in excess of the share's 'nominal value'. For example when the water industry was privatised shares had a nominal value of £1 but buyers had to pay a total of £2.40 to acquire them (spread over about a year and a half). The extra £1.40 is the share premium.

Software The coded instructions which the computer carries out.

Spreadsheet An application that looks like a very large sheet of paper with a grid drawn on it. Numbers can be entered into the boxes on the grid and very sophisticated calculations and analyses can be performed.

Sub-system A smaller part of a larger system. For example, there may be a despatch sub-system with its own set of documents and procedures.

Subsidiary A company under the control of another company, its holding company or 'parent'.

System A set of connected things. Systems are a way of organising activities. for example, a sales system may consist of documents and procedures used for: taking customer orders, despatching goods; invoicing; recording debts; and accepting payments.

Systems software Software which carries out the basic operation of the computer such as managing keyboard input and loading and storing disk files. The main part of the systems software is the operating system such as Microsoft Windows 95 or UNIX.

Terminal Equipment consisting of a VDU and keyboard used for accessing multi-user systems.

Trade creditors People you owe money to because you have bought things from them that go into making your product or service. (Other creditors include employees, the tax man, the landlord for rent and so on.)

Trade debtors People who owe you money because they have bought products or services from your business. (Non-trade debtors ('other debtors') are people who owe you money for other reasons: for example you may have earned 70 days interest on a bank deposit but not yet have received the money because it is only paid every 3 months.)

Turnover Another word for sales.

Univariate analysis Analysis which concentrates on reducing the raw data to meaningful figures and looking at what is typical.

Variable Something that can have different values. For example, the *number* of customers that come into your shop per hour is a variable: the number of customers changes, while the things it is measured against (your shop, per hour) do not.

Variable cost That part of cost which varies with the volume of production (or level of activity).

Variable overheads Overheads which change depending on how much is produced - for example, if the factory is running for longer it will need to be lit for longer.

What if? analysis A way of looking at a problem by considering what would happen in different circumstances (or 'scenarios'). For example what if sales demand is 10,000 units, or 20,000 units? What are the different implications for staffing the production department?

Wide Area Networks (WANS) Networks which can connect thousands of computers together. Their reach can be worldwide using the telephone system as communication links.

INDEX

REVIEW FORM

NAME ....

COLLEGE ....

We would be grateful to receive an comments you may have on this book. You may like to use the headings below as guidelines. Tear out this page and sent it to our Freepost address:

Clare Donnelly, BPP Publishing Ltd , FREEPOST, London W12 8BR

Topic coverage:

Summary diagrams, signposts, definitions, chapter roundups and quizzes:

Discussion topics, activities and assignments

Errors (please specify, and refer to a page number):

Other: